VIA Folios 159

Whaddyacall the Wind?

Whaddyacall the Wind?

Annie Rachele Lanzillotto

BORDIGHERA PRESS

ALSO BY ANNIE RACHELE LANZILLOTTO

Hard Candy: Caregiving, Mourning and Stage Light
Pitch, Roll, Yaw
L is for Lion: an italian bronx butch freedom memoir
Schistsong

for my sister

and

for the cugini, ancestors, *and* paesani *from Acquaviva delle Fonti, Bitetto, and Cassano delle Murge*

Cover art "Ribbon in the Wind on Lemon Tree" (acrylic, pastel, and marker on paper) and interior maps by Annie Rachele Lanzillotto.

Library of Congress Cataloging-in-Publication Data

Names: Lanzillotto, Annie Rachele, author.
Title: Whaddyacall the wind? / Annie Rachele Lanzillotto.
Description: New York, NY : Bordighera Press, [2022] | Series: Via folios ; 159
| Summary: "A poetic tarantella of the heart. Walk, tremble and fall in the Matriamia, cry for connection from alleyways up to open windows. Expose your heart. Know what it is to feel "like an errant puzzle piece... never to be found, never to be put into place." A New Yorker learns to walk on Sanpietrini, connects with gay community in the Matriamia, finds living cousins by hanging out in the village cemetery, talks to a Saint who sees ecstasy in stirring fava beans, learns of the Duchess who bit off the saint's finger, argues with Pulcinella, envisions the epic journey of a painting of La Madonna through four seas to get from Constantinople to Acquaviva delle Fonti, sells wind to sailors, avoids draughts, tangos Sciroccazzo, builds a bridge of hearts and asks the question: "What position do you want to be in for l'eternità?""-- Provided by publisher.
Identifiers: LCCN 2022024683 | ISBN 9781599541938 (trade paperback)
Subjects: LCGFT: Poetry. | Creative nonfiction.
Classification: LCC PS3612.A5885 W47 2022 | DDC 818/.609--dc23/
eng/20220729
LC record available at https://lccn.loc.gov/2022024683

Printed with Ingram Lightning Source.

Published by
BORDIGHERA PRESS
John D. Calandra Italian American Institute
25 W. 43rd Street, 17th Floor
New York, NY 10036

VIA Folios 159
ISBN 978-1-59954-193-8

TABLE OF CONTENTS

PART III. *Comu u Chiami u Ventu?*

PART IV. *Cum us Ce'ma e Vent?*

FOREWORD
by Edvige Giunta

FROM THE SUNROOM OF MY HOME in Northern New Jersey, I watch the unfolding of seasons and wait for spring. In my line of vision, "Grandma Rose," slender, lighter than last fall, opens her arms wide. I squint, looking for signs of new life. Five or six years ago, Annie carried her from Yonkers, a baby tree in a pouch. We planted her in my Teaneck backyard and, chanting, encouraged this child of Grandma Rose's bountiful peach tree, named after the mother tree, to grow strong roots.

I lean back on the old comfy blue chair, sip cappuccino, and listen. From the speakerphone, Annie's voice pours into the room. It booms and whispers. It sings. It chants my name. Annie is a name aficionada. Give her a name and she will repeat it, break it into parts, recompose it, make it a song, pull stories out of it. You can gather the names in this book, listen to their rhythms, string them together, make a rosary of Lucia and Franco and Giuseppe and Rosa and Timothea and Rachele and Annunziatina and Grace and Rocco and Carmine and Anna and Benedetta and Pulcinella.

Annie insists on pronouncing names the Italian way. She finds the beat in every name. Some twenty years ago, we held a presentation of *The Milk of Almonds: Italian American Women Writers on Food and Culture*, an anthology I edited with Louise DeSalvo. My mother, who had recently arrived from Sicily, sat in the audience, with no English and with much pride in her daughter. With a Sicilian mamma in the audience, Annie was elated. When her turn came to read from the anthology, she sang my mother's name: "Cettina, Cettina Minasola, Minasolaaaa Cettinaaaa." She sang high and low; she sang operatic and jazzy. My demure mother blushed and smiled. Who was this strange *Americana*?

Annie made sure to visit whenever my mother made the long trip from Gela to Teaneck to see her two daughters and their American families. The grammar of immigration is made up of coming and goings, hellos and goodbyes, a never-ending leaving of some place, a constant yearning for some other place. I have a video recording from one of these visits: we are sitting at the kitchen table and all urge Annie to sing for my mother, just like she did that first time she met her. The rest of us join in a chorus of whispers and laughter and *lalala*. After, my mother embraces Annie, the strange *Americana* she has grown to love. Annie is family, the rare American visitor we welcome in Sicily one summer when she travels all the way from Naples past the boot. As a family that reunites from different parts of the world, we jealously guard the little time we have together. Annie has joined our intimate circle. We sit around the table covered with oilcloth in the veranda. The smells and sounds of the Mediterranean mingle with the aroma and gurgles of the *caffettiera*. Annie clinks her tiny cup against my mother's. I know I will remember this moment.

There are periods when Annie and I talk several times a day, a habit I trace to the adolescent need to talk constantly with girlfriends, a tender, intimate practice that has survived through decades and over three thousand miles. We talk while cooking, doing the laundry, going for walks in the neighborhood. We talk of food, family, friends, Bianchina, her new washing machine, Donna Cuncetta, my pandemic stainless steel pantry cabinet. Our talk of the quotidian spills into— becomes—writing talk. Writing is the thick thread that connects us, as strong as our shared Italian origins—I, a first-generation Sicilian from Gela; Annie, a third-generation Pugliese from Acquaviva delle Fonti, Cassano delle Murge, and Bitteto. These daily talks must make do during the pandemic, when we lose the dinners, the parties, the sleepovers, the readings, the walks in the Village under full moons.

For over two decades, Annie Lanzillotto has been a key figure in a circle of Italian American women who value the conjoined power of written words and friendship. We are wandering women, eager to plant roots in familiar and unfamiliar gardens, deeply aware of the fragility and resilience of the most ancient roots. We understand that roots can be torn—and they may grow again.

I knew Annie Lanzillotto's name before I met her and felt the instant kinship that familiar names evoke, names that come from stories passed down through generations, names that have traveled great distances. I knew Annie's name before I had read her work or watched her glorious performances, like "How to Cook a Heart" or "Icewoman." Once I started reading and watching and listening to her, I quickly understood that Annie Lanzillotto spoke "Italianmericanese" like no other. Over the years, I have become a devotee more than a fan. As an Italian American feminist scholar and anthologist, I have been following Annie Lanzillotto's journey closely and recognize, like so many others, that Annie is not just a memoirist or a poet or a performer or a storyteller or an activist: she is a cultural force that should be ensconced in Italian American academic and cultural spaces. Observer, listener, recorder, and channeler of voices and stories, Annie is a literary anthropologist, an epic memoirist, a fabulist of intimate moments that would fade into oblivion were she not there to catch them in her fists and slowly release them to us, fortified by untainted love. Annie is not just a collector of stories; she is a lover of stories, no matter how hard, recalcitrant, painful they are. And if you have had the good fortune of partaking in the incantation of her storytelling, as reader, audience member, even character, you know exactly what I mean.

From my chair in the sunroom, from my kitchen, basement, bedroom, office in the attic, from all the rooms where Annie's voice accompanies me, I have listened to and witnessed the making of *Whaddyacall the Wind?* If *L is for Lion* is a book of beginnings and *Hard Candy* a book of endings, *Whaddyacall the Wind?* is a book of crossings—in the style of Persephone, mythical traveler, adept to comings and goings, to belonging to two places and none, juggler of loyalties and identities, descending and ascending, always on the verge of another departure, another season, another separation.

"Grandma Rose has some blossoms," I announce one April day, then walk outside, click FaceTime, and flip the screen for Annie to see.

"Hello, Grandma Rose," Annie says. "*Buon giorno. Come stai?*"

We exchange a few effusive words about our little tree, how beautiful she looks.

"Leave her alone," Annie says. "Do not touch her. Do *not* cut her."

Over the years, I heeded Annie's warning, but Grandma Rose had grown in so many directions, and now she had a fungus—so last fall, with much trepidation, I decided it was time to prune her. I asked my friend Nino to oversee the removal of excessive or sickly growth. She is looking well now in early spring. I am hoping for fruit this year or next.

Meanwhile, Grandma Rose stands in my line of vision, waits patiently for Annie's next visit—as do I. While we wait, *Whaddyacall the Wind?* carries Annie's voice.

You can hear it.

Edvige Giunta
Teaneck, New Jersey
May 10, 2022

PART I
WHADDYACALL THE WIND?

the

w
i
n
d

a
n d

y
o
u

b
e
s i d   e
e   m

i l
v
e
n
t
o

e   t e

a
c
c a
n
t
o   *e*
a   m

"Boccacielo / Mouth-Heaven / *Bocc'Ngjile"*

Napoli, May 22, 2018

I came to paint lemons
That's what I told myself
To cleanse my mind
Lemon juice the years
My soul has been away
Napoli
A *fait accompli*
The Bronx before she went through her changes
Alleyway after alleyway wet laundry
Awnings shield from raindrops
A hand painted sign:

> *ZIA ADA offre caffè, tè freddo, o limonata*
> *—in cambio di solidarietà.*
> *Le case per tutti.*

> Aunt Ada offers coffee, iced tea, or lemonade—
> in exchange for solidarity
> Housing for all.

The issues are the same in cities—people priced out

I just ate *melanzane* from a jar
It sounds incongruent.
A new product the hotel is pushing
Salvo the concierge, handed me a ticket
So I could eat a jar for free
Eating from a jar, warm, like eating baby food
I put the silver spoon in my mouth
Eggplant *parmigiana*, hot melts inside me
As I melt inside swirls of mozzarella

Pomodoro around my tongue
It's nothing you want to chew, just suck
And swirl, become part of the melt
They call it *Boccacielo*, Mouth-Heaven, *Bocc'Ngjile*
Microwave or boil the jar and all
In through the mouth
One spoon at a time

"Notes from *Napoli*"

May 22, 2018

NAPOLI YOU GOTTA LAND IN WITH YOUR MOUTH. There's no other way. As soon as the restaurants open at 8 p.m., I walk into the first open door. All the food at the buffet is laid out in ceramic dishes painted with embellishments of olive flourishes, lemons, green plumes and indigo waves. You serve yourself: *gnocchi,* zucchini flowers stuffed with *ricotta, insalate, fagiolini, polpette di pollo alla crema di limone.* This *gnocchi nella mia bocca*—my mouth stops in its tracks. I stop chewing and suck on each ball of potato pasta. *Gnocchi* melts in my mouth as I melt around *gnocchi.* Two big dogs, Nino and Sheila, come up and kiss me at the sidewalk table. I share my *polpette* with them. Dogs are off leash on sidewalks and in the piazze. Interactivity is here for the taking; dogs, people, barks and shouts, from balconies, down the street, up the street, a loud din from the sidewalk bar open all night, conversation everywhere, hands flying, a sense of freedom of expression. I am far from "personal space" and "boundaries" and "indoor voices." I know that no one in *Napoli* will ever tell me, "Keep your voice down," and this frees me, frees my voice. This is the chaos and interaction I've sought all my life. Vespas, people, the constant buzz, elders on motorized scooters. This is the loudness where I feel at home.

When I left New York yesterday, my sister Rosina cried on the phone. Aunt Grace cried when I hugged her goodbye. Faroukh cried in my arms. Friends were saying they were missing me already. What was everyone crying for? I wasn't going back to Italy as an American tourist on a European vacation. Aunt Grace would never cry for that, she's ninety-six, stoic and tough as nails. My sister Rosina would never cry for that, she worked all her life and now she's retired, a grandmother, with an awakened feminist spirit. I wasn't going back as someone on a vacation or honeymoon. These strong women wouldn't cry for that either. Not just as an American artist on a European tour. That wouldn't bring these strong women to tears. What was it? What was everyone crying for?

"Mother's Breath"

MY LOVE FOR THE WIND STARTED as my mother's breath, as a child, asthmatic, her kissing me and staying close, our faces, breath mingling. She took my temperature with her cheek on my forehead. Sometimes, especially now that she is gone, I wake up and feel her breath upon my cheek. The wind played a big part in our health. She protected me from getting draughts. Always a warning about draughts. She knew the distinction between a breeze and a draught. "Don't catch a draught!" as she wound a scarf around and around my neck to protect me, tucking the tail in like a Gordian knot. My mother spoke of the wind as a gift, as a visitor she would walk outside to greet, "*Ahh,* there's a fresh breeze outside." She aired pillows out the window, knew the sun as the best disinfectant, and the wind called for her. She'd step outside on the stoop, close her eyes, tilt her face to the sun, to the wind, and breathe in the universe, bask in this moment of life. The world breathes, and we with it. *Spirare.* The world blows in, the world blows out. Mother's breath.

As a child playing stickball in the street, wind determined our strategies. To estimate which side of the street the ball favored in the wind, I learned to stick my index finger into my mouth and pull it out with lips closed to wet the whole finger, then raise my arm high in the sky to feel which way and how forceful the wind blew. We took the wind into account when eyeing the ball, as it beveled the path of pop flies and pitches. My success as a player and respect by the boys on the block depended on me knowing the winds that swerved down our one-way street. I learned early on that cars and wind could come from either direction at any moment. After a play where the Spaldeen took an errant turn, we'd yell, "*Man!* Did you see how the wind carried that?" Winds that carried our home runs from the homeplate sewer cap down the block to Zerega Avenue, I call Zerega Wind.

At twenty-one, in Egypt for a semester, I experienced how winds can threaten your life, when climbing to the top of the great pyramid of Giza. Before starting the climb, we got a life-saving tip from a local who talked of the winds racing across the Sahara like a goddess whipping in a boomerang path around the pyramids, and how she blew climbers off the sides of the pyramids where they fell to their deaths. I pictured a giant goddess blowing on the pyramids like birthday candles. He said many soldiers died this way; climbers have been swept off since the pyramids were built 4500 years ago. As my friends and I walked around the pyramid debating which side to climb, he gave us this tip—Climb up the corner, this way you can block your body from the wind in two directions, and you'll always have a rock face to shield you. He was right. Especially as we climbed the equivalent of twenty, thirty, forty stories, the winds got ferocious. I ducked this way, then that, as the wind changed course, I clung with all my might to one rock, then scooted over the ledge around the corner of the pyramid to duck the other way. I think he called the wind the Sarqiyya, but I'll call it the Breath of the Goddess Wind, as that's what it is in my body's memory.

"67th and York"

Sloan Kettering feels like a rock in the wind
tonight. A wind bites both ways

A steady stream of traffic
and the breeze stopping with the light

Red red red red everywhere
Better run with the light

"Not in Service" says the bus
Green green green green

Walking in crosswalk

Tulips red and yellow
fallen open

"Whaddyacall the wind?" I ask wherever I go. I love when the wind
is talked about like an old friend with characteristic idiosyncrasies,
one who gets in your ears and drives you crazy or lifts your spirits
with relief or has a trickster spirit. I delight when someone knows a
local nickname for a particular wind. Most of the time, people don't
have an answer. It depends where you are. I love that too, having an
ancient question few today can answer. What do you call the wind?

Then, as always, we begin with an expulsion from Eden . . .

Chapter One. "Clues"

Yonkers, New York, August 2017

WOKE UP TO THE SOUND OF CHAINSAWS, squeezed my eyes tight to snap the sleep out, and scissored two fingers apart to peek through the slats of the window blinds. What was all the noise about? A man with an ax on his shoulder stood outside my window biting into a peach as big as his fist, cheek jutting out from the hunk in his mouth. Grandma Peach Tree lay on the ground, all the hard-to-reach, big-as-softballs, sun-blushed peaches at the men's feet. Peaches and work boots. A gang of nine men stood around, chainsaws and pickaxes, biting and chewing, necks and shoulders zesting sweat. Their deed was done. The landlord chopped her down.

It was late August. Grandma was full, and I mean full of peaches, stocked to the top branches two stories high. The buzz of chainsaws cut through the trunk of my gut. I wanted to run outside and tackle one of the men. I took a breath and thought it through. If I ran out there, they would've shrugged—*we're just following orders from management,* then I would've yelled and out of frustration might have grabbed a pickaxe and swung at somebody. I hadda get outta there. *Pronto.* In the words of Ignazio Silone, "*Che posso fare io?*"

I pulled on black dungarees, black t-shirt of Our Lady of Mount Carmel, black New Orleans Saints baseball cap with gold *fleur-de-lis,* black wrap-around sunglasses, grabbed my keychain and ran out of the building, blocking my eyesight with my right hand as I ran left to get out of the courtyard. I couldn't bear to look and didn't want to give the men the satisfaction of my tears. They relished the power of the kill, and were literally eating the fruits of their labor, chewing fresh peaches out in the hot open sun. I ran down the outdoor staircase cut into the hill, got into the car, growled a cry, smacked the steering wheel and sped up the street, my yells bouncing back off the windshield. Hyperventilating, I pulled over just a mile away, on Aunt Grace's block.

Aunt Grace was the last of my mother's like, siblings. Technically, she was my mother's cousin, which made her my second cousin, but since they were raised like sisters in one apartment, I called her, "Aunt," out of respect. They were cousins twice; their mothers were sisters, and their fathers were brothers. Tradition dictated that the girls be named after their grandmothers. They each had a sister. The four girls were named: Lucia, Lucia, Rachele, Rachele. To differentiate them, they needed nicknames. My mother was called Lilly, and her cousin was called Grace.

Their mothers, the Marsico girls, were born in Acquaviva delle Fonti and their fathers, the Petruzzelli boys, just three miles away in Cassano delle Murge. One road connects the two towns through olive fields and up onto the limestone plateau called the *murge*. They met over here in *l'Amereeq*, but I always wondered if they hadn't emigrated, if they would've met anyway over there in the fields or during the evening *passeggiata* in either of the town's piazze.

I walked up the narrow path of stones to the front door and rang Aunt Grace's bell. No response. I waited. Aunt Grace was ninety-six, it could take her a few minutes to hear the bell and come to the door. Her parents, Franco and Lucia, and my grandparents, Giuseppe and Rosa, had been part of the mass wave of post Italian unification immigration from the *Mezzogiorno* to New York. Back in the days of that first generation of immigrants, there were all kinds of relatives by blood or association, people who took care of one another and lived doubling up together to survive. My father's side of the family was larger, and it seemed there was always someone from the *paese* coming over, staying over, cousins, townspeople, you were never sure who was who or how you were related, different kinds of relatives or no relation at all. There were *paesans*, there were cousins like siblings, cousins who lived with grandmothers, *paesans* who were taken in by *paesans*—they got one another jobs and taught each other trades—cousins who married cousins, or, like all my grandparents, married *paesans* from the same province just an olive or fig field away. There were *paesans* of who it was said, "Grandma and Grandpa raised so-and-so," or "Grandma and Grandpa took hoodycall in like a son when he came from the other side." I innately understood though I didn't understand who was who exactly, just that there were a lot of hoodycallits around and I was required to kiss them all on the hello and the goodbye at family gatherings. Relations and relations of relations, we were all related in some way, and all linked back to the villages where our grandparents were born and connected through adoration of local saints. They left their country behind but never gave up their hometown saints.

I rang the bell again. At the top of the towering pine tree a black branch broke off and the V-shaped branch flapped, took flight and turned into a barking crow, slow black wings slapped sky. How could the peach tree be dead and gone, felled, on the ground? That peach tree was my grandmother, Rosa Marsico Petruzzelli. For seventeen years I'd pruned her branches and harvested her peaches, seventeen years since Grandma Rose spit pits into her hand and tossed them out my mother's living room window. Grandma Rose refused to throw away any pit or seed ever, and at one hundred years old, after she died, that tree burst up through the ground. It was miraculous spirit magic, Grandma transmogrified, and for the last fifteen years of my mother's life, Easter Sundays the tree brought pink blossoms right into her window like clockwork, and by the Feast of the Assumption my mother pulled peaches from the lowest branches in through the living room window, proclaiming:

"That's Mamma feeding us."

Gone. Gone. That was it. Gone. They all were gone. The peach tree was my last root to this place.

I knocked hard on the dark red door and called, "Aunt Grace!" up at the red bricks and windows of her gingerbread house with its peaked roof and chimney. Nobody came. I walked around the side of the house over the uneven stones and tree roots and knuckle-tapped her kitchen window. There she was, washing dishes at the sink, in her hand sewn orange, green and gold paisley apron and a crisp white linen blouse with eyelets. Classical music flowed from her solid-state radio. She was startled to see me at the window, rubbed her hands in a dish towel and pointed for me to walk back around to the front of the house where she could open the door. I took off my sunglasses and walked through the doorway. Aunt Grace was alarmed to see I'd been sobbing, "*Oooh* dear, come in, come in, I'll put on a pot of coffee," she laughed a nervous chuckle, "have you had breakfast? I can make a soft-boiled egg."

I waved off the offer of the egg, dropped my keychain on the table, cupped my hands under the faucet of cold water and splashed my face. My mother instilled in me the habit of shocking my face with ice cold water to stop the sting of crying. I downed two glasses of water as if to replenish the hot tears, sat down at her kitchen table, and took a deep breath calming myself by staring at the wicker basket of plastic fruit that had mesmerized me ever since childhood with its *trompe l'oeil* plastic banana, pear, red apple, green grapes, red grapes and tomato, true enough to color to fool me the very first time and fascinate me ever since. When I was twelve and couldn't decide if the fruit was real or not, I grabbed the red apple and to my surprise, it was light as air, hollow plastic, slightly discolored to look real. The pear had lumps and brown spots on its complexion like a true pear. The green grapes, pert and tempting on browned stems, made my mouth water.

"They cut down Grandma's peach tree," I growled murderously.

Aunt Grace flashed water into the coffee pot and put it on the stove to boil. "Why'd they do that?"

"They're afraid of bees."

"*Oh, for Pete's sake.*" She took out two thick white ceramic cups and saucers.

"Who cuts down a tree full of fruit? They couldn't wait a week for all the peaches to be picked? It's out of spite. They're trying to get rid of me."

"No, they can't get rid of you," she folded a white napkin into a perfect triangle and placed it on the table. "Fruit trees are a lot of work. They just don't want them on the property."

"That's true. One tree, a thousand peaches a year. I couldn't keep up with the pruning. They like things manicured over there. I like nature wild and free."

"*My*, that's a lot of keys. You look like a jailor."

How could I explain my keychain? My need for heft? How a keychain clipped to my belt loop and a bandana tied around my head and was my style ever since I was twelve? Or that I joined my mother's keychain to my own after she died? Or that having keys to the local recording studio and a lucky key to my friend's house in New Orleans gave me the feeling I could take off at any moment and follow my dreams of music? Or that I carried a set of keys to a friend's apartment where I could sleep over when I couldn't bear the sadness of returning to my mother's apartment so empty without her? Or my desire to get a new motorcycle and so I carried my snake lock key from the last? Or that with neuropathy I couldn't handle small keychains? Or that I tended to lose things even if they were right in front of me, so a big keychain with a steel link solved that problem? Or that a keychain clamped to your belt loop was a butch dyke signifier? Or that my keychain doubled as a weapon when I walked alone at night? Or that the more unmoored and lost I felt in the world, the more keys I wanted to carry to feel like I belonged somewhere? Or that the keychain made me feel I belonged wherever I was, as long as my hand could hold that cool nickel-brass and steel?

"What are all those keys to?"

"I dunno. Who knows?" I shrugged it off. "The managing agent wants me out, you know that bottled blonde. She wants to renovate, sell, turn the unit co-op. That's what they call homes now, units. I'm one of the last renters. They could sell it in a hot minute."

"Your mother always said she was snippy."

"Yeah, and my mother said whoever was mixing her blonde hair dye, put too much number thirty and not enough number forty. That's what she called her, "Too-Much-Thirty." Mom said she could have used more Topaz and a touch of Apricot."

"Lilly always had the knack for mixing color, ever since she was a kid."

"Yeah, whenever we were on the street, she would tell me the color combinations of people's hair dye. She was like a hunter for color. And just a couple of days after she died, Miss Too-Much-Thirty came to ask me, "How long do you plan on staying?" in that nasal tone, like a Terrier, "*Yippyyipyap.*"

"You tell her, forever! Nothin' doin'. She can't put you out. You have Shangri-La over there."

"Yeah, Shangri-La. That apartment with its thousand emotional triggers from my parents' divorce. I want to be anywhere but there. Maybe Miss Too-Much-Thirty is doing me a cosmic favor, cracking my heart with chainsaws to give me the push I need to move."

"Well, you just stay put, Annie, rents are outrageous. You have two nice size rooms. Shangri-La, you remember that. You stay put." She poured smokin' coffee into my cup.

"Stay put? Who wants to stay put?" I pinched one of the rubber green grapes. "Thank God for the State of New York, I have rent-stabilized housing. You're right. That is Shangri-La, a rent stabilized lease is a great inheritance. Maybe one day I'll feel a sense of home again, but for now, I do have housing, and that is a lot."

Aunt Grace cut up cantaloupe and arranged slices into beautiful smiles on a white china plate painted with red cherries and green leafy stems. She sat and adjusted her perfect posture so the dish towel she'd clothespinned to the lamp over the table shielded her eyes from the light bulb that hung just at the height to blind you when you sat. Aunt Grace was calm and steady, modest and precise, upright and attentive, utterly focused. She maintained her inner peace. Sunlight coming in from three directions in concert with the classical music, suffused her kitchen with a timeless serenity. She created peace of mind. Patches of rainbows popped and slid around the room onto the flowered wallpaper from a crystal hanging in a window. She meditated twice a day for decades and dished out ninety-six years of sage wisdom with absolute confidence:

"Just wait 'til next year. Things will shoot up again, I promise you. It always does. You'll see."

I didn't believe anything would grow again, but Aunt Grace knew plenty I didn't. My head shook side to side as my thoughts continued in my head: "You know," I confided in her, "someone told me this phrase. *Adult orphan.* It's stuck in my chest like a dart thrown. It's shocking to find myself all alone. Like everybody left at once. Grandma, my mother, everybody. The apartment is so quiet. I wake up, I'm like—Where is everybody?"

"That's life. At least where you are, you have sidewalks. You see a whole human being. Over here you only see people from the chest up. Here, they step outside their front door, I wave hello and they plop right into their cars. You don't even see a whole body." She shook her head in disgust and poured more coffee, "Do what I do. Play the classical music station. It gives you a sense of company. You'll be surprised. It fills the house." She was resigned to life and was solidly equipped to deal with it. I was restless. I had my sneakers tied tight and my passport updated, ready to run, to drive into the city, to create theater, music, eat with friends, start a new chapter of life. Aunt Grace delivered an omen, no pipe dreams, "You better get used to it."

"Get used to it? Don't you believe I can change my life? Start over? Write a new chapter?"

"This is life. We're born alone. We end up alone."

To fill her lonely hours Aunt Grace kept her hands busy; cooking, cleaning, sewing, baking masterpieces like her famous chocolate roll cake, raising focaccia dough in the basement every other Friday. "Go look," she'd tell me. "It looks like a corpse down there." What a system she had, the biggest lasagna pan possible, filled with hot water atop the washing machine, under the pan of rising dough, covered by a stack of blankets. Dough, like me, was prone to catch a draught, to its demise.

Aunt Grace pushed down on the table to lift herself up out of her chair and pulled a stack of crossword puzzles that she'd saved for me under her seat cushion. This was one way she'd helped me grieve my mother: conversations, cups of tea and coffee, sharing mutual grief, and giving me crossword puzzles she cut out of newspapers. I flipped through the stack and saw one of the crosswords was cropped tight, just boxes. No questions.

"Hey this one's got no questions! You cut off the questions. All I have is empty boxes. No clues."

"*Oh, for Pete's sake*, I'll be darned. How'd I do that?"

"That's exactly what life feels like. A crossword puzzle without any clues."

Chapter Two. "Erase Night"

ON THE WAY HOME, I pulled into the last gas station in the neighborhood which still offered the old-fashioned service of pumping gas. The guy working the pump was young, in his 20's, in a tight red shirt with a gold lightning bolt across his chest. I could tell he was Middle Eastern, so I tapped my horn, "*Ya habibi,*" Yo, my love. He broke into a big laugh, not expecting some middle-aged white lady pulling up to the pump who knew even a few words of Arabic. He matched my enthusiastic hello with a rousing, "*Habibti!*" In that instant, we made eye contact and forged a connection as electric as the gold lightning bolt. *Ka-boom!* I felt a jolt in my heart. There's a lot to be said for the art of the hello, the greatest art form of all time.

Faroukh carried himself like he was working in a fashion store about to help me into a new leather jacket. He wore distressed jeans with strategic rips in slashes, and red hi-top sneakers to match his shirt. Big brown eyes like my cousins and an impeccable haircut and shave with a hint of shadow above and below his full lips. His hands were strong, he'd done harder labor in the past. He said he needed to learn English. We exchanged numbers and planned to meet for coffee and language exchange. I'd teach him some English; he'd teach me Arabic. I was always happy to learn more Arabic. I had an ear for it from studying in Egypt back in college. Faroukh filled my tank, and I went on my way with the lucky feeling that I'd just met a new friend in the world.

The next morning Miss Too-Much-Thirty stood outside my window pointing at bushes with a congratulatory air, the word "clean" issuing forth from her mouth several times. She instructed the landscapers where she wanted a bush moved. Her face looked unnaturally elated as if she'd had a facelift overnight. *Yippyyipyappyyip clean yipyap.*

Beware the word "clean."

The crew of men came back over the next two days and bashed the ground with pickaxes uprooting flowerbeds all over the courtyard, a grass field the size of a basketball court. Neighbors came out of their doorways moaning: "The viburnum! My peonies! The purple irises!

Even the tulip beds!" We walked around in a state of disorientation. *No more Lee's buttercups. Poor old Lee, he was such a good guy, I loved thinking of him every spring when they bloomed. The yellow rose bush Sean planted for Rachel—they cut it down! The lilacs used to perfume right into Shirley's window. No more. So much money Florence put into spring bulbs. Down the drain.* It was all gone, our entire songline. Sparrows and robins flew around confused, not knowing where to go. Flowerbeds were shaved down to the dirt. Rabbits and butterflies, dragonflies and bees, vanished. The purple Belgian tulip bulbs I'd planted for my mother in her last years of life were trampled, bulbs sliced through. The men even carted away the rocks I'd brought her from all different states. Gone. All that was left was empty soil, burnt yellow August grass and squared-off hedges.

One neighbor wrote prayers on index cards and came to the stoop to hand me one. Three ladies walked the paths on their daily rounds. I called them The Angel Squad because they kept their eyes on things in the neighborhood and prayed for everybody. We walked the rectangular sidewalk around the grass court reciting the rosary. Another elder put a statue of the *Madonna* in her window, looking out, bearing witness with a look of pity on her painted ceramic face. The oldest and toughest lady in the court, *La Baronessa,* sat out on the bench with her arms folded in a show of strength, making her presence known. She was eighty-three, kept her hair dyed a shiny copper, wore floppy hats in every color to match her outfits, and still drove herself to work every day. I called her *La Baronessa* as an honorific because she said she inherited property and the royal title in Sicily. She worked for a flower seed company and could recite the names of all we lost: "Gerbera daisies, butterfly bushes, waxed begonias, bleeding hearts. Don't worry," she told me, "I'm Sicilian. I carry a knife in my pocketbook. That's right." She pulled one bottom eyelid down with her index finger, a gesture that let me know she was watching everybody. At the end of all our conversations, she looked me dead in the eyes, both lovingly and threateningly as she shouted an imperative to me that I better stay healthy, "*Stàtte bbuón!*"

The courtyard was dark. All the exterior lamps were out. The men had bashed the ground so hard with their pickaxes that they sliced through underground electrical wires. The court was now without lights at night. As you walked down the dead-end street and up the walkway you were greeted by a new sign that read: (odd) in parentheses, in gold lettering on a maroon rectangle of wood, giving a title to the vibe of the place. It took me a while to figure out that Miss Too-Much-Thirty ordered the sign to signify to delivery workers that the buildings on this side of the street were odd numbers, but the single word (odd) was never enough to communicate numerical logic to workers who needed it, instead cast confusion worthy of ridicule. "Welcome to the odd court," I told everyone who entered. My mother's voice and sarcastic wit was strong and clear inside me. Her spirit, verbatim, spoke. It was my lips that were moving, and the air over my own one good vocal cord formed the words, but my sharp-witted Bronx mother Rachele was doing the talking:

"Jackasses. Serves them right. Now they'll have to pay thousands in electrician bills."

I walked around with my head down, kicking the dirt. Between two boot prints in the soil, a thin peach tree shoot, about a foot tall, made its presence known, waving in the breeze with two leaves. How did it not get trampled? Saplings I'd learned to distinguish from weeds by reading leaves like thumbprints. Peach tree leaves are curved and long with a backbend and a central strong bifurcating vein feathered with bilateral veins. I dug up the tiny peach sapling and brought it into the kitchen to care for it undisturbed. New life. Hairy roots clutched the pit that gave it life. The baby peach tree would grow in the kitchen on my mother's windowsill, where she used to wave to me coming and going, a sprout of a peach tree taking root in the last of my mother's chipped white enamel pots. My mother's hand waving to me will always be framed in my mind by the white windowpane inset into the red brick wall. Her hand fluttered from this window as I came and went. The young do so much coming and going. On a bicycle or running to catch a train or driving to college or going to see friends, always friends. The baby tree I rotated every couple of days so all sides of the trunk, thinner than a pencil, got sunlight. This kitchen would always be my mother's kitchen, even though she'd been gone almost two years, the kitchen still kicked out all kinds of good home cooking.

I was the one doing the cooking, but it seemed Mom still was, or the kitchen was—my mother's magic kitchen. I felt her, sharp light hitting the frying pan as a *frittata* tilted, meatballs rotated, stuffed peppers' caves puffed with steam. Washed parsley in bunches hung from the knobs of the cabinets over the sink. This was the way she did things for years, and now I did things the same way. To the neighbors, I gave a kind word. That's what she did, sat on the stoop speaking kindnesses to everyone passing by, giving them nicknames. "Hello Miss Bling, I love the sparkle on those shoes." Others, she lifted their spirits. "Look up. You're the beauty of the court." And others, sarcasm, "Yeah, here comes Trick and Track." "Here's Shoulda-Woulda-Coulda."

The next months were dark in the (odd) court. Stars and planets hung a little bit closer in the solar wind. Jupiter, Saturn, and Mars made appearances with the moon. One night I looked up at the full moon and made a deal. Every night I would stand there for a moment, look up at her in all her phases, and write one image, one line.

"Moments with The Moon"

The cloud came across the moon
        like a moustache
            then a toupee

                    Pudding on her face moon

          Duck behind cloud cover moon

                    The staring contest moon

   Blindfolded moon
              One-eye gypsy moon

        The moon takes a breath before her swim stroke

Moon in my ribs tonight

        The moon peeks from behind her blue velvet curtain

                    Owl Eye moon

           Full breasted moon

Mamma moon

              The moon she winked at me

     Breastfed moon

       Half cup moon

          Two-toned guillotine moon

Sleepy eyelid moon

Veiled moon

Moon in the eye socket of the cloud

Boomerang ricochet moon

Moon in her pendulum slingshot

Disappearing moon

The moon is gone

The moon drowned

Moon sails shoeblack sky

Whispering moon

Gagged moon

Whistling moon

Echo moon echo

Snaggletooth moon

Moon sickle

The call to the moon to see
what other souls answer

Faroukh showered after his shift at the gas station, jumped in my car, and we went to *Slave to the Grind,* the local coffee shop where I loved to sit and write. Tattooed baristas played upbeat Alt-Rock music, volleyed conversation, and hammered espresso out of tiny steel baskets between shots. I handed Faroukh a red composition book and a Bic pen to get him started and asked, "What's most confusing in English that you need to know now?" He answered a jumble of things and we landed on trying to differentiate ordinal directions: 1st, 2nd, 3rd, 4th. How to explain the different endings for each number? We went over it a few times and then he taught me the corollary in Arabic. Very confusing stuff. Three Muslim girls wearing *hijab* walked in laughing, bought iced hibiscus teas and sat at a table across from us. An elder gentleman followed them as a chaperone. He sat at his own table to give them space to talk and took an interest in what we were doing in our notebooks. He asked us who we were to each other. Faroukh and I looked at each other and laughed as if to say, "We don't know yet, we'll figure that out over time." I told the man we were doing a language exchange, and Faroukh added, "Yes I need the English." The feeling in the air was that we were starting some kind of epic journey together commencing with ordinal directions: 1st, 2nd, 3rd, 4th, 5th.

When we left, we stood outside for a while talking. The air hung thick, hot, humid. Not a breeze to be found. Faroukh fanned himself, saying he needed to find a wife, a Muslim girl, and get on a path for U.S. citizenship. So, I stepped back inside and asked the three girls where they hung out, where young people met each other these days, and they told me, "At the mosque in downtown Yonkers." Faroukh's face was flushed, mortified that I had spoken to the girls.

"You tell me you want to meet girls and find a wife. How you gonna do that? Go to the mosque Friday night. Some girl isn't gonna magically appear at the gas station."

The next day, Miss Too-Much-Thirty had a bright halogen spotlight installed outside my window, turning midnight into noon. Light blasted through the window blinds all night, bright as the lamps installed on drug dealing corners to erase night. During the day, the (odd) court was devoid of pink and purple. Dry yellowed grass remained with box-shaped and conical hedges. I craved to be where life was allowed to grow. I felt a biological urge in my gut, a yearning for Italy where I remembered pink and I remembered purple towering above and around me, where pink and purple could reach their full potential, where flowered bushes grew big as houses on streets, alleys, highway medians, along walls, and dripping down balconies. After losing my mother, the imperative to get back to the motherland beckoned, if only to be surrounded by immensities of pink and purple. Looking out my window into the erased night sky, the thought struck me—this is what the landlord did. Erase. Erase night.

Chapter Three. "The Cinderella Call"

Yonkers, New York, March 2018

ALL FAROUKH KNEW OF AMERICA was the gas station. He collapsed after work, said his prayers, cried himself to sleep, got up and went back to work. I told him I was going to write him a tragic *aria*, "America is a gas station to me." He cried, describing his days as prison:

"All I know of America is the gas station. The gas station. Believe me, I am like machine, for two years. It's too hard here. You have to get papers, money, for what? Find the girl, see what she does. It's too much. I want to go home. It's a beautiful life. You don't need much. I am *fellahin*. I love these people. Pure hearts. I want to go right now."

"You can't just work in the gas station for two years then go back to your country. At least see New York City. There's a whole country here. So many beautiful places." He was insistent that besides learning English, what he most needed was to find a girl to marry and a Muslim community to fit into, so I took him out one night during Ramadan on a mosque expedition. He wore a red velvet blazer and slip-on sneakers with red, orange, and yellow flowers. I pulled up to 96th and Lex in Manhattan and showed him where to enter the big mosque on the corner. "The Imam is great in there," I told him. "I've heard him speak a few times." Faroukh ran across Lex. There was no parking, so I waited in the car. After ten minutes he came running out, saying the mosque was beautiful, but he didn't make any connections or pick up any community flyers. We headed downtown. The second mosque we drove to was on 9th Street in the East Village. While Faroukh went inside to see how he felt, I was content to write in my notebook and breathe in the action of the city. The East Village always felt like home to me. Streets you could walk without being judged. Faroukh came running out quickly again. He was like Goldilocks, no matter how many mosques we went to, he didn't find a mosque to fit him exactly right. As we drove around the East Village, we practiced ordinal directions in English and Arabic. "If you are looking for *haram*, this is the place to find it. It's all out here." I pointed at the myriad of folks in the crosswalk. "Whatever you want.

Haram. Look around. *Haram, haram, haram.* Whatever you want, it's here." He laughed, playing the naive village boy saying he'd never been kissed, and was afraid to be out in the city alone. I took him at his word, and was happy enough to shepherd him along, glad to have a friend to ride shotgun in the passenger seat that had been my mother's place to sit. The car had felt so devastatingly empty without her. I could still see her white sneaker tapping, keeping time, singing along as we blasted her feel-good songs: Bee Gees's "Stayin' Alive," Cyndi Lauper's "Girls Just Wanna Have Fun," and Sinatra's "Lady Luck." When my mother's foot was tapping, I knew everything was okay.

From the East Village I drove Faroukh over the Brooklyn Bridge to Atlantic Avenue where I rolled the windows down and waited 'til we heard the muezzin call to prayer. "Go!" I told him, "There's the door. That's where you go. Follow those guys." He disappeared into the building and came running out not long after, saying someone tried to steal his shoes.

"I ran inside. I eat the date. I take off my shoes. I go to pray, but as soon as I take off my shoes, a man asks me for money. I tell him, "Brother, I am here alone. I have no family." He said, "Brother, I am the same." I picked up my shoes. He goes to grabbing my shoes. I ran out of there. Enough with the mosques."

"*Alhamdulillah,* you didn't lose those flowered shoes, those are spiffy shoes." I could see he was shaken.

"Let's get ice-cream."

We went to an ice-cream parlor with a roof garden near the Gowanus Canal. As charming as it was, this was the gentrified Brooklyn I felt out of place in and couldn't afford. Brooklyn was my past life. I felt like a ghost walking these streets. I could hear the barks of my dogs who were no longer alive. I remembered the nights we walked down every one of these streets, my dogs marking their territory. Every corner was a place where I had memories of my girlfriend who was gone. Brooklyn felt out of reach and long ago and far away. I showed Faroukh the building where I lived for fifteen years and told him how we'd lost the lease to the apartment when the neighborhood flipped to the rich. I felt so alone even though my family had been in America for a hundred years. Faroukh talked of his parents' pressure on him to get married and start a family, and how he ached being so far away from his mother and father and siblings and cousins. It was an unimaginable challenge to grow roots in America out of thin air. He was all by himself. His paradox was that he craved a sense of freedom without the eyes of the village on his back, but at the same time he longed for the simple life of the village, embedded in family and culture and food and music and religion, a sense of belonging. As he talked, he exposed for me, my own desire to get back to my ancestral towns in the south of Italy. Twenty-two years had passed since I'd been in the *Mezzogiorno*. I'd first found many of my cousins when I traveled there after college, but I knew there were many more cousins who I'd not yet met; parts of myself I needed to retrieve. Faroukh and I both felt rootless, but at different stages of life.

As we drove back to Yonkers, we both had the feeling we were driving away from our lives instead of towards it.

A door kicked open. Out of the blue I received an email from Stan Pugliese, a historian and author I greatly admired. It was March 2018. Stan emailed a handful of us poets with news about, *"Napoli Città Libro,"* a literature festival in the heart of the old city. One of the organizers, Francesco Durante, invited Stan to bring Italian American poets to perform readings on a literary tour through the *Mezzogiorno*. "Francesco's only criteria," Stan wrote, "is that the events be delirious, wild, and joyous. I immediately thought of you."

It was a Cinderella call, long after I'd given up on Cinderella calls. I wrote back, "I'm in," clicked *send,* and fantasized about how the hell I'd raise the dough to get to *Napoli* in two months' time. Whenever I wanted to do something that required money I didn't have, a wave of heat wrapped around my gut. "Living beyond your means" was a sin in my world. Intergenerational poverty incinerated hopes and dreams. My mother's voice echoed in my mind: "Poverty is a thief who robs you of your talent."

Getting invited back to the *Matriamia* as a poet was epic enough, but *Napoli! Napoli* was the Bronx of Italy, where street interactions reigned, defining life. I'd felt most alive in the streets of cities where people interacted loudly, spontaneously, without any introduction: the Bronx, New Orleans, *Napoli*, and points unknown to me but that I imagined. Both *Napulitan'* Francesco Durante and *Newyorkese* Stan Pugliese were scholars who appreciated this *modo di vivere*. They'd dedicated their lives to the study of Italian history and literature, Italian American literature, and shared a devotion for the lifeblood of *Napoli*—the people in all their passion and raucousness. Stan and Francesco were dream Virgilian guides. Stan's scholarship threw light on subjects I loved—Primo Levi, Ignazio Silone, WWII history, and everyday life in *Napulitan'* neighborhoods. Francesco was a legendary *Napulitane* native son, writer, and literary scholar, with a mystique of folklore cloaked about him. He was the last person to be born *a casa*, at home, on the island of *Capri* in 1952 after which, women were ferried to the mainland city hospitals to deliver. Francesco's massive opus: "*Italoamericana*: The Literature of The Great Migration 1880-1943," collected a jaw-dropping eight hundred pages of writings of the great wave of Italian immigrants to America. Reading these works, you can hear the English cracking like walnuts in the writers' mouths.

Faroukh came over when I was in the middle of an art project. The living room was covered in paint, gaffer tape, Styrofoam, and cardboard. I'd cut a refrigerator box open, ripped sheaths were strewn about. I was sculpting a life-size prop bathtub for my book launch. Faroukh was flummoxed at what I was doing and amazed that someone would spend time in a self-directed way. "You do all this yourself? All your idea? Nobody tells you what to do?" In my mess of cardboard, tape and paint, I could see clearly the sculpture taking shape. From an outside eye it looked like I was living in an encampment inside a living room. I explained my idea to him, "The world throws parties called "showers" for engagements and pregnancies and so forth, so I'm creating a new type of party for when you give birth to a book. Instead of a "shower" I'm calling it a "bath," a "book bath." We're going to celebrate my new book." I didn't know if I was making sense to him. I continued, "People will get a book, step into the bathtub and two people, one on either side, will shake it, and a blue mylar curtain will rain over them while they are read to, aloud, from the new book. They come out transformed. It's a literary ablution." Faroukh laughed at the absurdity and whimsical nature of what I was doing.

I told him about Stan Pugliese's invitation to go back to Italy as an author. Faroukh gave me practical advice, "If you don't have the money right now, you can always save the money and go next year."

"That kind of talk makes me crazy. Next year never comes." My sword and shield went up. The concept of *next year* was alien to me. After surviving cancer after cancer from the time I was a teenager, then caregiving my mother until I made the hardest decision of my life—to call off the rapid response team as they snapped blue rubber gloves on to intubate her—that practical talk made me nuts.

"There is no tomorrow," I told him. "There never was. I feel this inner pressure like an air pump from the voices of my cancer buddies who died as teenagers." For anyone who *capeeshes* how to read Italian eyebrows, my expression was crystal clear. *Next year never comes.* Faroukh understood eyebrows. He said he was feeling miserable and trapped pumping gas to save money for a future he couldn't yet define or barely imagine. He was working for *next year.* He asked me to tell him how I felt. "I can never think a few years down the road," I said. "I never thought I'd live that long. We all have our inner clock. It's hard to express my inner sense of time. Time ran out long ago. The meter is already expired. You see this parking meter?" I showed him the parking meter I kept on my writing desk, my *memento mori* from the streets. "I feed this thing quarters" I told him. "A quarter an hour. Then I write. It reminds me, time is up. Look, it says *expired*."

The clock smells waste. An already expired meter. Whitman's imperative howled inside me, "Dismiss what insults your soul." I did a lot of dismissing every day. The calendar bled out. The voices of my dead friends revved inside me with a torque force pressure to *do* the most with my allotted time. I was a brass bell, and their words, the inner gong. Their voices each rang a note in my soul. Reverberations. Calls for urgency. Inner 911. The meter is always ticking. Beating in increments.

I told Faroukh two long stories about friends of mine whose voices pumped loudest inside me at that time. I'd made vows to each of them in recent months, to Athena that I would travel while I could still breathe on my own without oxygen, and to Timothea that I would get to Sicily while I was alive. Here are those stories, not as I told them to Faroukh, but more in detail, the written versions . . .

Chapter Four. "19"

Memorial Sloan Kettering Cancer Center,
New York, New York, October 2016

ATHENA WAS ADMITTED TO THE 19TH FLOOR of Memorial Sloan Kettering Cancer Center. She messaged our Long-Term Hodgkin's Disease Survivors' Group that she wanted visitors. I just happened to be in the building, which wasn't rare, not rare at all. I'd been a patient there since I was eighteen, and had a doctor for every organ system: lung, heart, blood and lymph, breast, vagina, thyroid, skin, colon, kidney, eyes, ear nose throat, sleep, a physiatrist for my irradiated neck, a paralyzed vocal cord expert, a specialist in long-term late-effects of radiation and chemotherapy, plus specialty surgeons for boutique parts, and finally other doctors so hyper-specialized I wouldn't know how to classify them—over seventeen doctors at any one time. Sixty days a year I averaged being on-site, for tests, and follow-up appointments. Every couple of years there was something growing inside me that the surgeons cut out: tumors, a schwannoma, suspicious lumps, cysts, organs gone awry, whatever. I was always grateful when they could do something about it. Lucky. Lucky to breathe. Lucky to walk out of there. Sloan Kettering was my *Hotel California*, "You can check in any time you like, but you may never leave."

I messaged Athena that I could come up and visit. That day I was at Sloan Kettering as my mother's caregiver. Mom was on 12, and Athena on 19. Sloan truly was our second home—and in many ways, our first. It was the only place my mother and I ever had our own two beds. At home, one or the other of us slept on the couch, one arm hanging off the edge. And it was the only place our whole lives together that we ever had a river view with soaring sunrises.

19 was the VIP floor. No one could access 19 unless you were announced and buzzed up. I got into the elevator. Thoughts swerved through my mind about all of us around the world who'd survived Hodgkin's Disease as teenagers and who corresponded with each other. Athena and I had never met in person. My heart was racing, I was meeting a long-lost sister. We knew each other in the deep way

trench mates do—an innate knowledge of each other's ordeal—no questions asked. It's a rare compassionate intimacy of vulnerabilities down to our bone marrow and vagus nerves. We experienced the same range of regimes of chemotherapy, radiation and surgery, and suffered similar ravages from the treatments. Grateful to be alive, we had trouble breathing, swallowing, feeling the tips of our fingers, holding our heads atop fibrosed necks, and our lungs and hearts had borne the brunt of radiation and chemo.

The elevator opened. Hospital pastel hues swapped out for hotel cherry wood furniture, a crystal chandelier and hand-painted blue china. 19 had a mystique about it. The concierge behind a mahogany desk like a hotel, told me to wait. I hadn't been up to 19 since 1981, thirty-five years earlier, when 19 housed experimental bone marrow transplants and I waved at friends in sealed off rooms through see-through walls off the corridor. I don't remember if they were glass or plastic at the time, just that there was a dusky blue glow permeating the west end of the floor. Friends reduced to peach fuzz skulls too heavy for their necks, friends who dreamed of breathing blessed street air once again—anything to get back out onto asphalt and cement. We once were teenagers with blood and lymphatic cancers, now, those of us still alive, one by one by one, had hearts failing and lungs seizing. We were the first generation in human history to survive these cancers and these treatments. Nitrogen Mustard, the fourth of eleven chemotherapeutic agents that I'd received, was developed after a WWII German bombing of twenty-eight Allied ships on December 2nd, 1943, in the port of Bari—my ancestors' neck of the woods. Mustard gas leaked from U.S. bombs secretly stored on the SS *John Harvey*, resulted in the torturous deaths of an untold number of soldiers and civilians; thousands died. The scientists who observed their low blood counts under autopsy were brilliant enough to seek other applications in cancer treatment from the Nitrogen Mustard, thus inaugurating cancer chemotherapy. These agents were given to us Baby Boomers and over the decades, refined. Some of us outlived early predictions and best hopes. Gifted with decades of survival, we suffered stripped immune systems. My Infectious Disease doctor had once told me point-blank: "Your chest is World War III. Nuked." My oncologist told me, "We'd never do today, what we did to you then." A specialist told me, "You're a prisoner to the medical machine." The cardiologist told me, "You got away with murder." Ensuing generations benefitted from the studies done on our bodies and collectively, that felt like a boon. We willingly signed up to be part of randomization trials to add to the data to save the next generation. Our bodies were red carpets for the next ones coming down the pike.

An escort met me at the concierge desk and walked me down the hall directly toward Athena's room so I wouldn't wander into some celebrity's room. A nurse once told me that medical care wasn't any different or better on 19 but you got amenities *beau coup*, a private room, and architectural details that softened the fact that you were in a hospital. A couple of thousand bucks extra per night got you a stay up here. As we walked down the hall, it jarred me, the comforts money could buy. All the details hit me at once: the hallway carpeted in a lush blue and gold floral design, no names on any of the room doors. Privacy! In a hospital? *That's* luxury. My body and life had been splayed open my whole adult life here, as split open as a flimsy hospital gown. An open doorway flashed a vast room with gold tieback drapes, gold painted moldings, a white couch with striped olive, rust and gold throw pillows like a fancy hotel conference room. Individual room doors themselves were dark wood, mahogany or cherry with shiny brass lever handles and kick plates.

The escort knocked on Athena's room door and waited for her to answer. She was sitting up in bed. It's easier to breathe sitting up. Long-term survivors know this. We prop ourselves up with extra pillows and neck supports. Athena had a striking elegance about her, intelligent wide-set Jackie-O brown eyes, neck tendons pumping like pistons to breathe, and a thin neck that was our signature from radiation fibrosis. We both opened our arms toward each other as if to come in for a long-awaited landing, but I quickly said, "Let me wash my hands first." This was *de rigueur* for us, the immunocompromised. The bathroom had soft marble earth tones and a chic sliding door with a stack of soft towels folded hotel style, a back-lit mirror and a lavender scent, it didn't smell like a hospital; the soaps, shampoo, everything was upscaled.

I pulled up a cushioned wooden chair, sat beside her bed and we rested in a gentle hug, holding on for dear life, breathing, as our hearts knocked at each other's ribs. It was a relief to find someone *who knew.* Athena was ahead of me in terms of post-radiation lung fibrosis. I was looking at my future. How far away was anybody's guess. We both teared up as we talked, affirming all we'd survived and the thousand times our bodies had been poked, prodded, pricked, cut open, scanned, beamed, infused. I took it all in, a vision of my future. Tethered to oxygen, laboring to breathe, Athena talked only of things that counted. Our calcified coronary arteries and scorched lungs gave us urgency. "Travel while you can," she urged me in her hoarse voice I knew well from fibrosis, "while you're not tied to an oxygen tank."

"I promise."

These words and phrases passed between us: "We made it this far." "We're here now." "Now's all there ever is." "You take care of yourself." "Get your rest." "Drink plenty of water." We talked about the effects of treatments we'd undergone and a little about the cancers themselves, all the tumors that got lost in the shadows of our conversation because this far down the road, the ramifications of treatment overshadowed our wild anarchic cellular overgrowth. We held each other knowing this was the only hour we would ever share together breathing on this earth, though we'd been in and out of the same exact machines and doctors' offices and hospital doorways for decades like a carousel—one gets off the other gets on. There was no pretending, *let's have lunch,* or wishful thinking, *hope to see you again.* We knew too much. Too much for any of that. I felt her ribs as we hugged, intercostal muscles pulling with all their might, taut as rubber bands.

The details of the room stung me. Out of all of it: the plush bed—not standard where the sheets pop off the plastic corners and you slide off the edge, the bronze reading room lamps set in the walls to be easy on the eyes around a giant flat screen TV, what absolutely stung the most was the guest pull-out bed in the wall for caregivers. It's impossible to quantify the suffering this would have alleviated for us over the decades. Each floor had portable convertible chair-beds, but there were too many nights even these weren't available, and my mother or one or another of us passed out, exhausted, neck bent at a right angle in a chair, or two chairs pulled together and nowhere, after a three-day stint, for a caregiver to shower. All caregivers need a place to rest, not just caregivers who can afford a place to rest. So much suffering, in the end, had been completely unnecessary. There were solutions for necessities like sleep we'd done without. But no comforts or human amenities could soften the hard truth: Athena would be tethered to oxygen for the remaining weeks of her life, every single breath a struggle. We held each other strong and long, the life force pulsing through and coursing around us. I wished I could have given her my oxygenated cells. My lungs were tight but working. Athena repeated the message: "Travel while you can breathe on your own without oxygen." She was adamant. This was a warning. A clarion call. *This is it kid.* The word "travel," rang in my heart. This was soul talk. Her words engraved on the marble tablet of my heart.

"I'll travel," I vowed.

Athena died weeks later, and my mother—months.

Chapter Five. "Three Pens for the Road"

Massachusetts, August 13th, 2017

ONE MORNING I WAS AWAKENED with a clear thought, loud like an alarm: "Go see Timothea." It was a year after Athena and my mother died. I hadn't seen Timothea in nine years since we'd each been caregivers to our mothers, she in D.C., me in New York. Both our mothers suffered heart failure among other things, and we each stayed with them until the last breath. Timothea was a Marxist community organizer, an adult convert to Judaism, painter, photographer, wise woman, and now she'd been in a nursing home in central Massachusetts for sixty days. How someone so beloved, who had worked her whole life building up communities and had given so much to so many, ended up in a nursing home, angered but didn't baffle me. The world is inside-out. This is exactly what happens in our society if you're alone, aging, poor, and sick. Poverty is a killer that erodes you over time. As it rushes time along. The cracks in the system are indeed crevasses, and in a glacier, a crevasse like a moulin can be hundreds and hundreds of feet deep. You fall, you're gone. Into the ice.

It was a good day for driving, a clear bright powder blue sky, the kind of crisp air that's perfect for flying single-engine planes; wings are responsive in cool air. Driving with the windows all the way down gave me, in a small way, the sense of risk and adventure I'd felt in my twenties when I got licensed as a private pilot and felt everything was possible as long as I was breathing. I inhaled deeply, howled into the wind, and cried for the mercurial loss of that feeling. Where did it go? I asked the wind.

Timothea texted me a list of what she called contraband—snacks and treats she wanted. I hit a couple stores, grabbed double whatever she'd asked for, and on a whim bought a gorgeous pot of deep purple bluebells. I kept driving. I was looking at about three hours of road in front of me. She'd given me explicit instructions to go to the Kentucky Fried Chicken just up the street from the nursing home so the mash potatoes and gravy would be steaming hot when I got to her. As I drove, I listened to horrifying news on talk radio; Virginia was in a state of emergency over a white power march the night before in Charlottesville. My heart beat fast. I gripped the steering wheel with tension. At 75MPH I turned off the news and changed the station to blues.

Thoughts catalogued in my mind, back to how Timothea and I had met eighteen years before in privileged circumstances as Rockefeller Foundation fellows, and the hopes and dreams we'd had for our lives and work. Over the course of five years, the foundation had brought over a hundred of us together, innovators from every sector, class, race, you name it, and offered us opportunities to self-organize around projects furthering democracy and social justice. Timothea was famous in the group for saying, "We're not supposed to be in the same room together," pointing out the potential power and explosiveness of the collisions of all our differing politics and world views. Gorgeous debates and clashes began. Both Timothea and I loved a good debate. I believed that argument was an opportunity for creative conflict, and that that's where the gold was to be found in a pluralistic society. Everybody, potentially, could benefit. The trick was to create the conditions where everyone rose above division for division's sake, to make room for the vast array of perspectives.

Timothea and I, as part of a sub-group of artists, visited communities with arts and social justice initiatives. All history is women's history erased. So, I'm writing the names of the artists here: Cara Page, Liz Canner, Kathie deNobriga, Pam McMichael, and our facilitators— Elizabeth Kasl and Doug Paxton. While we were on the road, I met activists who opened my mind. I struck up a conversation with Ramona Africa on a street corner in Philadelphia on the anniversary of the day the city dropped a bomb on the MOVE house she was in, killing eleven. And at Highlander, Tufara Waller Muhammad sang into the wind coming off the Smoky Mountains under the stars one night around a fire. Tufara was steeped in the tradition of songs from the civil rights movement, and she organized initiatives throughout the south and Africa. She would become a cherished friend. There are nights in life I want a thousand of, but I'm lucky if I get one in a lifetime. That night of Tufara singing on the mountain at Highlander was one such night.

Timothea and I got to know each other on the road driving to Appalshop in Whitesburg, Kentucky. We talked about going to Sicily one day as an extension of this quest. Sicily and the *Mezzogiorno* were a crossroads of Africa and Europe. The goal was always to change the world, to change ourselves, to cause a shift. As Timothea said to the group, "Helping children find their voice doesn't keep people from being evicted." She tagged her emails with a Miguel de Unamuno quote. "My job is to agitate and disturb people. I'm not selling bread; I am selling yeast." Some letters she signed with her new Hebrew name first, then her birth name in parentheses all in lower case: *Ruth Elisheva Bat Avraham v Sarah (timothea howard)*. She was focused on, as she said, "bringing up the next generation of Marxists." As the years went on, she expressed feeling more and more alone in the struggle as some of her key comrades died and, "Others ran for the cover of respectable jobs, politics, and the suburbs." She said she felt "orphaned," as they "left the stage."

The nursing home was tucked away on a quiet road on a couple of acres of land in rural Massachusetts. Grass. Trees. Breeze. Quiet. As I walked under the green awning of the entranceway carrying big heavy brown paper bags in each arm, a man in a wheelchair looked up at me, asking, "You havin' a party?" And we did. Bedside. I covered the hospital table with a purple tie-dyed cloth, arranged the pot of purple bluebells and set out the feast. Timothea sat all the way up in bed, legs over the side, a blue, green and gold kente cloth over her shoulders around her Wedgewood blue hospital gown, embodying the wise regal queen she was. She was a mountain of a woman with soft graying dreadlocks and insatiable curious eyes behind round eyeglasses. As we hugged, I rested my head on her softness. The bluebells sparked her smile:

"I know what I'm gonna do, tonight I'll draw a picture of these. What a color! *Oh,* I need this today, you don't know how I needed this today."

We talked about Charlottesville and the state of the country. Timothea was less shocked than I. We spoke of the hubris, whereas the Klan used to be hooded, now white supremacy groups were out in the open, marching through town carrying tiki torches, gathering at the statue of Robert E. Lee, taking selfies of one another, and posting on social media. Their faces spread all over the world within minutes. There it is, there are the faces clear as day. Blonde boys with a vacuous hunger in their pale eyes. We shared the unbearable feeling of being too fragile to be out on the streets with other activists. Timothea was sidelined, bedridden. We shared the toll caregiving had taken on our health, on top of grieving the losses of our mothers, and agreed, "It's time we take care of ourselves now." Timothea came to this conversation like all our conversations, even though I felt we had fallen far as a society, she shared an urgency to move the world forward, and the assertion—*we are moving forward.*

"The young are picking up the struggle."

I spread out her banquet, over which she recited a prayer in Hebrew and invoked our mothers' names, Ella and Rachele. We talked about our mother's lives. Timothea asked me to bring the cranberry juice and some of the treats to the nurse to put in a fridge for the coming days, and the nurse at the station was happy to oblige. When I came back into the room, I saw on the other side of the curtain her roommate was out of it, no movement, no sound, not an utterance. Timothea acknowledged her with a sweeping gesture in a sign of prayer to include her too in the supper blessing.

As we ate, Timothea inquired about practicalities first, "And you're covered? Health insurance?"

"Yes, right now I have Medicare and straight Medicaid. I need four legs under the table. Medicare and Medicaid are two."

"That's it. That's why I'm staying in Massachusetts, you know, the health care. I hope to plug into more life-saving services."

"Yes, I *capeesh. Capeesh tutto.*"

"*Brava.* I know you *capeesh!* We gotta get to *Sicilia!* And you have housing?"

"Yep. I fought to get on my mother's lease before she died, you know, so I wouldn't be in a housing crisis right after. Too old to couch surf."

"Tell me about it. Rent stabilized?"

I nodded.

"That's it. So that's three legs under the table. Now we gotta get you a fourth leg."

We laughed. "Well, I got Disability. That's four."

"You're all set!"

"No one wants to live like this, but I thank the Goddess every day for my mother who kept this lease, and for the United States Federal Government and the State of New York and the City of Yonkers. Without their programs and protections, I'd be out on the streets. I mean . . . the lengths we go through, with disabilities, to get health care and keep health care. It's ruined my career in so many ways, you know, people always say, "Why don't you teach as an adjunct professor in some college?" They don't realize, with part-time work, I'd lose everything, all the benefits, *poof!*"

"Health care is a right and should be covered across the board. Period."

"I know, I know. I kept working and getting pneumonia, going into classrooms to teach and getting pneumonia. Every time I had a job, I got pneumonia. How many dozen times can one pair of lungs get pneumonia and still be walking around? When I applied for jobs, I had to think, is it worth getting pneumonia? Worse, if you're sick and poor in this country, it's like you're a criminal. And if you got my Bronx accent, *faget it*, people assume you're thieving."

"And you're not even black!" And we laughed even harder. "I want you to remember something. When you're working in community, when you're teaching, or out in the streets, remember this. This is what I tell the young ones coming up. Give, but not to the point it hurts you. Give your time when it makes sense and can significantly change outcomes."

"That's not always so easy. I grew up believing in sacrifice. My mother, my father, all they did was sacrifice for others. My mother didn't have a selfish bone in her body, and my father was cannon fodder. His health, his mental health, all was sacrificed in the war. Forget working-class, he was part of the sacrificial class."

"But don't sacrifice *you*. We need you in the game. Get it?"

"I got it. It drove my father nuts, civilian life. He couldn't cope with the self-serving nature of it all."

"I'm takin' that in," Timothea closed her eyes for a beat, "considering how much damage he did, out of the damage done to him. It's important to see history, to understand history." Then she said something that changed the trajectory of my attention forever. "If you want to know the true history, the people's history, read song lyrics. That's the history I trust. It's all written in song. Folk song."

We ate and talked about music and survival. We talked about the poet who wrote "Strange Fruit," Abel Meeropol. I sang her a couple of the songs I'd written for my mom after she died. Timothea encouraged me to keep writing songs and poetry. Then we got back to the practicalities of life, and the process of getting on SSD, Social Security Disability. I told her all about it:

"To get on SSD, you gotta go to the SSD doctor. They got their own doctors, their own psychiatrists. You gotta go to *their* doctors. What a *fiasco*. He sees on my chart it says, "neuropathy." So, you're not gonna believe what the creep does. Wait, *yeah*, he sweeps my hair off my right ear with his hand and says, "*Aha!* But you can put on earrings!""

"*Whaaaat!* He touched your hair?"

"*Yeah*, at the time, my hair covered my ears. Of course, I didn't have on earrings, I can't put on earrings, if you see me try to put on earrings it's like watching a dog put on earrings with his paws. Can't be done. I can't snap my fingers; I mean try being an Italian entertainer and you can't snap your fingers. No fun. Imagine Dean Martin if he couldn't snap his fingers. If he couldn't snap his fingers, there'd be no Dino Martino. I can't button, can't tie shoes, I have trouble with keys and zippers. I told him, "Doc, I can't put on earrings." *Fagetaboutit.* And my eyes are always red 'cause I don't have a thyroid, so they assume I'm stoned. I cough a lot cause the radiation knocked out my salivary glands and paralyzed my left vocal cord. So, I'm coughing, dropping things, and my eyes are red, and I have this Bronx accent. This doctor's looking at me like I'm a criminal Dago trying to get away with something. He asks me if I can lift ten pounds and carry it three feet. The Social Security Administration still defines work as Work = Force x Distance, the formula we learned in grade school. So, I gotta tell him, "No, I absolutely cannot carry ten pounds three feet," because that's the definition of work and then I am able to work full time. I'd like to see him try to survive in my body. *Fagetit.* Anyway, everyone gets rejected at first. So, I hadda go before a judge. I didn't bother getting a lawyer, I just had Sloan Kettering print out my medical chart and a list of my appointments for the year, it was two reams of paper. I handed the whole stack to the judge, which in effect was carrying ten pounds three feet, but anyway, the judge was an intelligent man, an elder with a full head of thick white hair. Judges can be very wise. His name was Lazarus. He looked at my file, and shook his head, "I'm so sorry, you've been through so much," and he apologized that they'd rejected my application, and he immediately approved my case. Lazarus resurrected me."

Timothea laughed, and the name Lazarus prompted a talk about death. Timothea laid down a plain simple truth, "They say things like, *he took off his overcoat,* or *she's transitioning,* or *he's in a better place.* No, you die. Plain and simple."

I told her about my old friend Elias, a Rastafarian street poet in Providence who said that of the dead—*he took off his overcoat.* "Coming from Elias it sounded good back then. Maybe death is *taking off an overcoat.* That's one way to look at it. Though, part of me thinks death is an ending and Heaven a cover-up. You know, we look up to an imagined Heaven because we're going down into the earth. No, let's talk about going down into the earth, becoming earth again, and wind. Giving our matter back to the earth and our spirit back to the wind. On the other hand, there's this old part of me that fully believes angels have wings and the wind is the Divine Mother's Breath. It goes back to childhood. My mother's breath was my first sentient experience. When I feel a soft breeze on my cheek it brings me back to my earliest experience of my mother holding me cheek to cheek and feeling her exhale out her nostrils onto my cheek. When she rocked me in the maple rocking chair, I felt the wind on my neck, her breath. The wind is my mother's breath. The wind, I am sure, will take me. Wind comforts me for death. I wanna be the wind. In Divine Mother's Breath. Whaddyacall these bones on your back? Do you call these angel wings? On your back, whaddyacall those bones? My mother called these angel wings. Did you grow up calling them that? Wings are the way to know wind. The heft, the body of wind.

Sometimes I dream I have wings, grand magnificent silvery wings, and when I wake up, I can feel them. She always told me those bones were where our wings were clipped."

"I think those are called the scapula bones," Timothea smiled. We laughed, ate and jousted. "As they tell me at the synagogue—you give good drash—meaning midrash, a debate over exegesis of the Talmud." Her eyes widened and her hands opened like she was tossing an idea into the air. "You know, something bothers me! I keep thinking—why are Annie and I in this situation? Why? Why! I keep thinking, how are me and Annie gonna make it to Broadway and to Sicily? What do we have to write to get to Broadway? How are we gonna get to Sicily?"

"Yes Sicily, Sicily, *ahh Sicilia*," I chimed in. "*Sicilia's* gotta be next. Spirit list. Gotta get there. Gotta happen. *A Sicilia!*" Considering the straitjacket of health and finances, I figured I better lead us both there right in the moment. "Timothea, let's close our eyes, go to *Sicilia* right now. Close your eyes. Deep breath. Feel the breeze. *Andiamo a Sicilia, 'iammo 'iamm 'iamm.* We just landed in Palermo. We're walking. *Cammina, cammina.* I see a hill. Terraces, clotheslines, lemon trees, a road leading downhill to the sea. The houses are white. *Terracotta* roofs. Fishing boats bobbing. Blue, green. A red flashing light reflecting in the water. I hear the water slapping the ribs of the boats. What do you see?"

"I see waves. Laughing, I hear children's laughter. I breathe in the sea air. I feel the sun on my face. There are people all around. A bicycle. And motor scooters, those Italian Vespas."

"I am walking up the hill from the water. I see white low houses with flowers on the balcony. All kinds of flowers."

"Yes, flowers. Flowers everywhere. And seagulls. I hear seagulls. I see seagulls eating. I'm tossing them good Italian bread. *Ayyy,* they're loving it. And *mozzarella.* I love *mozzarella.* All the birds are coming."

We laughed. Went deeper. I saw lemons. "I'm setting up to paint still life portraits of lemons. I'm walking up a hill, carrying yellow paint and a paintbrush. I'm gonna paint lemons, that's all I'm gonna do from now on, paint still lifes of lemons. I feel the wind coming off the sea. I wonder what's the name of that wind. Whaddyacall that wind?"

"It's hopping up from Africa."

"Yes, the wind off the Sahara. Up from Africa."

"*Oooh* a warm breeze, and I hear drums. I know what I'm gonna do. I'm gonna paint these bluebells tonight."

I opened my eyes. The bluebells seemed the most beautiful garden in the world, a regal purple, that deep blue purple like stained glass windows, like ancient royal robes, like rosary beads.

We wrapped our arms around each other. Hugs are never long enough. Then she opened her bedside table and pulled out art supplies: colored pens and pencils and markers and her notebook. She turned the pot of bluebells to see all sides. "Let's see, I'll draw from this direction. *Hmmm,* the perfume." She spread pens on the purple tie-dyed cloth. "Take three," she said. Giving out cool pens was one of her missions. Every time we'd ever met over the years, she'd offer me three pens: interesting pens, calligraphy tips, fountain pens, ballpoint pens, all color inks. She was a collector of cool pens. Choosing three made me feel special. This time I chose a tiny silver pen that fit in the palm of my hand like a silver bullet, a purple pen, and a fountain pen that looked like a green water pistol on the outside and was fun to hold. This was Timothea: handing out pens full of ink and salient questions.

As I walked out of the room, she said to me what she always said, "My arms are always around you."

A wave of cool night air whooshed upon me as the front door slid open and the stifling heat snapped back inside the yellow halls of the nursing home. I stepped out into the bite of night. Cool darkness was a lot better to drive in than a blinding sunset. My heart capsized with the wish to get her out of there and back to work in the world, plan an adventure while we both were still alive, and join the protests in the city streets. The cold air smacked me awake as I drove west.

The next day I received word from a mutual friend. Timothea died that night.

Deep purple was the last color she drew. Deep purple was the color Timothea went out on, deep purple blue purple.

Chapter Six. "Blue Onion"

Yonkers, New York, March 2018

I SAT IN MY MOTHER'S APARTMENT ALONE and stared at the floor, wondering what to do. I thought about Stan and Francesco's invitation. Athena and Timothea's voices ricocheted inside me. "*Travel while you can. While you can breathe on your own.*" "*How we gonna get to Sicily?*" "*Listen to folk lyrics if you want to know the true history.*" In the last year of her life, my mother marveled at her blue onion patterned floor, "Imagine? This linoleum lasted all these years. Never even wore down or pulled up." At the time, I wasn't exactly sure what she meant. She knew lots that I didn't, like what happened to floors over time. I looked down at her blue onion linoleum. She picked it out in 1975, and after she died in 2016, the floor began to wear out in the middle, as if it missed her gentle shuffling footsteps. The floor chipped and kicked up under my feet, under the chair legs, split with a cracking sound like I was stepping on crab shells. The motif separated from the base and left a fossil imprint of ghost lace. Was the floor protesting my lumbering heavy walk? For over a year, I'd been stepping on crab shells. "It's gotta go, now's the time," I thought. In that moment, I pulled the whole floor up with my bare hands, dragged it outside and began to lug the sheaths down the hill to the dumpster, but when the sunlight glazed it, the beauty of the pattern magnified and I realized how irreplaceable it was, you couldn't find such vintage linoleum like that anymore. Suddenly I could see my mother clearly and remembered how she adored that blue onion pattern, how she'd scrubbed it on her hands and knees and waxed it to a shine with soft white cotton rags, scraps of old t-shirts or socks or pillowcases that had graduated to take on the bigger jobs. I remembered how I ran and skidded in my booties on the days Mom waxed the floor, the maroon with baby blue trim booties Grandma Rose had knitted for my feet. I pictured my mother sitting on the kitchen floor reorganizing canned tomatoes, *cannellini* and *ceci* beans in the bottom cabinets that served as her pantry. That floor had brought her joy.

I dragged all the sheaths back inside the apartment. My hands were blackened from the filth on the underside. I laughed at myself. I remember having this realization: nothing would please my mother more than if I sold her old floor to raise money to go to Italy. I laughed hard. Either I was losing my mind or onto a new art project. Or both. I flicked the blade of the gray box cutter my father had bequeathed to me long ago when he'd given me his old, rusted tools, and began to slice the floor into roughly six-inch squares. I sliced and snapped, sliced and snapped, careful to keep all my fingers. It took me all day. I put the hundreds of squares into my mother's white porcelain kitchen sink and soaked them in soap and bleach, in batches. I blasted Sinatra and the Bee Gees, her favorite songs, and cried. The squares curled in the water. Blue onion on white diamond squares.

My mother Rachele/Rachel/Lilly, had loved blue onion patterns her whole life, hunted for plates, cups, candle holders, bric-a-brac, whatever she could find. I'd joined this search with and for her. When I was sixteen in 1979, dusting place settings for $2.60 an hour in Roadside China on Central Avenue in Yonkers, I saved my weekly pay envelope and eventually bought her a complete set of four blue onion place settings: dinner plates with beveled edges, lunch plates, bowls, cups and saucers. And in 1986 in San Francisco when I was working as a bike messenger, I found three blue onion china canisters in the Salvation Army on Valencia Street in the Mission District and carried them all the way home to Winchester Ave in Yonkers, without breaking one. This was our safe house—our rifle—Winchester—like we had our own cavalry, and we did—Mom's front door, to shut out violent men, all threats, closed, secured and triple locked. In 1975, I was twelve when the workmen laid this blue onion linoleum down in one sheet on the kitchen and foyer floors and with their big iron cylindrical roller, went back and forth until it lay perfectly flat, even along the edges where the floor met the walls. And now in 2018, I'd cut it all up into pieces and washed the old floor in her sink. Was I nuts? Was I just like my father? He'd spent the better part of his last decade systematically taking things apart in the boiler room workshop of the mental home where he lived. I couldn't—wouldn't tell anybody what I was doing. Wet from the sink, I spread the 6"x6" tiles out, layered paper towel and flattened them with boxes of books, my new book I'd just gotten from the publisher. After four days of working in isolation, I told a few friends over the phone what I was up to, more as a mental health check than anything else. I convinced myself I was in the middle of an art project and happily I continued my task. After a week, the squares were dry and flat. I used one as a drink coaster as I stared at the squares wondering what to do next. I finally answered the phone and told some friends stories about the floor. Faroukh dropped by and again asked how I thought of these things to make. I couldn't explain how my mind works.

I typed up the story. The life of the floor. I arranged the words into a diamond shape, printed and cut out the diamond shaped texts, so they would fit onto the back of each square, one corner pointing up. Each problem was one step forward, each obstacle, a challenge of design. How to get the story laid-out in a perfect diamond? How to adhere the paper to the back of the linoleum? How to protect the ink from smearing? How to finish the edges? How to hang these on the wall? I laid all the squares out over the whole apartment and polished each one with floor wax. Then with my father's wooden handled awl, I hammered a hole into one corner of each tile and pulled a strand of Mom's ocean-blue scrap wool through with her tiny crochet hook. The squares of flooring now hung as "Story Tiles." It didn't escape me—I was polishing my mother's floor almost two years after she was gone, and hanging pieces of her floor on the walls, yet I was *faccia contenta* doing it, and the result was stunning. I wanted my mother's floor to shine forever, the way she had made life shine. Transformative. Gorgeous. Sparkling. This once in a lifetime floor. It is my mother's floor I stand on. I always will. A once in a lifetime floor.

I called my fundraising effort, the *"Bafanabla!* Campaign." *Bafanabla,* my father's go-to curse word, means "Go to *Napoli!*" or "Go make (or do) it in *Napoli!*" It's a curse only outside of Naples, equating Naples with Hell. I sold and auctioned off the "Story Tiles" as artifacts of our life. The fundraising campaign worked. Everyone was very generous, and soon there were pieces of my mother's floor hanging on walls in all my friends' homes, and I bought a plane ticket to *Napoli.* That vintage blue onion motif lived on.

In the apartment, underneath that layer of linoleum, the original flooring from the 1950's was revealed. Two things stunned me, "floored" me you might say. First, the underneath layer of flooring had a particular lay-out; the center of the floor was marked with a four-foot black rectangle with half-moon cut-outs in each of the corners. In that instant of seeing the floor I had a flashback to a ward in Sloan Kettering where I'd waited for echocardiograms. I'd stared at that floor for years, but I never knew why it captivated me until I ripped up my mother's linoleum and found the same geometric pattern; a rectangle with half-moon cut-outs in the corners, and inside, all the tiles positioned on angles as diamond shapes. And now seeing it, memories burst through the erstwhile fog. This floor was there when I'd first stepped into the apartment when Mom and I moved in over forty years before, when she'd escaped my father. This floor is what I bounced my Spaldeen on, tested out the bounce and echo of the new apartment and our new life alone on welfare together. The second thing that surprised me was the long straight cut marks in the flesh of the floor that I remembered making when my friends and I roller-skated around the apartment. One friend came in after falling off her skateboard, a rock embedded in her knee. I remembered the blood again now on the floor and squeezing her skin to get the rock out of the open wound. My mother became the hero that day when she came home from work, sterilized a pair of tweezers and pulled the rock right out. She had a delicate steady hand. Those skate marks were part of the reason we needed new linoleum in the first place. Once the blue onion linoleum was installed, I took off my roller-skates in the hallway.

The night of my "Book Bath" where I sold "Story Tiles," Faroukh took the train into Grand Central Station by himself for the first time and walked all the way to West 12th Street to where I was performing at New York University's *Casa Italiana Zerilli-Marimò*. But I never saw Faroukh. Later he told me that he'd stood in the back of the auditorium, and although he didn't have the words to express it, I could see that he'd felt so alone and estranged that he couldn't break through the crowd to join us. So, he walked back the way he came and slept on the train back to Yonkers. He was getting closer to throwing his body into the city with surrender, to enter wholeheartedly the anonymous chaos of the city streets.

A couple of weeks later he called, miserable and out of breath. "Whatsamatta?" I asked. He was despondent and couldn't put two words together. "What?" I asked, "You gotta move in with me?"

"Can I?"

"How long do you need to pack your stuff?"

"Two hours."

"You can stay here. But remember, I'm immunocompromised. So, if you get sick, if you catch a cold, you'll have to go to another friend's house. I can't be around anyone who is sick, or I get very sick."

"I understand. No problem."

I picked him up, gave him the couch and played him the song from *Hello Dolly!* where Cornelius and Barnaby want to get out of Yonkers and into the city. Faroukh laughed cathartically and promised next time he caught a train to Grand Central Station he would stay and explore the streets. He came to New York from a small agricultural village in Yemen, with a restless spirit, a hunger for freedom, and youth and health enough to take a risk. He woke up before the sun, worked all day, was eating packaged food at the gas station and was depleted. He kept catching colds. I embraced him as family with home cooked meals, connections to immigration attorneys, contacts for jobs, school, and wove him into my circle of friends. One night, he came downtown with me to La Mama Experimental Theatre Club in the East Village where I was acting in a play with a large gay cast. Faroukh had a penchant for singing and fashion, and I thought there was a budding artist inside him. He continued to insist he was looking for a wife, so I asked a group of friends that included young women his age, to sit with him in the audience. He'd been encountering Islamophobia, and he didn't want me introducing him with his Arab name. I assured him, "That won't be an issue with my friends." Still, he wanted to be called something else, and chose the name George.

I guess, when in a new country, if you want to fit in, pick the name of the first president. I said, "Well, you look like a Giorgio, let's call you Giorgio." I donned him, Italian. My grandmother always did that. I'd say, "Grandma this is June," and she'd say, "*O! Angelina!*" She gave everyone an Italian name, especially the names of her siblings who she'd left behind in the *paese*. Audrey, the woman who I was in a relationship with for many years, Grandma called, "*Oggi,*" which means "today." Oggi lived life very in the moment, and the name fit. When my cousins in Italy met her, they asked me to explain how her name could be their word for "today." *Ahh,* the circles of life, and the need for translation of translation.

Faroukh easily passed as a Giorgio with big brown eyes and olive skin. My castmates thought he was my cousin. At the cast party after the show, one of the actors flirted with him, sharing French fries. He looked at Faroukh like he was a young cupcake. I felt protective of Faroukh, like a son. I also was afraid he might reject me because of his faith, if he got hit on the very first night he hung out with me and my merry band of queer actors. "Giorgio, Giorgio!" I said, intervening between him and the guy, slinging my arm around his shoulder and opening their French fry vibe up to include the whole table. Later that night I asked him if he knew that guy was flirting with him and he played dumb, like he had no idea.

Nights after work, I'd hear him sweeping the living room, singing Arabic love songs to himself, full of the yearning of long riffs of howling vowels. He reminded me of my grandfathers and father, always sweeping and hosing down the sidewalk. He was amazed by simple things they didn't have back in his village. One night as I was cooking dinner, he tried to cut Saran Wrap with a pair of scissors. I said, "Watch this," grabbed the box and in one quick motion snapped the sheet off the built-in razor edge. Faroukh yelled, "No way!" He was so surprised, like I did a phenomenal magic trick. America America. Just by being a New Yorker, I felt full of magic.

Chapter Seven. *"Arrivederci* Pedicure"

AUNT GRACE MADE A LAST REQUEST, "Will you do me a favor and give me one more pedicure before you go to Italy?" I went to her house armed with peppermint soap and lotion, lanolin, a foot pumice, nail file and clipper, and clear nail polish. We decided to take a walk first then do the foot bath. On her block there were no sidewalks. We walked in the middle of the street, linking arms, "like they do in Italy," I said, "for the *passeggiata.*" Aunt Grace always decided the route, she liked a couple of neighborhood circuits. This time we strolled down her street across Bronxville Road where cars went faster than they should, and down a quiet block where she knew stories of neighbors who used to live there years ago, and how she'd watched this one magnolia tree grow and develop over her many years in the neighborhood. We turned the corner at a white picket fence and walked back up a hill past where one of our cousins used to live, and further up where an oil tank had spilled. At ninety-six, Aunt Grace could outwalk me with my bad left knee. She had stamina. No cane, nothing.

Back at the house, I filled her basin with hot water and Epsom salts. Aunt Grace's feet worked hard her whole life. I'd massaged plenty of Petruzzelli feet before, on both sides of the ocean; it was one of the more relaxing offerings of relief I could give to elders. My mother and Grandma Rose had characteristic bunions. Aunt Grace's bunions were less pronounced. Bunions ran in the family, plus these women had all worked on their feet their whole long lives and had walked many a mile on Bronx cement. Aunt Grace was a seamstress and in her later years volunteered at Lawrence Hospital's Bargain Box, a thrift store which had earned millions of dollars for the hospital. Aunt Grace clocked nine thousand hours of service, nine thousand hours on her feet, and she outlasted that place, forcing her into retirement at ninety-two when they shut their doors. It was just in the last year that we got started with pedicures and foot massages. One day we were having tea and she tells me—I have no pep. I say—Put your feet up. Do you have an ottoman or something? She says—No. I say—No? Don't you put your feet up? Ever? She says—I never thought of that.

I say—You're ninety-six and you never thought of putting your feet up? And she says—No, it never occurred to me. And then I thought to myself—when it's said, "they don't make 'em like that anymore," this is exactly who they're talkin' about, they're talkin' about Aunt Grace.

I placed a towel on her kitchen floor under the basin of hot salt water and set out a pumice stone and nail file. She took off her good brown leather shoes, unsnapped her garter belt, pulled off her stockings and soaked her feet in the hot salt water. The first time we did a foot bath, I was surprised that garter belts had only two snaps. I'd never seen one before. Aunt Grace had grown up in a whole different era. She raised one foot then the other onto a towel on my knee so I could do a good job with the nails. She said she felt like a queen. A foot massage was a rare luxurious indulgence for her. My mother had trained me how to delicately push back cuticles. She always told me to be careful with cuticles, as they're the site of blood transmission, where infections can go right into the bloodstream. I was extremely careful.

"Do you wear pants, ever?" I asked Aunt Grace. "Or only skirts?"

"Just skirts."

"Did you ever wear pants?"

"No. There was no need. I've had these denim skirts, *geez,* since I was in my twenties."

"Seventy years?"

"I guess so. I have the same waistline as when I was in high school."

My life was a rollercoaster compared to Aunt Grace's steady even keel. She resisted even the trend to wear pants, although she'd lived through the years when pants became acceptable for women. My grandmother also never wore pants. These women had a formality about them, just like their cousins in Acquaviva delle Fonti who all dressed with *la bella figura;* your Sunday best all the time. If only Aunt Grace could have met her cousins in life, they would have been so compatible with one another, all these women who lived into ripe old ages, well beyond their marriages. I wished I could have taken Aunt Grace to Acquaviva delle Fonti where her mother Lucia was born or Cassano delle Murge where her father Franco was born. I mourned that the separation of immigration was a separation for lifetimes.

I was going back for all of us.

I dried and put lotion on her feet and brushed on a clear coat of nail polish. As the polish dried, I washed my hands with soap, then made tea, boiling water in a small saucepan, and turning the light on above the stove, shifting the blunt knife blade she had wedged in the knob to keep the light on. I knew the tricks and idiosyncrasies of her kitchen. We'd been sitting like this, one-on-one, at her kitchen table, at least once a week for almost two years, and before that, with my mother. I told her about Faroukh. "The kid at the gas station is going to stay at the apartment while I'm gone." She was cautious, asking about his trustworthiness. I told her that I'd introduced him to the neighbors and was glad to help a young immigrant. He needed a place to stay, was respectful and a hard worker. I told her how he reminded me of my grandfathers, and her father too, who had been a shoemaker. "I'm sharing Shangri-La."

She expressed heartfelt pride that I was taking care of myself after caring for my mother so devotedly. As I left, she said, "I'm so glad you're taking time for yourself. It's about time. You deserve it." Then asked, hesitantly, "How long do you think you'll be gone?"

"About three or so months—'til the money runs out."

Her eyes dropped. Three months felt like eternity. Each year the brutal August heat and humidity was a mortal threat for elders. She pulled the two sides of her sweater together, pearl buttons shining like teardrops. She stood half in the doorway, half out, we gently hugged, and she got choked up and cried. Then I cried. I told her I loved her, and she told me she loved me too, and she held her palm up in a wave of goodbye and blessings.

Chapter Eight. "The Boot Inside Us Kicking"

FAROUKH CALLED FROM WORK to say we had to have a talk before I left town. That night, as soon as he walked in the door, he stood tense with excitement as if he was ready to parachute out of an airplane. He braced himself and blurted out, "I not told anyone in the world this, but I feel safe to tell you. I am gay. I like the boys. I am gay man."

"*Alhamdulillah!*" I shouted and hugged him. "I'm gay too. What a relief! How could I not have known this? *Madonn'!*"

"No way!"

"Yes! I should have known. The spiffy flowered shoes, the way you clean the house and sing love songs, something should have tipped me off."

"I was afraid to tell anybody. My family, they want me to have wife."

"And I was afraid too. I thought you wouldn't want to be my friend, you know, because of religion."

"*Wallah!* Life. She is too crazy. So where is your *habibti?*"

"I don't have one right now. I was with Oggi for a long time. Then I took care of my mother."

"No way! She's so cute. *Halas!*" He clapped his hands as if to say it's time to move on. "We need to find you wife."

"Well, let's stop looking for a wife for you."

"Yes please."

"And let's get you a boyfriend. Do you know Tinder? Grindr?"

"No, what's that?"

"This is going to be so much fun. Here, give me your phone. You'll have a boyfriend in five minutes."

Faroukh was astounded at how many boys were on the Apps. As he swiped, he kept singing, "Where is he? Where is the boy for me?"

"He's out there," I told him. As my grandmother used to say, "Take a chance on love." Faroukh knew exactly what he liked and what type of guy he was looking for. He wasn't as naive or sheltered as he'd pretended to be. Looking back, I should've known he was gay, and should have left him alone with the actor with the French fries. I'd taken him at his word, and I had to account for my own internalized homophobia, how afraid I was of being rejected. I'd done one thing right; I'd introduced him to my queer world at the theater and left the door open. My hope was that he would walk through in acceptance of me and my world, and instead, he came out. It made perfect sense, why we were drawn to each other. He felt he was on safe ground to step forward and speak his innermost secret. He took a big leap.

Faroukh's New York dream was the freedom to walk holding hands with a man in public. To kiss in public. The ultimate freedom that New York streets afford, to walk down the street as you are. Nobody cares. You can dress how you want, act how you want, believe what you want, eat what you want when you want, love who you want, how you want. This is the freedom he craved and what drove him to New York. He wanted to become himself. He'd left all his family and was heartbroken about it, all to get away from the stifling village where there was no money to be made, everybody watched everything you did, and the price of deviating was at best to be ostracized, at worst, to be gay-bashed and killed. Emigrating is a break-up for everyone. His mother was heartbroken. His father was heartbroken. He was heartbroken. He talked with his brothers often and like all immigrants I've ever known, worked to send money home to save the family. He said he didn't know it was possible to be gay as a lifestyle, that in his village there were men who had sex with men but that it wasn't considered gay. He said he never saw anyone with an out gay life, who was out at work and respected and integrated in community. He didn't know that being gay could be socially acceptable and that men could get married. He didn't know that being gay wasn't against Allah. That being gay wasn't a sin, or even a choice. I played the song for him that saved my young gay life, that gave me the words to begin to have pride and melt away shame. "I Was Born This Way," sung by Carl Bean. We played it over and over. I told him that Carl Bean was a Reverend and we talked about how radical it truly is to live out and proud of who you are. "A song can save your life," I said. "Listen to the words."

Over the next weeks I took Faroukh on a whirlwind tour of gay New York. We went to gay clubs old and new from The Monster to Boxers, and we found a gay Muslim social group. I was his lesbian Mamma, a trope in the gay community, a mentor. I'd sit at the bar while he pranced a lap around the club and could find me when he felt afraid. I sent him off with these words: "Be careful. Remember the men out there are gonna look at you and see a cupcake."

It was May and still chilly out. I filled two suitcases with life-saving medications: antibiotics, nebulizer, EpiPen, and Trach Kit for laryngospasms since my vocal cords sprang shut at the slightest provocation cutting off my airway, dramatic but common in the life of a long-term survivor of mantle radiation. I packed enough meds for three months and three seasons of clothes, from down vest to bathing suit, but really, I would need clothes for five seasons: the hat, scarf, zip-up fleece and down vest season, then the long sleeve blazer days, then short sleeve days and long sleeve nights, then shorts and t-shirts round the clock, finally so hot you lay down all afternoon from just after lunch to early evening. I packed copies of my books, CD's and bumper stickers to give away.

I held my maroon *passaporto* in my hands. I'd put a good deal of effort into getting Italian citizenship, and now I finally would use my *passaporto* to cross the ocean. Because my mother had been born in the Bronx before her immigrant parents became U.S. citizens, by law, our chain of Italian citizenship was intact, our *cittadinanza* had never been broken. I just had to prove it. I'd ironed out the consonants in my grandfather's name, Petruzzelli, which was spelled differently through the chain of documents: birth certificate to passport, to declaration for U.S. citizenship, to marriage certificate, to my mother's birth certificate, to death certificate, to gravestone. There were all kinds of variations in spelling: one "t," two "tt's," one "z," two "zz's," and an "s" added on the ultima syllable as in the original Greek version of the name. I chose one spelling, with the double "zz's" and got the rest of the documents legally changed to match. I loved handwriting the double "zz's." Still, my own last name is spelled wrong. That's part of being American. Originally, the name was Lanzillotta. An Ellis

Island mis-stroke of the official's pen turned the final "a" to an "o" and I've left that final "o" as a scar on my name representing the change that occurred in the ocean crossing. I'm a scrappy American with a misspelled name and messy hair.

My plane ticket to *Napoli* was open return. I kept saying to myself: "I don't know when I'm comin' back, if I'm comin' back." It turned into a blues song in my mind. *"I don't know when I'm comin' back, if I'm comin' back. Since you're gone, no place is home. I'll walk 'round Italy, cruise 'round Sicily, sidle up to things to see—what sticks, yeah, see what sticks."*

I telephoned my sister Rosina to say goodbye and she cried. First Aunt Grace cried and now Rosina. I told her, "I'll be in the south. You and Rocco come meet me and I'll introduce you to the cousins. We can go to Acquaviva delle Fonti together. You're retired. Your kids are well. You've never been to Acquaviva. What are you waiting for? Get a ticket and meet me there. This is your chance. Grandma Rose's niece Annunziatina is still alive. You'll be so happy meeting her. I'll be done with the book tour in a month, and I'll make my way to Bari. Talk to Rocco. Get a couple of tickets."

I pulled on the blue and brown striped wool hat my mother had knitted for me, tossed Faroukh his own set of keys, and walked out the door. He pulled my suitcases out of the apartment, past the stump of the peach tree and out of the (odd) court, down to a taxi. He gave me a big bear hug and thanked me for everything. "I love you," he said. "You are the best person in the world. The best American I ever meet. I swear. You saved my life. I never forget you or what you did for me." He cried in my arms. The driver closed the trunk.

Before I stepped inside the airplane, I pressed my lips against the plane's cold steel chassis, then smacked my hand on its body the way you encouragingly pat an athlete about to go out onto the court. In the seat in front of me, a little baby girl, not quite two years old, was held by her mother. The little girl kept looking back and staring at me with big wide dark cherry eyes, long eyelashes, and a ponytail up on top of her head like a fountain spout. *"Ciao,"* I sang to her. *"Ciao bella, ciao."* She scrunched her hand open and closed. She was secure in her place in the world, in her mother's arms.

As the double bells rang, I clicked the seatbelt into place, lights flashed, and the engines revved. The plane slowly pivoted, made its way around the tarmac, waited its turn for takeoff, then lined up the nose on the centerline of the runway and picked up speed. We shook with the vibration of the tires against the asphalt, then suddenly everything was smooth beneath our seats as the nose lifted. We leaned back and rose into the sky. The buildings of New York got so small so quick, so many little houses in Queens and the vast gray twinkling metropolis behind. I too was overcoming gravity, as the plane broke through the layer of clouds into the stratosphere, the feeling overtook me that I had no life to come back to. Above the clouds, the sky was radiant, blue, promising a clear path to the sun. Reality, like the troposphere, is nothing insurmountable.

My goal was to empty my mind and see what comes. I carried a blank notebook. I closed my eyes and took deep slow breaths. I never know what will come. Songs? Stories? Poems? What would *Napoli* inspire in me? Breathe and empty. Breathe and empty. I was going home and hoped home still existed.

I thought of Aunt Grace wiping tears from her eyes and holding her palm open, blessing me for the journey ahead, and of Rosina and my friends crying over the phone. Were they crying, in part, for the ceasefire between cancers in my body? For the luck of surviving for a chance like this? For the victory of taking that chance? For my defiance of poverty and illness and all that held me down? What did it mean to return to the villages where my grandparents had little choice but to leave a century ago? And what of the root canal of the heart—the long curved nerve that is the *Mezzogiorno* throbbing with all that had been lost in the split of immigration and Americanization, the killing of that root and the saving of that root, the deep place carved out inside us? The root of the boot of Italy reaching down that kicks the center of my gut? All the loss. The boot of Italy inside us kicking.

It was as if an angel whispered: Come find that lost part of yourself. Come breathe the air of the *Mezzogiorno*. I was going back to bask in the languages of our ancestral tongues, to weave in loose threads. Only a handful of nights throughout a whole lifetime have I felt whole and at peace, woven into community, rare golden nights when I could hear the moon's crazed laughter echo inside my ribs, and I could grieve losses, some named, most unnamed. Reconnecting with the *paese* years ago changed me integrally, every notch of Italian I *capeeshed,* every phrase I learned to speak, every hour I listened to a long-lost cousin's story, every *canzone, soprannome,* and *sfraganizze* that could roll off my tongue—ratcheted up my soul. I had an intense desire to find cousins who I'd not yet found and who if I didn't seek out now, would never find, not in this lifetime. I was alive in a pivotal moment in history. My parents and grandparents were all gone, and my parents' generation was just about all gone. The connectors, gone, the people who knew of each other, gone, who knew the dialects, recipes, stories, proverbs, prayers, songs, saints, nicknames, the dead, gone, the ways of the land, the language of leaves and trees and roots and crops, gone, the knowledge of hands, how to make every single thing: *vino, olio, formaggio, terracotta, cavateel,* walls, houses, all of it. Gone. After one hundred years since my grandparents immigrated from these towns to the Bronx, all the links were about to be severed. I had a sense of duty. And anyway, I was curious. As the *aria* says, *"Sono una poeta!"* I am a poet and the daughter of a U.S. Marine. *Semper Fi.* I thought—If I don't do it, nobody will. I'm that third-generation artist you hear about. The first generation of landless peasants knows the ways of the land, knows animals, comes to the Bronx, carries block ice and coal, sews in Manhattan sweatshops. The second generation knows cement and tar, carries ice and shovels coal from eight years old on, fights in the wars, installs oil burners, gives expert haircuts and manicures. The third generation writes poems and songs and remembers to fulfill the ability to bring our Bronx stories back, back, back, into the *murge* . . .

PART II
COMME SE CHIAMMA 'O VIENTO?

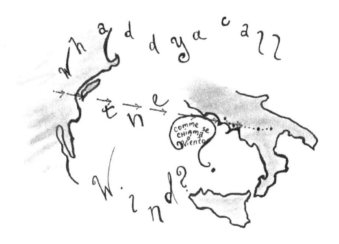

I long to be

part of a flock

of
s
w
o
l
l
a
w
s
when

they
d
i
v
e

It's hard to be
a
l o n
e

just glad to be
a
l
i
v
e

a
l
i
v
e

"Naples is like having ten lovers"

in through every orifice all at once
the boys swim team warms
up under the volcano

Dormant? Surely
the way they swing their arms
and spin their torsos in preparation

for the butterfly stroke, stirs and heats the blood
of the land. For now, it's an amazing act of insanity
we look at Pompeii's bodies

in contortions under pumice and ash
and believe we don't share a common fate.
Pulcinella points at me and laughs

trips me in alleyways.
Finally, I can play the most difficult ancient *lazzo:*
Spaghetti alle Lacrime, Mangia Piangia! Magna Chiangge!

Now, every *marinara* makes me cry.
Sunset, I cannot look. My heart afire
pink and orange setting sun,

the bronze nose
of the bust of Pulcinella on via dei Tribunale
polished by millions of luck-seekers' touches,

measures from my belly to my head.
I ask Pulcinella to reveal these alleys of *Napoli* to me
to slow my New Yorkness down

Pulcinella, Pulcinella,
Napulitane saint as prevalent as The Crucified One
without the tragedy and apotheosis

just a trickster spirit
who acts stupid when he's smart
then pretends he knows everything when he doesn't.

Pulcinella over *Port 'Alba* watches
a handstand in *Spaccanapoli,* Pulcinella
held at a gunpoint by *La Verità*

Pulcinella does a chicken dance
around the *guglia* through the Bubonic Plague
atop the plague tower kisses *San Domenico*

holds the long note from a balcony
through the tragic news of the centuries
Pulcinella eats spaghetti

with his hands
and for all the ages
weeps

"Gimme a *Napulitan'* Street"

any street where *Sanpietrini* checker
the path uphill at impossibly high angles
any alleyway an old woman leans out into
from the top half of a saloon style door
joining her living room to the street
so I can hand her a *caramella* and whisper
"*Buonasera,*" in my hoarse *Mezzogiornese* voice
where the laundress tells me:
       "*Stai qui e apre 'na libreria,*"
       Stay here and open a bookshop,
where Pulcinella laughs all night long
the moon dancing cartwheels around the piazza
youth balancing cigarettes on wet lips
where the young mother smacks
her son to tears then snaps
her fingers loud as firecrackers
for her daughter to follow her
through the doorway where the waitress runs
into the arms of her lover
cradling a beer bottle up the street
where snaps and kisses are *O!* so loud
where there's a relaxed acceptance of humanity and sexuality
and the cross-street swoops all the way up the mountain
Napule!
I can't wait to wake up again
to walk the alleyways of *Spaccanapoli*
where the lava of *Vesuvio* melts the mozzarella inside me
at the 1847 Pizzeria Capasso in Porta San Gennaro
Napule!
Does anyone staring at *Vesuvio* not see Sofia Loren's *scollatura*
in the double peaks? Seriously,
Napule!
slow me down

I walk slow or trip
talk fast or be misunderstood
Napule!
my words rush into phrases and hand motions
yells and cut off exclamations
one glance can slit your throat
where people smoke as much as talk
ashtrays overflow
men with crutches and casts
cough with rhonchi and rales, and lower lobe atelectasis
one *nonna* on oxygen in an alleyway
her family all around her fanning, batting,
belting, smacking, waving desperately night's air
to stir to stir the wind
into Mamma's breath

Chapter Nine. "*Gnocchi* Seduction"

Napoli, May 2018

NEVER LAND IN ITALY ON A SUNDAY. Not in the south, anyway. Everything's closed. The taxi driver from the airport charged me double for "the holiday." *Uè! Benvenuti a Napule.* Sunday is God's day off, so the meter—you pay double. It's the nature of money to change hands. This is the south, the *Mezzogiorno*, the place whose nickname means "midday," and like "high noon," fills you with so much intensity it makes you stop everything, lie down and sleep through the heart of the day. From the taxi, I pushed two heavy suitcases bumpety bump over *Sanpietrini* stones through an alley leading to a small arched doorway. My suitcases were too heavy for me; a lousy way to start a trip, but I was just getting my sea legs again. Inside the hotel lobby, a split-level terracotta tile floor tripped me, and I fell all the way down flat, my cheek smacking the floor. What was a step doing right in the middle of the floor? I levered myself up on an end table where a statuette of Pulcinella stood, hands on his belly, laughing. *Azzo Pulcinella! Te scamazzo a coccia! So that's how it's gonna be, you playing pranks on me now that I'm on your turf? Ridi eh Pulcinella? Ma staje pazziann! Grazie frà'. Ti vedo. Ti vedo. You're on.* Pulcinella and me had history. I got to my room, took a shower, and a nap.

Sanpietrini are not New York sidewalks. My Gotham feet, fast with purpose, zigzagging around strangers to stay on course, proved dangerous in *Napoli*. As soon as I crossed my first street, the toe of my sneaker caught a groove between two stones, and I fell down, flat to the ground, this time face to face with the *serci*, the black volcanic basalt blocks inlaid into roads. *Azz'! Pulcinella 'Nzevato! Sfaccimm'! Te spacco a copa mammalucco!* Pulcinella loves falling, like a child, loves spinning and falling. That's his gag, pratfalls and tumbles, down ladders and stairs. Now he's trippin' me for sport. I brushed myself off and walked on. *Pulcinella, basta con gli scherzi!* Two falls in one day. *Basta!* I saw him everywhere I walked in *Spaccanapoli*, statues in windows, graffiti on walls, a giant bronze statue in the street. Pulcinella walks down the hill then disappears.

Sanpietrini slowed me down. The beveled tops of the stones rise under the foot's arch. The Irish blessing, "May the road rise up to meet you" is literal here. I had to navigate curves and ruts, shake the New York walk out of my legs and get my *Spaccanapoli* stride on. My New York footfall lands in the center of one square of sidewalk cement, then just over the line of the next square. In Manhattan they flattened the earth to build the grid, leveling as much as they could. In *Napoli* they built right into the mountains, they didn't level the mountains. Manhattan you can walk miles of sidewalks without a hitch, set a pace and tack and *fagetaboutit*. For sport, you can find paths on diagonals, walking swiftly across cement then asphalt then cement, on side streets and through intersections from corner to corner, ignoring crosswalks completely. In the boroughs you gotta keep an eye out for cement squares pried up on angles by tree roots. The earth of course is dynamic, moving; cement cracks and keeps workmen in business. Asphalt gives in to sinkholes. Cars have been swallowed whole by the street. *Sanpietrini* respond to the earth and are eternal. A workforce of specialists, the *serciaroli*, rhythmically tap their brick *mazzapicchio* hammers, *tktook tatoo tuk, tktook tatoo tuk, tktook tatoo tuk,* adjusting and replacing, stone by precious stone, *serci* by *serci*, tooth by tooth. The most skilled worker can set thousands in a day, setting new stones where old ones were uprooted. Only these *serciaroli*, and children who create street games, and the fallen, like me, with a bad knee or fast gait, get *faccia a faccia, guancia a guancia* with the *Sanpietrini*.

I changed the arc my legs inscribed from hip flexors and knees, slowed my steps, rocked heel to toe, heel to toe, with a kick and pause at the apex of the forward foot, before bringing the heel down on the next stone. In physics you might call this point the *apogee,* the foot is going up—the foot is coming down, that point in spacetime where direction changes, gravity takes hold, the suspension in air of the foot before the heel comes down to find the next stone. *Cammina cammina.* I walked down a curved alley and came upon a most interesting activist sign, handwritten in marker with whimsical black lettering curled with embellishments. Red, green and yellow slashes energized the message:

> *ZIA ADA offre caffè, tè freddo, o limonata*
> *—in cambio di solidarietà.*
> *Le case per tutti.*
> Aunt Ada offers coffee, iced tea, or lemonade—

in exchange for solidarity.

Housing for all.

I'll trade solidarity for a coffee. Vendor stalls lined both sides of the street—all blanketed and closed. Sunday afternoon. *Tutto chiuso.* To find out who made the sign, I'd have to come back when the vendors were around. I noted where I was. Long white sheets written with protest messages in bright red paint hung beneath the windows on the facade of a building. I walked back the way I came to trace my steps as a point of reference. Shaken up from having fallen twice, I looked for a place to sit down. In piazza Dante I drank *acqua minerale* and wrote in my notebook as life bubbled around me with the same effervescence as the *acqua.* A festival was happening, the Sri Lankan New Year—*capo d'anno.* A group of young teens stood in a circle kicking around a soccer ball. The ball popped up high and landed on a balcony. In three seconds flat one of the smallest lankiest boys scaled the building onto the balcony and retrieved the ball. He didn't even take his backpack off, just wedged one foot into a carved groove on the stone facade of the building, grabbed a higher notch, then a pole, shimmied up, held a wire and flung himself up over the second story railing. He was on the balcony within seconds to the cheers of his friends, threw the soccer ball down and descended even faster than he'd scaled up, and the game resumed. Without a thought or plan or hesitation, a hand here, a foot there and up and over. There was a time I had that marvelously adept dexterity and faith in my body, to climb into apartment windows when friends forgot keys, or when my mother worried about an elder who didn't answer their door—even into my forties I hopped fences to play basketball and climbed vertical ladders to get onto Brooklyn rooftops to picnic and salute the sunsets, but age had caught up to my knees this past spate of years and now I aimed to just stay vertical, to not trip on *Sanpietrini* and end up face down in an alley. Arm wrestling, like climbing, was another thing I used to love to do. Everywhere I went I'd roll my sleeve up over my shoulder, steady my elbow on the hood of a parked car, desktop, table, somebody's bent back—whatever hard surface was handy, and challenge someone to it. Arm wrestling is holding hands. Arm wrestling is struggling at the apex when it can go either way. Arm wrestling is gut wrenching, takes all you got. Arm wrestling is holding on, not giving in, then just when your opponent thinks he has you, bursting with umph to pin him down. Triumph, or get pinned.

This Sri Lankan boy had a touch of Pulcinella inside him. It's said amongst *commedia dell'arte* actors that every *Napulitane* has a trace of Pulcinella, and that Pulcinella touches you, chooses you, you don't choose Pulcinella. I found this to be true when I joined a *commedia* company in New York, not realizing the journey of consciousness I'd signed up for as I made and donned the mask, white flour sack hat, oversized white clothes and entered the *lazzi*. The toughest *lazzo* for me was *Spaghetti alle Lacrime* which I interpreted as *Mangia! Piangia!* or Eat! Cry! *Magna! Chiangge!* The skit is this: get on stage, eat spaghetti and weep profusely, which I tried to do for years to no success, usually ending in laughter or mock tears. My mother was alive at the time, and there was an endless supply of her gravy. When she died, *Mangia! Piangia!* happened spontaneously when I ate the last of her gravy that had been in the freezer and wept inconsolably. Pulcinella had finally broken through. I would never be the same.

Sitting in piazza Dante, drinking *acqua minerale* exquisite as champagne, I bent my head back and opened my mouth as if to drink the wind. I had the rare feeling of wanting to take all life in, all the life in all the alleyways, all the little bookstores, all the bars brimming with conversation, all the lifeblood coursing through *Napoli*, and all the wind; the northerly *Tramontana*, the easterly *Levante*, the southwesterly *Libeccio*, the westerly *Ponentino*, the northwesterly *Maestrale*, the southeasterly *Scirocco*. It is the winds I call. Winds from all directions. Breath, come inside me.

The name of the street I was staying on, via Santa Maria di Costantinopoli, brought me back two thousand years. *La Madonna di Costantinopoli* is the patron saint of Grandma Rose's town, Acquaviva delle Fonti, and I knew the miraculous story of how she arrived there. I'd first read the story in a letter Grandma Rose received from one of the cousins, and it grew in my imagination over the many years. In 1453 when Constantinople fell, Ottoman Turks burned the city down and destroyed Christian icons or threw them into the Sea of Marmara. This painting of *La Madonna di Costantinopoli* was hurled into the sea. She floated on the water and rode a fast current coming from the Black Sea speeding through the Bosporus Strait through the Sea of Marmara southwest into the Aegean Sea. The sun and the moon aligned to make the waters rise, and with the push of a swirling *Scirocco*, *La Madonna* was carried into the Ionian Sea and up the Strait of Otranto. There she sailed a counterclockwise current north into the Adriatic Sea nearing Dubrovnik where she spiraled back toward Bari. Two *Barese* fishermen out one early morning, saw *La Madonna* floating in the water and considered it their great spiritual fortune to lift her into their boat and dry her in the sun. The two fishermen carried her to shore and decided to escort her to the cathedral in Acquaviva delle Fonti, which had been holy ground since ancient Greek times when a temple stood on the spot, and where, in the fall of 1900, Grandma Rose had been baptized. This painting became known as *Santa Maria di Costantinopoli*. Local silversmiths adorned a frame around her and covered an altar with ornamental sheets of silver, which amazed me the first time my cousin took me down into the subterranean level on an insider's tour of the church. The silver altar lit up the basement, shining in all directions as if *La Madonna* herself was the source of illumination of this underground silver cave.

The street sign, via Santa Maria di Costantinopoli, gave me a sense of place in the cosmos, connecting me back eight hundred years to Constantinople, and almost two thousand years since Saint Luke was alive. As one version of the story goes, it was Saint Luke himself who painted this portrait of Mary while she was alive. Luke never met Jesus in person, but he got to know Mary after Jesus' death, and she influenced his writing of her son's life, which became the gospel of Saint Luke. It's said that Luke painted this portrait of Mary while he was interviewing her about Jesus' life. As the story goes, angels brought Luke the boards on which to paint. I picture Luke asking

Mary questions while he painted this portrait of her, somewhere between the years 33AD and 40AD, around one thousand, nine-hundred, and seventy-eight years before I happened to be walking on via Santa Maria di Costantinopoli. By all accounts, Mary didn't live long after Jesus. Does ascension qualify as death? Jesus, of course, lived until the year 33AD, and Mary seven or so years after. She did a lot in those years, talked with the apostles, and wrote letters as part of her mission to inspire people all over the world. I wondered if she had any other children.

I took a right off via Santa Maria di Costantinopoli down via Port'Alba where I tripped and fell a third time on the downward slope, this time catching myself on the far wall of the alley, and who was there, but Pulcinella, in a graffitied portrait on the wall, laughing, pointing his right index finger right at me. *Azzo Pulcinella! You gotta be kiddin' me, vafamocc' a mammeta!* I smacked the wall. My New York walk didn't work on these stones. I had to learn to lift my feet, make some kind of adjustment. *Pulcinella ma cche staja faccend'? Chiann' chiann'.* Slow. The pace and rhythm of my feet had to change. How long would it take me to slough New York off?

I focused on walking slower. My *Napulitan'* stride began to take over my legs. Center on the back foot, lift the front foot and kick out, let the front foot pause at the apogee of the kick before coming back down, heel first, as the bevel of the next *Sanpietrini* rises to meet the arch of the foot on its landing, let the toe traverse the gap to the next stone. After a few steps, my legs were getting the hang of it. This walk seemed familiar to me. Why was this so familiar? I looked down at my legs, and thought, who am I walking like? Then it hit me, the walk was exactly Michael Corleone's walk after he returns from *Sicilia* and gets out of the car to find Kay outside the schoolhouse. He walks like he's on *Sanpietrini*, keeping his balance on his standing foot while the front foot kicks out in front of him with those shined black shoes the camera picks up on. Pacino walks the walk. Corleone metabolized cobblestones.

Chapter Ten. "Francesco"

TOO EXCITED TO SLEEP, I jumped up out of bed, knowing that one of my dreams was about to come true. I was scheduled to read my poetry in Francesco Durante's class at *Università degli Studi Suor Orsola Benincasa*, and had to take the *funicolare* to get there. I couldn't help singing, "*jammo 'ncoppa jamme jà . . . Funiculì Funiculà!*" I downed an early espresso and *cornetto alla crema*, walked down via Santa Maria di Costantinopoli, took a right on via Port'Alba and warned Pulcinella to not even think about tripping me this morning! *Uè guagliò! Non ci pens'! Checazz'!* I cut across piazza Dante on a diagonal and walked up via Toledo which was flat and even, asking a woman, "*Dov'è u funicola?*" Her arm shot up in the air like I had miles to walk, "*Sempre dritto! Cammina, cammina!*" The *funicolare* in my mind was like a ski lift over a cliff, my feet dangling over a steep rugged abyss, the wind fierce against the steel cable. I expected to be strapped into some kind of cable car up the mountain, but when I arrived at *Funicolare Centrale,* the cars were indoors, like a subway on a steep incline. Pulcinella cackled at my misconceptions, and I laughed with him, climbed the stairs, and got into one of the cars. My Italian American mind was wrong about so many things about life in Italy. I'd been expecting an outdoor steel cable pulling me up into the sky, but the *funicolare* was just a diagonal subway where my feet stayed on the ground the whole time. We went slow and smooth six hundred feet up the mountain, Pulcinella roaring.

I exited and walked in the direction everyone walked, away from the cliff. On one corner, an outdoor *caffè* jutted into the intersection. Outside sat an elegant man, drinking espresso, a cigarette and full ashtray before him. I knew instantly—*that must be Francesco Durante.* He had a softness and intelligence about him, inquisitive eyes behind tortoise shell rimmed glasses. This man delighted in the world. Tall and lanky, he sat with his legs easily crossed, his thoughts swirling around him. Expressive wisps of graying light brown hair feathered a graceful air about him. He dressed in a classic style with a suit that flowed, a light gray button-down cotton-weave shirt, open at the collar. He seemed to be taking it all in—the river of life: sky, wind off the mountain, street, his newspaper and thoughts, conversation with people and the waiter hustling around him.

I stepped across the intersection, "*Ciao Francesco, sono Anna Rachele.*" He jumped to his feet and as we hugged, he asked me how I liked my coffee, motioned to the waiter, his finger circling the air to bring me an espresso, and he another. I thanked him, telling him that this day, this trip, was, "*un sogno realizzato,*" a dream come true. He smiled and responded with a question:

"You say this is *un sogno realizzato. Perché?*"

I let that question hang in the air as my mind raced, building a litany. "Gimme a few days," I said, "and I will tell you."

We walked down sets of stairs cut into the mountain between umber and sand-colored buildings to his classroom as he told me the history of the university which was once a monastery founded by a mystic nun, Suor Orsola. As it turned out, Suor Orsola had died on my mother's birthday, three hundred years prior, and was born on my Cure Day—the day I celebrated the end of my first cancer, when a mass was removed from my mediastinum. Whatever the forces were that got me to *Napoli*, to this university atop the mountain, for this one day in life, felt like an extreme blessing. I wondered about young Orsola the mystic nun, who received a vision, founded an order, and created a monastery up in the mountains over the bay of *Napoli*.

In Francesco's class, the students craved to hear my Bronx English. A Bronx accent was something they'd heard in movies, songs, online, but never in person. Francesco picked one my poems, a short simple one I'd written in the voice of my father, "This is the Bronx," a verbatim story my father told me about his childhood—well you can't call it a childhood, he was a laborer, an iceman at eight years old. The poem expresses the essence of street soul that is both Bronx and *Napulitan'*. Francesco performed a live translation in *Napulitan'* as I recited the poem in my mother tongue, *Bronxese*. He echoed my Bronx vernacular street tongue.

The students asked questions about New York. I told them that in a sense, as the poem says, I too am always "driving in reverse," going backward to go forward, looking to the past, taking the difficult route, bucking the system, defying rules as simple as street signs. It's the heart of who we are, throwing ourselves behind the wheel of necessity, improvising, veering toward then swerving away from collision and the ultimate *finale,* ducking and bobbing Death's swing of the scythe at every turn.

I catalyzed writing and improv exercises with the class. Some hours of life have a magnificent luster. This was one. I shared a dream poem, and as I articulated it, I came to understand myself. My dream mind had made swirls of paint in Italian paintings into an alternate reality, a parallel universe. I shared this question with the students, "*Dopo la morte di mia madre, dov'è sogno che sia la sua anima?*" After the death of my mother, where do I dream her soul is?"

I told the students how my mother Rachele believed in colors and utilized colors as her keys to healing, to reignite her sparkle after years in an abusive marriage. She'd told me that colors transported her in life. She'd picked up the pieces of her life and regained her sparkle, through working with colors. She was a manicurist, hair colorist and hairdresser, knitter, and gardener. She focused on colors in everything she did, even the way she cooked and set the table, ironing tablecloths with floral patterns and positioning statues of angels everywhere. She wore outfits of deep purple, with scarves and hats and gloves, all purple. I'd experienced her applying masterful brushstrokes of nail polish, one careful brushstroke at a time.

"This is the Bronx"

Worked all my life.
Haven't taken a vacation since I was twelve.
Learned to drive at eight years old.
You know how I learned to drive?
You know how I learned to drive?
My father puts me on the truck.
He says Drive.
I say Pop I can't drive.
So he socks me.
He says Drive.
And I drove.
Not only that, I backed out the driveway.
Learned how to drive in reverse.
That's my life in a nutshell.
Driving in reverse.

"*Chest è il Bronx*"

Agg faticat tutt a vit.
Nun m'agg pigliat na vacanz ra quand tenev dodicc ann.
Agg mparat a guida quann tenev iott ann.
Tu o saje comm agg mparat a guida?
Tu o saje comm agg mparat a guida?
Patm ma mis ngopp a nu camion.
E dicett Guida.
I ricett Ba' nun sacc guidá.
Allor iss me rett nu cazzott.
Ricett Guida.
E ì guidaje.
Nun guidaje sulament,
in retromarcia 'ngoppa a via 'nnanzi a cas'
Me mparaje a guida a retromarcia.
Chest è a vita mi nda na nocciolin.
Guidare in retromarcia.

"Renaissance Heaven / *Il Cielo di Rinascimento*"

My mother shows me Heaven one night in a dream
and in my dream, Heaven is as it is, in Renaissance paintings.
Exactly like that. Angels swirling in glowing white and orange robes
creamsicle colors. We fly vertically my mother and I,
fast we fly up a tunnel of colors, pinks and purples
up greens, up blues, purples, pinks,
up oranges up golds, up yellows up whites,
everyone is smiling and waving at us
from the rings of the tunnel
happy to see us together holding hands.
Vertical flight is ascension.

When I dream of my mother in Heaven, where do I locate her?
In a Renaissance painting. In Italy. Not in the Bronx. Not in America.
In Renaissance brushstrokes. Inside brushstrokes of colors.
In a purple brushstroke, surrounded by all the colors.
In *Italia*. The *Madreterra*.
My mother in Heaven is a purple brushstroke
inside a Renaissance painting.
Her soul is the colors.
Renaissance paintings are literal, angels and all the colors
my mother always believed in.
All the colors. Her spirit swirls in pinks and purples,
blues and golds, yellow and oranges, all shades of oranges.

I realize why all these paintings are up so high
in churches, in apses, around rings and menisci of *cupole*.
You must look up, bend your neck all the way back
feel the disorientation that comes, the vertigo,
when you squeeze the cervical vertebrae.
Look up into the vortex of the dome, of the heavens,
and let it make you rise.
It is practice
for your own ascent.

After class, one of the students, Tomasso, walked me back to the *funicolare*. He was burly and strong with handsome dark eyes and a cap like my grandfather used to wear, and like I wear. On the walk he told me about his father's farm *in campagna*. Tommaso's hands were muscular with the knowledge of olives and grapes and figs and sheep and goats. We said goodbye in the tunnel and went in opposite directions, Tomasso further up the mountain, and me, down.

Back on via Toledo, I veered off onto side streets without paying any attention to where I was going, turned a corner and walked toward the sea, ending up in a magnificent glass mall with a glass dome ceiling—a *cupola* of glass. Gold angels kept watch from way up high. Grand. *Stupendo!* I sat for a cold *acqua frizzante* and cut slices of cantaloupe. A tall man with a thick wavy white head of hair arrived, stood by the wall and sang a set of tenor *arie*. Another man showed up, sat next to him and played mandolin. The space was vast. I wondered where I was. I texted Tomasso a photo of the place and he wrote back: *La Galleria Umberto I.*

A table of kids in their twenties sat with arms around each other, thin cigarettes balanced on their lips. Their whole bodies shook when they laughed, blowing smoke out their wet lips up to the vaulted glass ceiling. The youth looked at each other, dripping from their eyes. What age does seduction find the eyes? It is everywhere here. *Napulitani* of all ages seemed comfortable with their sensuality. The body seemed an expression of life force. I admired their carefree youthful beauty and freedom of expression. I hadn't felt that free in my body in a long time. As a teenager, sex scared the hell out of me. It was a mystery nobody talked about. The nuns taught us sex through flowers, pistils and stamens. As a kid I was very confused. I remember wondering after their lectures if I could get pregnant by eating an apple.

A family of three arrived and sat at the table next to me, mother, father and a college-age daughter. They naturally included me in their conversation. The mother ordered a big orange drink. She tells me it's a "Spritz." I was fascinated by the orange glowing color and the big size and what refreshing relaxation it offered her. "This is the *aperitivo*," she tells me. "The right time of day to have a Spritz." They brainstormed a list of the things I *must* do in *Napoli*, and the daughter wrote the list in my notebook. The list was three pages long. It would take a lifetime to complete this mission.

A group of about forty school children appeared, all wearing yellow baseball hats, running for the gelato stand. I shouted out—*Di dove siete?* Where are you all from?

"Altamura!" one shouted back.

That's in *Puglia*, very near my family. These are my *paesani*. I asked the boy, maybe eight years old, how to get to Altamura from *Napoli* and he abandoned his quest for gelato and stood there giving me step by step instructions, moving his arms in the air describing the hills and turns to Altamura. He gave me detailed directions for twenty minutes. It's more than a three-hour drive. This kid will never know how enheartened he made me, *rincuorato*, with his enthusiastic directions to the hill town he was so proud of coming from, his hometown, Altamura. He welcomed me. He obliterated the word "stranger." Listening to his directions made me feel at home in the world. If I could get rid of one word and one concept in all languages, it would be, "stranger," the intense separateness humans put onto each other where we don't recognize each other at all. The little adorable *ragazzo Altamurese* gave me a feeling of okayness and belonging in the world. He healed a part of me that needed healing. The last time I'd said hello to a kid I didn't know was in the East Village in Manhattan some months before. I was walking down 2nd Street feeling alive and interactive, and I said hello, like a *Buongiorno*, like—*Beautiful day to be alive, isn't it?* I addressed this hello to a man and his kid sitting on a wall enjoying the sunshine and a cool drink. The father got angry with me for saying hello. "We don't know you," he admonished, modeling for his kid the desired behavior. It was against the rules to say hello to "strangers" in the gentrified Manhattan. I was an old school New Yorker, and I didn't know where my New York had gone. I felt shot in the heart, out of place on the very streets I'd always felt at home. The "Stranger Danger" campaign in the 1980's spread the idea that children were not to interact with strangers—defined as *anybody who you don't know where they live.* Still, I grew up playing and roughhousing in street games with kids who I didn't know, even as an adult. Kids knew how to play; cars respected our street play. I could walk through New York, join a double Dutch jump rope game, turn the ropes for a while with kids I didn't know in neighborhoods not my own. We spoke the language of play. Street play was our mother tongue, Spaldeens flying overhead, basketballs speed bouncing between us, the streets were our playground, the streets were alive. I could intercept a ball or grab a kid who was running away from another, and join the game, pointing out where one was hiding in Hide-and-Seek. The language of street play as I learned it, is as extinct a dialect for me as the *Acquavivese* Grandma Rose spoke, but in both languages I hunt for someone to speak phrases with, to play catch with, someone who *capeeshes*, who remembers, who volleys, and I do find these people, everywhere. Francesco Durante was one of those people. And so was this little *ragazzo* from Altamura.

"*Perché*"

for Francesco Durante who asked,
"You say this is un sogno realizzato. Perché?"

Perché?   I can barely speak anymore
         American, every syllable—an affront.
         There's no word in English for anything
         I truly want to say. That's why I write poems
         To shred language and line breaks
         Until some meaning comes

Perché?   *Limoncello* by *il mare*
         For the first time in a hundred years
         Soothes my irradiated throat

Perché?   For *l'eternità* Pulcinella
         In spaghetti weeps

Perché?   Volcanoes inside me

Perché?   Eruptions disruptions divisions schisms isms is mmmm sss

Perché?   So much is left out of consciousness
         Like the puzzle piece fragments of mosaic
         Of the one-eyed eagle
         Up high on the white plaster wall
         To the right of the altar in the *Duomo di Salerno.*
         O San Matteo do you lay here?

Perché?   Once we starved right here

Perché?   I am that spiked blond boy
         On the scooter on via Francesco Caracciolo

Perché?   Cravings of freedom

Perché? The heart broke so many times
You can see the marks
Where it's been tenderized, pulverized

Perché? For screams and moon howls long enough and loud

Perché? For wanting to be woven in instead of weeded out

Perché? To cut the line of this goddamn emergency brake
I've had on all my life

Perché? We will never come this way again

Perché? We haven't hung laundry *nel vento*
since we lost "private property"

Perché? *Mezzogiornese* sun sees I am American and slants on me anyway

Perché? We haven't had enough days like this
Or hours of the night eternal

Perché? Bullet shots of *caffè* how many times a day *caffè?*

Perché? *Perché?* *Perché?* *Napoli* is the freedom I crave

Perché? *"Vidi Napule e po' muore!"*
See Naples and then die!

Chapter Eleven. *"Un Momento di Luce"*

I WAS EATING CANNOLI, standing at a counter at a *caffè* and a guy walks in, doesn't even have to order, just nods at the barista, and says to me, "Why are you eating cannoli in *Napule?* If you want cannoli, you go to *Sicilia*—then you're finished. You're in *Napule,* you eat *apizz',* you eat *sfogliatell'*—and you're finished. Eat *la Riccia.* That's the one. My mother likes *Santa Rosa,* but *la Riccia,* that's the one." He bit into his sfogliatell', licked the powdered sugar off his fingertips, and pointed to the waiter to bring me *"la Riccia"* too. I thanked him and said I'd be in Palermo and Messina in a couple of weeks.

"This time of year, you go to Messina you get granita—and you're finished. Granita you get on the water, you want cannoli go inland, go to the mountains, but never in summer." He finished his sfogliatell' in three bites, downed his espresso, wiped his mouth with complete satisfaction, and hurried out as quickly as he came. He'd left his taxi running, parked on an angle up on the curb. Technically I knew the guy was right, but I realized that if you live that way, you'll never be finished. In traveling, there's always a push to go see the next thing and the thing after that. Someone's always gonna say where the best pizza is, the best pastry, the best museum, the best ruin, the best church, the best sunset, whatever, and if you listen, you'll always be on the run to the next thing and never be where you are, so in effect you never get anywhere, because you never arrive, you're always coming or going. I'd go to Caltanissetta for cannoli and just as I was about to take a bite, someone would say, if you really want cannoli you gotta go to the lady on top of the hill just out of town whose got her own sheep, her cream is the freshest on the island, but only go when the sheep are full of sweet grass between *La Festa dell'Immacolata* and *La Pasqua.* And I'd go to that lady, and she'd tell me her sheep were sick all fall, and if I really want cannoli I should go across the valley where the young sheep are. I told myself—*you'll never be where you are if the best thing is always somewhere else.*

So, I did the opposite. I made this deal with myself. Every day would be better than the last. A commitment. An intention. Not to do bigger, better things, but rather, in small moments—to be here now. To create *un momento di luce*, a moment of light, a oneness. These came in the most mundane tasks. Every day I found a moment to say, this is where I am, hand rinsing my clothes, biting into this *cornetto alla crema*, talking to this person in the street. Breathe. Be here now. Take it in. Notice all around you. Distant sounds, the light, the wind, scents, the white cat running across the top of the old stone wall as lightning cracks. Feel joy now. A moment of light. A poet's moment. A freedom moment. Vertical time, where time stands still and takes on the luster of a still life. Be here now. It's a poet's way to wrangle moments. Lasso a moment. Lend words to a moment in time. Live the haiku. Make this the best moment of the day. Feed the moment. Feed time. I thought back to my old parking meter on my writing desk in New York, an hour cost a quarter. You had to feed time. Now I had a task, an intention. To feed time. Feed eternity. Eternity in the cleft of seconds. Live the still life of it all.

Stan Pugliese and Jennifer Romanello arrived in town. As we walked through the streets, I linked arms with one then the other. Walking arm in arm meant I wouldn't fall again. Maybe that's why Italians started walking arm in arm in the first place—so as not to trip over *Sanpietrini! Uè Pulcinella, whaddyathink, a ccussì?* From via Santa Maria di Costantinopoli, we cut through piazza Bellini and took a left down via San Pietro a Maiella passed the music conservatory. We were headed to a joint they knew to have dinner, *La Loconda del Grifo.* Stan had *Sanpietrini* down, he had the walk; heel toe, heel toe, kick up—pause, find the meniscus of the next stone with the arch of the foot, let the toe roll forward over the space between the next stone, step by step by step. I told him, "You got the walk. Look how you are walking! Like Michael Corleone in that scene with Kay and the school children." We all laughed. Stan and Jennifer fit right into *Napoli*—a handsome *Mezzogiornese* couple. Jennifer was down to earth with long brown hair and a flowing warm welcoming vibe. Stan dressed sharp in casual suits. He had a perceptive look in his eye as a witness to history. He knew *Napoli*. Walking with him made every century come alive at once. One afternoon we joined a tour group in Pompeii, and Stan graciously whispered addendums, clarifications, and contextualization to us about what the tour guide left out. After the tour, we did Stan's extra tour. One lucky moment happened on the official tour. The tour guide asked if there was a singer in the house. Stan pointed at me. I said, "What singer, I'm no singer," thinking they'd expect some lyric soprano. Reluctantly, I walked down the stone rings of seats into the bullseye of the ancient amphitheater. I took a deep breath and chanted a vocal improv in *terza rima*, the rhyme scheme Dante created for the Divine Comedy. Waxing on the moment, I recited the syllables of Stan and Jennifer's names, both of whom had awesome powers of listening and receiving, and enjoying; open souls, open ears and open hearts, as open as *l'anfiteatro* itself. My voice amplified off the acoustics of cut stone rising in waves around me. I had an overwhelming feeling of belonging. This is where I felt at home, standing in the center of the basin of the stage in the amphitheater in Pompeii, releasing my voice to ricochet up off the rings of stones. Now, I had a locus to refer back to whenever I felt lost and alone, a singular moment where I felt cosmically connected.

We continued on our walk toward *La Loconda del Grifo,* walking down the curved hill of piazza Luigi Miraglia, where once again I saw the hand-painted sign on the wall that had captured my attention. I stopped and pointed out the fanciful lettering, embellished with colorful dots and slashes of color and that unique message, the best activist sign I'd seen in all my life with its personal offer:

> *ZIA ADA offre caffè, tè freddo, o limonata*
> *—in cambio di solidarietà.*
> *Le case per tutti.*

> Aunt Ada offers coffee, iced tea, or lemonade
> in exchange for solidarity.
> Housing for all.

I yelled up at the windows, "*Zia Ada! Zia Ada!*" The building was a pale sandy yellow with gray window frames and shutters. Above the signs, the shutters were painted red. Under a span of three windows a long white sheet printed with a protest message in red lettering waved in the wind. All the windows on three floors were wide open—which was strange. Italians avoid draughts at all costs, the infamous *colpo di freddo*, attack of the wind, that only affects Italians—that's why we wear scarves even in summer, to block the wind from hitting the back of our necks. The wind attacks on an angle, not at the spine, but three quarters back on the neck, the vulnerable spot only the wind knows how to find. Even worse, *la corrente*, the flow of the wind, spirals all over the earth from the solar wind down to us terrestrials and causes *cervicale*, when the wind gets inside and between your cervical vertebra where it seizes the muscles of the neck and upper back. Italians take extreme precautions to keep the wind out of our chests, so to see all these windows wide open was radical. Who were these people?

Sheets hung below several windows, with red block lettering:

MOVIMENTO PER IL DIRITTO ALL'ABITARE
MAGNAMMECE O PESONE
CASE REDDITO
SALUTE NAPOLI
       (Movement for housing rights
       Eat the rent!
       Houses for Income
       To the health of Napoli)

Mai Più Senza Casa
Movimento Per Il Diritto All'Abitare
       (Never Again Without Housing
       Movement for The Right to Housing)

La Casa a Tutti!
       (Housing for All!)

I yelled up at the windows again, "*Zia Ada! Zia Ada!*" No one answered. I yelled louder, more insistent. One thing I knew how to do with my Bronx voice was how to shout at buildings to call for people, joining the long tradition of pushcart peddler cries ricocheting in alleyways up at windows. I thought of all the women of my Bronx youth who saddled windowsills with pillows so they could lean out their perch and commune with the street, all the windows I'd yelled up at to call for my friends, a Bronx tradition rooted in these very alleyways. My voice was made to bounce off stone like a Spaldeen and ricochet off *Sanpietrini* where voices have echoed for fourteen hundred years of *Napoli*—Neopolis—New City. "*Zia Ada! Zia Ada!*"

"*ZIA ADA*" Stan said informatively, "is probably an acronym of some kind. *Zona Industriale . . .*"

"*O,* I thought it was a lady. Aunt Ada." *Uè Pulcinella, rumpo cazzo! Madonn' couldn't you clue me in!* I shouted up at the open window again, "*Zia Ada! Zia Ada!*" and a woman appeared on the street walking directly toward me.

"*Sì, sì,*" she said, almost concerned and as if to say, "Why are you hollering so?"

"*Tu sei Zia Ada?*"

"*Sì, sì,*" she aimed to calm me or find out what was the matter with me.

Young, hot, voluptuous, with blue laser eyes, long black hair, a silver stud in her top lip—she didn't look like any "Aunt Ada" I'd pictured. Meet Benedetta, *la Napulitana più bella,* the consummate Neopolitan woman.

"*Ti offro la mia solidarietà,*" I offer you my solidarity. Hands on my heart, "*Dov'è il mio caffè?*" Where is my coffee?

Her eyebrows sharpened in questioning decisive angles; she didn't know what I was talking about. I pointed to the sign and repeated my declaration.

"*Ahhh,*" she laughed and hollered up at the windows until a redhead appeared. They yelled up and down until they agreed, I should return the next day at the proper hour to have a coffee: "*Sedici,*" sixteen hundred—four o'clock. The redhead yelled down to me, "*Mo facce nu caffè, a doman'. Piacere mij.*"

Benedetta was gracious and generous. She told us about the housing crisis in *Napoli*. Locals were forced out of their homes as apartments were being rented through Airbnb to travelers instead of locals. Landlords made quadruple the rent if they rented short-term, creating a housing crisis. Benedetta told us passionately, "*Senza Napulitani, Napule è finita.*" Without Neopolitans, *Napoli* is finished.

I told her the same is true for New York. "*Senza Newyorkese, New York è finùd!*" Without New Yorkers, New York is finished.

Benedetta explained that she and thirty-four others, including ten children, moved into this building which had been empty for years. A developer was trying to get them put out into the street, so he could turn the building into another hotel. We talked about the Catholic church being one of the biggest real estate owners in the world. Benedetta said they owned a lot of properties that were empty, that they didn't pay tax on, and they didn't use for social programs either. Families seeking emergency housing occupied some of these buildings and aimed to negotiate to rent. Meanwhile the church courted commercial real estate deals. Neighborhoods were foundering as locals were pushed into homelessness, for more hotels and Airbnb. Where do locals go?

Sitting with Benedetta the next day, I bent my mind around the Ouroborus message of the name of their housing movement: *Magnammece O Pesone.* Eat the rent to survive. If the choice is to eat or pay rent, then eat the rent. If you eat the rent, you can't pay the rent. These thoughts spun in my head. Must we eat ourselves to pay the rent? When poor and faced with the choice, people ate the rent and were eaten by the rent, from the combined effects of poverty, gentrification, unaffordable rents, low wages, and the housing balance tipped in favor of transient international elites. Benedetta and the rest of her community all appreciated tourism for the good of the city, but not at the expense of their city. No one wanted a *Napule* theme park. Eat a pizza, sing a song, ride the *funicola'* and go home.

Every day I visited with Benedetta at her outdoor stall where she sold African soaps, natural creams, scents, incense, henna, lipstick, and eye make-up. As much passion as I had for *Napoli*, Benedetta had an equal passion for the Bronx. Our conversations were filled with housing issues and the refugee crisis in the Mediterranean. She asked me how much I paid a night for the hotel, and told me that on my next visit, if I wanted to stay longer, she knew of cheaper accommodations. I told her how in New York we had the same housing problem, and that I too was priced out of where I'd lived in Brooklyn. Artists, the poor, and the working class lost plenty of New York housing as a gentrified Manhattan became more a city for international elites. She wasn't shocked to hear that about one out of every hundred New Yorkers is without stable housing and thousands sleep on the street, in the subways, and in shelters, every night.

One day Benedetta had to leave the stand to get her son at school, so I watched the stand for her and felt completely at home on this curved street in an activist community in the heart of *Napoli. Uè Pulcinella wanna buy some soap?* A customer came to smell soap fragrances and I chatted her up until Benedetta returned.

Chapter Twelve. "Portals through Time"

TO GET TO PIZZERIA CAPASSO, I meandered for hours through a maze of narrow alleyway streets on my way to Porta San Gennaro. On via Consolazione, I offered a candy to an elderly woman leaning out of her street level window. The street was an extension of her living room. "*Buonasera Signora,*" I said, "*vuoi una caramella?*" With an outstretched arm, I handed her a candy that I had in my pocket. She broke open into a toothless smile like a child, "*Grazie,*" taking the candy, unwrapping it and putting it right into her mouth. *Un momento di luce.* I felt at one with the world, bringing me back to all the times in life my mother or grandmother handed me a piece of Italian hard candy, or butterscotch balls or green mint jelly leaves. A piece of candy is an offering that lasts just long enough, and for as long as it lasts, everything is alright.

I walked through the gate of Porta San Gennaro, a stone arch entryway in the old section of the city, and joined Stan, Jennifer, and Francesco at an outdoor table up on a raised stone platform outside the pizzeria. As Stan poured vino, he pointed out that the arch of the gate showed a fresco of *San Gennaro, La Madonna* and other saints who saved the city from plague in the 1600's and that this gate was the oldest in the city, first built by the Greeks on a lava field that determined the layout of the streets, back as far as when *Napoli* was Neopolis. I drank the *vino* and listened. The gate was a portal through time.

Peter Covino arrived. As he walked up to our table, I got a flashback to twenty years before, when he walked toward me one night after I finished reading at a podium. Peter embodied elegance both in his poetry and in the way he carried himself. It was 1998 when we were at Teachers & Writers Collaborative off Union Square, in a room surrounded by polished oak and glass-paned doors. That night, I was being honored with a poetry award from the Italian American Writers' Association. Peter walked toward me with his arms open, in heartfelt congratulations. He was finely dressed in a blue suit jacket, and as he walked, the world softened around him. He gave me the Italian double kiss hello. I remember introducing him to my mother. Now, twenty years later, we were in *Napoli* and here comes Peter, and it was as if the moments joined, and that wherever I would be in the world of poetry, Peter would be there walking gracefully toward me. We were slated to give readings back-to-back from town to town. Massive serendipity, the opposite of a heart attack, whatever that would be; an all-of-a-sudden out-of-nowhere heart lift.

At Pizzeria Capasso, we dove into an ocean of pizza. I floated in it, head back, staring up at the sky. Pizza makes me feel alive. The Capasso family was one of the oldest *pizzaioli* families in *Napoli* and the world, and it is true, this was the best pizza of my life. Eat pizza at Capasso's and you are finished, for life. The pizza is alive. The dough grows even as it goes inside you. The living pizza inside you, bubbling like the volcano. We met three generations of Capasso *pizzaioli*. Iole, the granddaughter, joined us and made the introductions. She was a photographer and would document the literary festival. As I sat there, I pictured my grandparents as teenagers running through the stone arch and eating this same pizza margherita con *funghi* one hundred years before, when they could have eaten here on their way to embark for America. Pizza is a throughline. It was good for me to think of them young and laughing with pocket money to spend on pizza, and not as starving peasants who had to go work in another country to save their family from starvation between the two World Wars. The true truth I'll never know, although I did question Grandma Rose all my life, and record her memories. She was sick and nauseous on the boat and couldn't bear to indulge remembering it. The crossing was full of pain and suffering for her. In life, as I knew her, she kept in the moment as much as possible, kept focused on what needed to be fixed and mended, cooked, cleaned, sewn.

Napoli Città Libro was a weekend long, at San Domenico Maggiore. Francesco was excited to have Italian American poets with him, and his pride showed. He introduced us to editors and scholars, with the plan of getting our books translated into Italian. He considered this tour an epic return of the literary eye back to the homeland. I buttoned my navy blazer's brass buttons and blended in with the men, who wore dark blazers. A life-size statue of *La Madonna* in the center of the courtyard inspired me to pray an *Ave Maria* at her feet, and upstairs in the grandest room, the *Sala del Capitolo*, a giant painting of the crucifixion gave me pause. I stood there in silent reverence before this visceral larger-than-life crucifixion scene which depicted the drama of the labor of lifting the cross; an effort which took five workmen. One man up in a tree pulled a rope with all his might, tied to the top of the cross. All his muscles engaged as he pulled the cross to a standing position. On the cross, an already unconscious Christ. Four men pushed from below. Gray clouds swirled through a pale blue sky. I wondered where the animals were to witness the scene. There was a white horse of a Roman soldier. Where were the birds? The goats? The lamb with a compassionate eye? The donkey? There had to be animals there. Animals are always depicted at the birth of Christ in nativity scenes, they had to be present to witness his death. The animals would have come.

We performed readings outdoors in the cloister, the central interior garden of the monastery. The walkways around the garden were covered with white scalloped ceilings with archways. It was easy to imagine monks walking these halls in the 1200's. Francesco read my bio and announced the names of my books, translating the titles, except for the word "butch." I interrupted him and asked, *"Scusatemi, c'è una traduzione per la parola* butch?"

"Not directly," he said, *"forse maschio?"*

That didn't sound right to me. Being butch was not just about masculinity. It was about rejecting the role assigned to women as being snake charmers to the phallus, and it was also about being a woman. There had to be words in Italian. Italian had better words for everything, I expected nothing less of the word "butch." Francesco, being a natural performer and fourth wall breaker, asked the audience. One of his students in the back row offered, *"Camionista."* Truck driver.

Now I had a new question to take on the road. Is there an Italian translation for the word, "butch?" Are there words that come close?

Are they all derogatory? What are the proud words? There must be a word.

Francesco requested I recite, "This is The Bronx," in English, while he performed a live translation. This poem is about learning to drive a truck! *O Madonn'*, I guess I was playing the *camionista!* I opened my mouth and swung the bat, connecting with the crowd. When I had to choose what to read next, I looked at the audience and thought about where we were: the monastic courtyard of San Domenico Maggiore where Saint Thomas Aquinas received his life-changing mystical vision in the 1200's, when Jesus on the cross spoke directly to him. After his "vision of the cross," Thomas, who had written vast amounts of theology, declared he would stop writing, and a year later, died. I was filled with passages of his work on the necessity of suffering for the soul's development, which to me, made a lot of sense. I always thought that without the cancer stripping everything away when I was eighteen, I might have become some right-wing prosecutor. Could have happened. I knew I had to speak and write, who knows what turn this would have taken if I didn't go through the furnace of illness. The audience was attentive and spread out under the loges in the open night air. I looked around and thought, what can I bring to this place at this moment? I chose a lesbian poem to read, "Licking Batteries." The stark counterpoint of the place and the poem was lost on no one. And it was fun for me to watch Francesco improvise a translation.

Francesco organized what he called our "Welcome Home Tour," and joked it was our "Red Hot Chili Pepper Tour." He'd been a front man in a rock band in his youth, and some nights he belted out rock ballads in English after our gigs were over and the *vino* flowed. He was powered by his intellect and passion for artists. He had a rock and roll spirit, drank bullet shots of espresso, smoked cigarettes continually, charged through the day, sang to our audiences at night and was the last to turn in at day's end. He treated us like rock stars. I stayed a couple of days at his house, making *i momenti di luce* hanging my clothes on his pocket balcony with all the others on his street hanging clothes on their balconies, winds gushing over the tall staircase built right into the side of the mountain, like a waterfall of wind. I learned the hard way, the secret of why *Napulitan'* laundry doesn't drip on pedestrians' heads. I hung my wet clothes out and someone yelled up from down below that my shirts were dripping on people. Francesco's daughter Libera showed me the way. Wet clothes are not hand-wrung, but spun effectively, or put through the wringer enough times, so there's no drip. A secret revealed.

Francesco had a world of books at home, floor to ceiling, many he'd edited, translated, organized the publications of, and his walls were full of original works of art. He showed me a black and white Keith Haring painting, and told me his adventure getting it:

"In the '80's I was getting on a subway in the West Village, and I spotted a Keith Haring graffiti on a poster on a wall. I stepped out of the subway car and went *shhhhhrrrrrp* and ripped it right off the wall." He gestured with two arms up in the air and showed me how he stripped the wheat-pasted painting off the wall in one decisive motion. "I rolled it up and got back on the train." This was one of his prized possessions, framed in his living room, and emblematic of his passion for the street, for art, for living artists making their mark on the street, for the real, the palpable, the grit, the true.

Francesco, Stan, Jennifer, Peter and I performed readings from town to town. Peter and I stayed for the whole tour from *Napoli* to the University of Salerno at Fisciano, to Matera, Potenza, and Salerno. On the eve of my fifty-fifth birthday, the moon was just past full over Matera. Other forces were at work. It seemed my ancestors were orchestrating this trip. My younger cousin, who I cherished, came from Acquaviva delle Fonti to our reading in *Fondazione Sassi* in Matera. To give a recitation inside a cave like a grotto imbued with spirit, with my cousin in attendance, felt like an overlay of lifetimes; the significance of our intersections through time was greater than my comprehension. All I know is that we were smiling and hugging inside a cave fixed with lighting and a sound system, where our ancestors had lived for millennia. Matera is said to be one of the most ancient habitations on earth, with life dating back to the Neolithic era over seven thousand years ago. I breathed deep and took it all in, squeezing my cousin in a bear hug and filling the cave with my voice. The next day, on the mountaintop of Potenza, novelist Paolo Albano and his group *Letti di Sera* threw me a birthday feast, the likes of which could never be reciprocated, not in a thousand lifetimes. There was a spirit of meeting the moment in life, a generosity, as if everyone understood this moment would only come around once in a lifetime.

Francesco drove, and when I was hot and tired, he pulled my massive suitcase, which he monikered, "the corpse." Peter and I went for long walks, one night we drank a quiet Aperol Spritz through the sunset on the waterfront in Salerno. I found *un momento di luce*, sipping sunset. Francesco introduced us to literati in every town, and the *Mezzogiorno* came alive through the words of these writers. Peter's poems were exquisite and vulnerable, summoning his mother in the act of calling him from the other room, and visions of *La Madonna* and ancestors. The relationship of his poems to the spirit of the *paese* was palpable. Peter was born in Sturno, about an hour outside *Napoli*, and had immigrated to the States as a child. His recitations gave the audience a nuanced ride where they could hang onto his beat and breath.

Time slowed down when we were on the road. New poems came to me every day. I had *i momenti di luce* every day, and never wanted to be anywhere but where I was, day by day. I was grateful to whatever forces were at work, whatever wind, whatever power, that had paired up Peter and I to represent America on this tour. Although this was a once in a lifetime road trip, I couldn't help but be filled with the feeling that I would return and have lifelong relationships with the writers we met, for however long life lasted. I knew I would think of them the rest of my life. I also knew there'd never be a way to reciprocate the level of welcome and hospitality we received, whenever they made it to New York in the future. New York felt out of my reach. After losing my housing in a wave of gentrification when apartments were boosted to "market value," I'd lost my sense of place and home, my connection to my town was severed for me in the gentrified New York. Long ago, when I was a kid in the Bronx, I felt that irrevocable bond to my block, my neighborhood, but no longer. I thought back to emails from members of *Malia*, our Italian American women's writers' collective, "Does anybody know a good inexpensive place where we can meet, eat pizza, drink *vino* and talk for hours?" The inference was—without it costing forty bucks a head? New York had left us flat.

Our last night in *Napoli*, a bunch of us sat at a table drinking *negroni* beneath the obelisk in the middle of piazza San Domenico Maggiore. As the conversation in Italian went over my head, ashtrays filled, and the *negroni* took effect, I felt the tilt of the piazza. We were sitting on the downward slope, and although the grade wasn't noticeable as we walked in, it steepened during the second *negroni*. The piazza was a giant ashtray at night buzzing with action, people coming and going, smoking and talking, laughing and communing, drinking and kissing, breathing through cigarettes with burning orange tips and flicking them in arcs onto the *Sanpietrini* where they settled in cracks, smoke curling upward from the stones until they died out or were crushed under a foot or were picked up by a straggler who walked on with his treasure, smoking like a man who could afford indulgence. Life was good. The obelisk towered above us, lit up, like an ivory femur from a giant.

"What's the significance of the obelisk?" I asked the table.

"*Ahh* the *guglia*," someone said.

"It's a plague column. An ex-voto. It was built as a vow to protect *Napoletani* against the Bubonic plague of 1656."

Half the table got involved in this conversation. Sit at a table with writers and historians, ask a question and you'll get history, a debate of conflicting histories if you're lucky. A fragment of the story stays in my mind and magnifies into full blown dialogue. I don't remember who said what, or even who was at the table, just the bone-colored obelisk towering above us, and that I expressed my love for studying global epidemiology in college; how plagues shaped the world and the outcomes of wars, that I read closely such texts as, *Plagues and Peoples*.

"Back then plagues spread slowly by ship. The Bubonic Plague came to *Napoli* in the spring, probably from a ship from Sardinia. There was one doctor who noticed people were dying by the dozens and had the *coglioni* to talk about it to governing powers at the time. No other doctors wanted to come forward.

"You report it, you get blamed for it."

"Exactly."

"Then everyone panics, and you have mass hysteria on your hands.

"And the powers that be, don't want that."

"Upsets the status quo."

Pulcinella, you were there, whaddya have to say?

"One man, Dr. Giuseppe Bozzuto was at the *Santissima Annunziata,* a hospital for abandoned children and unwed women who were ready to give birth. There should be a statue to him. He named what was going on as a contagion. People didn't want to hear it."

"You gotta remember this was all a kingdom. *Napoli* was the seat of the capital of the Kingdom of Two Sicilies. And who supported the hospitals? The nobility. And the nobility did not want to hear about a plague coming to town. Nonetheless, Dr. Bozzuto came out with it, he got a reward—they imprisoned him."

"Imprisoned him? What happened to him?"

"He died in prison. Of the plague. No one had any idea what caused the disease. Since it was spring, it was Lent, when everyone ate fish. Meat, of course, is forbidden during Lent. No one knew why people were dying by the thousands. Some concluded it must be all the fish everyone was eating."

"Blame the fish for the contagion."

"So, what did they do? They threw all the fish back into the sea. There were riots right here where we're sitting now and all over the city. Chaos. They did bloodletting, they made poultices, they forced vomiting, they fasted to the point of starvation—nothing helped. Priests rang the church bells for the dead until the bells of *Napoli* never stopped ringing, and the nobility clamped down and said, "No more bells. No more counting the dead.""

We toasted the dead, gave thanks for our health, emptied our glasses, and lifted a glass in *salut'* to the many saints pictured on the *guglia,* some of the usual suspects: *San Antonio, San Tommaso, San Caterina, San Domenico, Sant' Agata, Santa Rosa.*

I lifted my glass. "Cheers to the dead, to all who have passed, may your souls get to Heaven fast."

"Poor Dog of Pompeii in a Steel Chain"

Legs twisted up to *Vesuvio*
Tortured for *l'eternità*
I hear your howl
For Apollo
Who *Alas!* was only made of bronze
and could not could not unchain you

"Chips of Moonlight"

on the pavement
like stars

you navigate your walk home by
walking surprisingly quick

from stone to stone meniscus
under the curve of your feet

that's why you don't step on the cracks
your mother's back actually did break when

her toe ripped in the ridge
between two broken stones

you are resolute to not falter
your feet feel for the center of each stone

a simple system, millennia years old
embedded in the ground: white tiles, stones, shells

for the moon to find
to make a path of footlights

chips of moonlight guide you home
from meeting your lover in the forum

in the nameless wind
under Apollo's

chiappa

"The House of the Tragic Poet"

Sitting on a chalky stone wall in Pompeii
il sole Napulitane a heavy piggyback

white cotton t-shirt wrapped around my head
like a sheik to soak sweat and shield

me from the volcano sun
Stan Pugliese walks on, *Virgilio*, leads us:

"Just a couple more mosaics
I want you to see."

Pugliese tugs us back two thousand years
to the snarling black and white dog

inset in tiles
Cave Canem, Beware of Dog

two-thousand-year snarl and bark
We hear you

as we stand at your *portico*
where you felt earth's rumble

where you guarded the door
moments before

the volcano blew black curtains
over the sky

"Bubbles"

Lemons big as footballs
we sat under, lemons of Vesuvius

nursed on volcanic ash.
A chair in the shade is such a welcome relief

after walking the streets of Pompeii
staring at twisted petrified remains

Pompeians in their final moments,
in cowering angled postures.

Plates and glasses and conversations overflow
Lacryma Christi vino and *acqua minerale*

Stan Pugliese, Jennifer Romanello and I,
mountains of *gelato*, whipped cream spirals

cherry syrup drizzles lava patterns
around our white china plates.

Everything is effervescence
streams of bubbled light

from bottles pour
steadily into our glasses.

Stone walls are bubbled pumice
filled with pockets of air.

Frizzante, inside us and all around,
air bubbles buzz as they rise.

Che piacere respirare insieme adesso
Proprio adesso
in questo momento
in una vita
Una volta

What a pleasure it is to breathe together now
Right now
in this moment
in a lifetime
Once

"Clothespins"

The flags of *Napoli*
shake the wind on rope and wire
from windows and pocket balconies
by each *Napulitan'*

Who am I screaming to
to help me forge a life?

Is it all back to the interminable cry in the crib?
Adults talking around the table
convinced my cry is best left unanswered?

I know they hear me
I know they think I will stop
but the cry has only gotten stronger
over fifty-five years, more insistent

I see a man, he looks so free to me
without a shirt, pinching his bed sheet to the line
on via Giovanni Bausan, a *Napulitan'* street that begins
as a staircase cut into the mountain

My silent cry reaches the sea by scooter
over cobblestone alleys where you must go faster
or your front wheel will get caught in a rut.

Going slow is more dangerous than one would imagine.

My cry speeds up
gains power in the knowledge
it is heard in the din
and I will never
hear the answer

"I See You Pulcinella"

Mask
in a marble notch on via Alessandro Dumas Padre
but you forgot something
and hurried back up the hill
before returning
to mask at sea

What did you forget, Pulcinella?

"I want to dive"

into the sky
and circle the courtyard
le rondini Salernitane / the swallows of Salerno
are having all the fun
more than *i ragazzi* on scooters
bands of them
too many to count
and some of them
are calling

"Tomorrow my *cugini*"

have "organized themselves"
to come hear me recite poetry in a cave

under a moon just past full, in Matera
on the eve of my 55th birthday.

This confluence is beyond anyone's planning.
My mother Rachele I am sure is our tour manager

organizing it all from above as Grandma Rose
conspires with angels. Can you hear the laughter

of ancestors in the caves?
How long can an echo last if you keep listening?

In death they have accepted all of me
the writer who opens her mouth like a crack in the earth

to let the pressurized sulfur out
and the butch lesbian who will carry their seed no more.

No more *Racheline* or *Rosina* coming from this body,
just the stirring in my soul of *il campanile a sei e mezza*

the song of the swallows celebrating
the heat of the day subsides

the peach pit I take from my mouth
to pinch back into earth

"*i Fosforescenti* / The Phosphorescent Ones"

Was it Jupiter or Saturn under the red moon
that night we three poets sat on the low wooden wall
of *Spiaggia Santa Teresa* in Salerno, debating

names of planets over the bay?
Peter Covino, Giorgio Sica, and I,
dangled our legs over the wall

swayed gently with the sea
drank *vino vulcanico sotto la luna rosa*
watched tangos swirl couples

over wooden slats of the boardwalk
one leg at a time stretching up to kick stars
then slowly sweeping arcs across the floor.

Vocal tracks with trilled *rrrr's*
passionate vowels intimating love
rode accordions and violins

in Italianate *arpeggi* like bird cry
over the sea by three fast fingers
the old song shook loose

three poets mourning divorce's brutality on children.
Three fishing poles stood vertically in the sand
pointing straight up at the planets

One pole was directly in line with, was it Jupiter or Saturn?
On top of each fishing pole, LED lamps,
phosphorescent as fishes, purple and green lights.

I wish there were more nights like this in life,
three poets and three fishing poles—*i fosforescenti*
tipped with light, poised to catch what comes

"When I wander"

no inclination to walk
in one direction over another
I follow someone.

Today I follow a family with little kids.
It's Sunday, *la Domenica,* they must be taking their kids
somewhere beautiful. They lead me through a park
to a beautiful seaside road.

I stop for *acqua minerale e apizz'*
via Francesco Caracciolo
The air is good here.
Il vento, the wind, a relief.

Pedal carriages, people cycling
their Sunday four at a time along the sea.
Onward. Go for a walk
Go. Let the winds

take you where they may. Five directions at once.
Pulcinella, Comme se chiamma 'o viento?
Whaddyacall the wind
that finds my face and flutters?

The wind that skips over the sea
and bends around
me?

"*La Madonna di Libertà*"

Green face like the Statue of Liberty,
her copper countenance once shined,
when Grandma Rose left *Italia* from this port of *Napoli*

Immacolatella

The last *Madonna* Grandma Rose saw
before *La Madonna di Libertà* at Ellis Island

Immacolatella

stands on a serpent with the head of a bulldog

Immacolatella

Her first angel holds left hand on heart, mouth open in adulation.
Her second angel sits in clouds, feather
in hand, turning toward her.
Her third angel points, directing us to her.
Her fourth angel raises an open palm over us,
blessing and warning at the same time,
just as my mother did whenever I left the apartment
standing by the door, "Be careful!"
"*Mi raccomando!*"
A serpent is hiding, poised to attack
from between the fourth angel's legs.
The fourth angel seems to control the serpent's ferocity,
almost rides it.

Immacolatella, Immacolatella

A salute to the sea where you were born.

"*Caríssima* Grandma Rose,"

I STAND WHERE YOU STOOD when you boarded the *Duca degli Abruzzi* in 1919 with your sister Lucia when you were teenagers. I'm looking up at the copper statue of the *Immacolatella,* and I realize that she was the last *Madonna* you said a prayer to, until your arrival in New York where the copper Statue of Liberty seemed like a giant *Madonna* to you, rising up out of the ocean. *La Madonna di Libertà.* That miracle moment, to be greeted by the biggest *Madonna* you could ever imagine and right there, in the water, her face and torch and book and long robe, as your ship pulled into the harbor of your new life. A prayer answered. The grueling crossing was over.

How must you have felt at nineteen, so full of hope and bravery for the unknown? So willing to work. I wish I knew you at that age. What did you do with the fear? Did you have a few hours in *Napoli* before you shipped off for New York City? Did you eat pizza in *Napoli* before you got on the boat? I'd like to think you did. I'd like to think you ate at Pizzeria Capasso in Porta San Gennaro where I ate a hundred years later; that you ate pizza made by the grandfather, and me by the grandson. Who knows? Pizza was poor man's food. It's possible.

I still have the little plastic Statue of Liberty you gave me forty years ago that you stole from Liberty Park. I laugh when I think about what you said. "There was a *tavola. Tutti free.*" And how you and your senior citizen tour group took everything on the table, and my mother figured out what happened. "That poor vendor must have gone to the bathroom for a minute and when he came back everything was wiped out." We had a good laugh over that. You came home with pennants and statues. I painted my writing room Liberty green. It was unintentional really, I was mixing paint, and that's what I came up with. Then I saw that it matched the Statue of Liberty you gave me. That color of oxidized copper, green with a silver overtone, still subconsciously gives me hope for new beginnings, and so as I write, that is the color of the wall I stare at.

I think that for you, immigrating was going to work, a practical decision, going to where the jobs were, sending money home, saving the family. You were a master of staying in the moment, in the here and now. Always productive, your hands busy. I know my life made no sense to you; it makes little sense to me. Embroidering words. The needlework of punctuation and spelling. Hours staring into the light of a screen. I woke up today and before I opened my eyes, behind my eyelids I saw lines of words scrolling after one another. What am I doing to my brain? Staring into light. And all the contemplation. I remember you teasing me, "Make a few more pages," as if I were wasting my time. I'd like to live more like you, more hands-on, hands on something. When I was born you were already a senior citizen, yet now I think of you as a youth, running to New York City to your factory job, saving, saving.

I'm so glad you got back to Acquaviva once to see your sister Maria and her daughter Annunziatine. I imagine you both in your eighties, seeing each other for the first time in sixty-five years. Did you talk about the fact that she was supposed to be the one who went to America instead of you? That if The Great War didn't interrupt the plan, she would have been the one to go? I know you instantly knew each other's eyes and voices. I bet you wanted to stay in Acquaviva at that point. It could have been sweet to live out your years in the *paese*, walking in the piazza, shopping in the open-air market. Instead, you came back to the Bronx at eighty-one, and did your shopping across White Plains Road alone for the next twelve years, crossing four lanes of traffic carrying plastic bags on your arms. It's hard to imagine the displacement you must have felt, especially after going back. And the hostile aggressive traffic zipping around you. No wonder you told me, "Life is a dream." I am beginning to understand. With loss, and death and the way life doesn't make sense. What is a dream? You close your eyes and your mind creates a world. You exist on another level, someplace else behind your eyes. The people you know make appearances, and other people you imagine. You wake up and it's over, and sometimes you remember what happened, sometimes you don't.

I'm grateful I got my mother to Acquaviva to meet her cousins. Those few days in Acquaviva made all of life worth living, all the suffering, all the loneliness, poverty and disease, abuse, and hard times—all rendered worthwhile by a couple of days when she walked arm in arm with her cousins through the piazza and got to see where you were born and baptized. We only had a few days on earth together with the cousins in our homeland, but what a miracle it was, a modern miracle of medicine and surgery and peacetime and privilege and technology, aircraft and credit cards and dollars. You'll be happy to know, I've convinced Rosina and Rocco to meet me to go to Acquaviva. We're meeting at the airport in Rome and getting a connecting flight to Bari. Then we'll drive over to meet Annunziatine. I'm so grateful. And all in your honor and memory.

I remember the first time I drove into Acquaviva after college. By the time I got to Zia Annunziatine's house, she already knew I'd taken a wrong turn and had to circle around twice. Some lady looked out her window and told another lady on a balcony and word spread like that, lady to lady, window to balcony, that a red car on its way with an American to Annunziatine took the wrong turn. Every woman was a lookout from her window. And that's how Annunziatine greeted me, pointing out that I took the wrong turn. She had ladies keeping an eye out for me, from the road entering town all the way to her house. I might have been the first American to walk down her street, via Leandro Pecci. That's how it felt, the return of the American—let's see what they made of themselves over there . . .

Acquaviva delle Fonti has a lot to be proud of, it's become a sophisticated town, and has grown so much, with the best regional hospital, the ancient and still best source of *acquadolce* drinking water for miles around, and of course the phenomenal giant red onions. That's another thing I didn't understand when you were alive, your onion calzone, *madonn'* that thing was heavy as a cinderblock and sharp with provolone, but boy do I wish I had it now. You made the best crust, the lightest crust I ever had in my life.

> Thank you for putting life and a light touch
> into everything you made, including me.
> And for the sparkle in your eye,
> in my eye now,
>
> Annie

PART III
COMU U CHIAMI U VENTU?

This
is
the
food

I

w
a
n
t

on
my
death
bed

Gnocchi
alla
Sorrentina

Let
earth
quakes
come

Let   o
Etna   t
roar   a
            i
I felt   g
            n
the breeze   a
            m

 of Death's
  scythe   ho
   before   *Gia*
     Let   more
    her s w i n g once

Chapter Thirteen. "The Love in Your Eyes"

STEFANIA TAVIANO, A PROFESSOR at the University of Messina, invited me to Sicily ten years before I arrived. We'd first met in Manhattan when she was researching Italian American performance artists. I told her to meet me at the crossroads of Bleecker and Carmine Streets at 6th Avenue, an intersection that had vestiges of New York Italian culture: *pasticceria*, church, pizzeria, and a park with a fountain where you could toss bits of your pizza crust to pigeons and sparrows. My routine was to sit and write over a cappuccino and a pasticciott' at Rocco's, and since I was a New Yorker I could have a cappuccino at a blasphemous afternoon hour of the day, then after a few hours get a slice at Joe's Pizza where three men with fast hands and pivot action worked around each other like a basketball offense under the boards dishing out pizza, grabbing dollar bills and yelling, "Next!" to the line of customers streaming out onto the sidewalk. I'd eat my pizza at the fountain in the park, toss the shy sparrows crumbs away from the aggressive pigeons, then walk into the cool dark nave of Our Lady of Pompeii Church to talk with Saint Rocco or whichever saint I needed, and finish down the block at the old anarchist bookstore where I'd browse or buy a new notebook and an old title. This was my pilgrimage, a place where old New York could still be found within new New York. Some variation of that ritual had been going on for generations.

Stefania's smile could disarm anybody, she had curly hazelnut hair and dimples deep enough to make problems disappear. We'd talked about my performance-art at The Arthur Avenue Retail Market in the Bronx. Somewhere in our conversation on that bench by the fountain, she invited me to Sicily. Ten years later, I arrived.

In Messina, Stefania welcomed me into her home embracing me in the daily life of her family. On her balcony overlooking the bay of Messina, I experienced the wind in a way I never had before. The wind was a visitor that blows in to change your life. I stared out at *la Madonnina* guarding the bay, a golden *Madonna* commemorating the handwritten letter that Mary wrote to the citizens of Messina, rolling her letter as a scroll, tying it with a lock of her hair, and handing it to Saint Paul to deliver. In Messina, on Stefania's balcony, I thought long and hard of the Blessed Mother Mary as a writer.

Stefania organized a book reading for me at *Sicilia* Queer FilmFest. We sat in an open-air yard in the shade of low brick buildings, outside a film screening room. A group circled up to hear the New York poet. Stefania translated, having fun with the Bronx street parlance of my texts, and how my phrases translated better into Sicilian than Italian. The festival was a queer safe zone; everyone was there expressly for the film festival and to be in each other's eyes. In that sense it reminded me of the gay gathering spots in New York of the 80's, like the Christopher Street piers. We went to out-of-the-way places along the edges of the city where we could gather outside the harsh eyes of "the norm." There were no passers-by. At *Sicilia* Queer FilmFest, I felt like the older lesbian Aunt returning to tell a bedtime story, a much-needed inspiring tale, a dyke Marco Polo with a message of coming out and breaking through the prejudices and hardships of living in the straight world. I continued my query, asking the crowd for words in Italian that came close to "butch." The list was getting longer, but no word hit the mark. There was a word in Italian for everything. Except "butch." I had *camionista* / truck driver and *maschia* / masculine. The young *Palermitane* added to the list: *maschiaccio* / very masculine, *baffosaffo* / hairy Sappho, *mascula* / masculine with an insulting edge, *cazzuta* / fearless, *cozza* / a mussel, and *fricatrice* / one who rubs.

As I read, I saw the relief of laughter across the faces of the youth. I was from another time and place and had already jumped many of the hurdles they were about to face. While they looked ahead, dreaming of the life that was to come and wondering how they would navigate the challenges, I looked back and remembered that feeling of holding onto your lover like a life-preserver in a storm-tossed sea. I was on the other side. I'd lived through the family confrontations, the homophobia, the confusion, the anger, the rage, the realization that I was not something to be fixed, the disgust in people's eyes, the family still hoping I would grow out of becoming myself, the spiritual wrestling with the Catholicism I'd been steeped in as a child, the questioning if I should become a nun, the coming to terms with whether I was worthy to be alive, the adamant pride, the realization that the world was gay and didn't know it, that people fell into the roles assigned to them, the A.I.D.S. movement and feeling my voice as part of a throng, the protests, the marches, the deaths, the clubs, the desperate breakups, the abandonment, the push through to a modicum of defiance as simple as—Here I am. I'd lived life, written life, and read my life. I had *Death in Venice* moments, plugging into the eyes of the gorgeous young queers who gathered to hear my Bronx voice. Some were in love, and lust, clothes barely staying on their bodies. I read questions into their eyes that latched onto me, eyes full of passion, fears, wounds, desires.

After the reading I connected with one young butch/femme couple who shared with me, their plight. Their Catholic mothers weren't accepting them. After all this time? After everything the movement had accomplished? Everything we'd fought and protested for? Put our bodies on the line for—in the streets? Their mothers were my age. I understood how these two felt and how they suffered. I knew this struggle.

I came out in the 80's at the beginning of the A.I.D.S. crisis when homophobia was rampant. People had true fear. I remember people thinking gayness was something catchy and that A.I.D.S. was a scourge against gays from God that could be transferred by spit. I was lucky in one sense. I had just survived my first cancer, Hodgkin's Disease, after a year of surgeries, chemotherapy, and multiple rounds of radiation. My family was grateful I was alive. They could have lost me. My teenage cancer buddies died after weathering treatments too strong for their hearts. Any one of those mothers would have given anything to see their kids live. Being gay, paled in comparison, to being dead. So, I didn't have a problem with my mother, not that she was thrilled, but she learned to cope and was accepting of my girlfriends. In her they found a very loving "mother-in-law." Really, they hit the jackpot. I wasn't so lucky on the other end. Mothers of girls never understood their daughters falling in love with me. My presence was tolerated, sometimes accepted, and in some cases, celebrated. I got lucky with the grandparents of my first lover and with the father and stepmother of the woman I was in the longest relationship with. They were truly loving; those relationships were lifelong gifts.

To see the heartache written on the faces of these young gorgeous *Palermitane,* gave me shockwaves right back to the 1980's. Over the decades, the movement achieved phenomenal strides for the next generation, but every time a gay youth, or a queer at any age, suffered isolation and persecution, or committed suicide, I felt a sense of personal and collective failure. We hadn't done enough. The next generation would have to match and better our stride.

I wrote their mothers this letter . . .

"Caríssime Mamme Palermitane,"

June 29, 2018

TO THE MOTHERS OF THE BRILLIANT and stunning young lesbians of Palermo. Don't lose out. Don't make your daughters suffer. You are making yourselves suffer also. I see the pain inscribed in your daughters' eyes from your rejection, your hesitancy, your holding onto old ways. Do not drive them away any further—you are destroying the greatest joy of your life. Your daughters are your sacred bond. They fell in love. Deal with it. Celebrate their love. Above tolerance, above acceptance, is celebration. Celebrate love at all costs. Do not make love a problem. You will have other problems in life, real problems, health problems, diseases, deaths, accidents, tragedies, catastrophe, war, poverty, job losses, real problems. This is not one of them. It is your privilege you are wasting, these years of their youth and health when all is truly well, so well, you can choose to create a problem where there is none. Know life's problems when one comes. Love is not a problem. Let it be.

Time is life's precious blood. Time spills. Time leaks. Time falls. Time ruptures. Time bursts. Don't waste any more time. You have wasted years already, drenched your daughters' souls with the battle fatigue of being gay and not being accepted, not being celebrated, by you. You will never get this time back. Your daughters will always remember. Don't waste any more of these precious years which you will look back on and realize that everyone was healthy and that these are the years you should have grabbed onto hard, not let them slip through your fingers. You don't get many of these in life. You must celebrate these years. You will never get this time back. Your daughters will always remember the stern eyebrows of judgment. The days and nights you shut the doors on their lovers, these closed doors are never erased.

It's time to turn it around. Invite them in. Invite their circle of friends to your table. Invite all of them. Your children love you but cannot be other than who they are. No sooner could they change the color of their eyes.

Pardon me if my language is antiquated. Update it as you will. This is the language of my generation, and it is how I think and speak. I can only tell it as I see it.

To the Mamma of the knockout femme,

Rest assured your daughter is holding the reins. She's being treated as a queen by her butch lover. Embrace her girlfriend. Now you have two daughters. Take her in. Get to know her. Look beyond what you perceive to be a tough exterior. A good butch is hard to find. I know just a moment ago your daughter was in pigtails. You think your daughter is not truly gay, that she's under the influence of her butch. Nothing is further from the truth. Resist the urge of boxes. All of us can be many things in life. Maybe you too would've had a girlfriend, if you weren't so convinced of who you are, if you were young today, if you didn't fall in line with expectations projected upon you.

To the Mamma of the beautiful vulnerable butch,

I know you think she works too hard, runs in circles supporting her femme. She has so much to give. Her love is endless. You cannot control how she loves. Do things with the girlfriend, plan a surprise party for your butch daughter. Above all, don't pressure her to dress or cut her hair differently. Let her be. She will stay close to you if you let her. Protect her from the stupid pedantic comments of family. Stick up for her. Don't choose your boyfriends over her, ever. Protect her. Love her. Remind her to take care of herself too. She will always be there for you when you need her. She needs you now even if it doesn't seem that way. Give to her endlessly. Tell her how beautiful she is, as she is.

To each of you,

Don't miss out on the best party of your life. The goddess has given you this gift. Don't miss the party. Be part of it. Celebrate their love. Your daughters are gorgeous and in love. Congratulations! Make a lasagna. Celebrate. They know you love them but there is nothing more painful than a mother's approbation—the drawing back of the head with the tight lips of disgust, dismissal, a cold shake of the head, subtle messages that add up to: *the "don't exist" injunction.*

One of the best times I had with my mother was bringing her to a Gay Pride Parade. My girlfriend and I brought her everywhere. I'm so thankful we made that day happen. It was the best parade she ever went to in her whole life. She met interesting artists and had the time of her life. Let your daughters love you, let them include you in their life. Meet their friends. Cook for all of them. Knit for them. Do the things you do, for them. Be their hero. Love them unconditionally.

Remember:

She loves. Her eyes are brown. She is healthy. She loves a woman. These are facts. Celebrate your daughter's life, not the picture in your mind of your daughter's life but your daughter's life. For she lives. She aspires. She is building a life with a foundation of love. Get to know the woman she loves. Enter the conversation. Dive in. Open. Embrace her love and you will gain a friend for life and another daughter who loves and sparkles for her.

Years from now when your heart opens in sickness or old age, you will grow to regret the days you now waste. Years from now, when you call your daughter's name, when you need her, she will be there to catch you when you fall. Let her come to your bedside remembering you were always there for her, rooting her on, cheering her, supporting her, guiding her, lifting her soul.

Today is your opportunity. Today you breathe. Your heart beats still. Life is over before you know it. Invite your daughter's lover to talk and walk with you. Hold your head high. Open into laughter. See how your daughter's heart smiles.

When she was young you taught her to push the orange square block into the orange hole, the yellow triangle into the triangle hole, the blue circle into the circle. Now she teaches you. Learn the lessons you taught her decades ago.

> You could no sooner change her
> as you could make the ocean break
> in the opposite direction.
> You could no sooner change the color of her eyes.
> All she wants is the love
> in your heart and in your eyes.

It's raining on the shore,
Annie

"Pride Piazza"

Kicking around the ruins
Footprints of buildings in place
Amidst dry grass. I step on stones
that once were the foundations of houses.
But how long ago? Epochs or decades?
I sit for *apizz'* on the side of the square, thinking
          "This ruin, this ruin, is not ancient.
          What happened here?"

As the Pride crowd grows
I recognize the friend of a friend
Eating *apizz'* at another table
This is Pride, my tribe gathers
I ask the history of this ruin.
One among the group enlightens me:

          "WWII. The Americans bombarded *Sicilia*.
          General Patton. The city was in ruins.
          This neighborhood was flattened.
          Carpet bombed. B17 Flying Fortresses
          dropped 180 tons of bombs on Palermo.
          The funds never came here to rebuild.
          Mafiosi took and took. Built vacation homes.
          Instead of rebuilding this district they turned
          it into a piazza. Really, it's a bombed-out neighborhood,
          Welcome to piazza Magione."

Strobe lights from the bandstand
Hit the trees in rhythm
Flash like the memory of bombs
The drag queen lip-syncs
Tosses her glittery blue superhero cape
Up to the full-breasted moon

Flutters her giant sparkle eyelashes
Mafiosi roll in their graves, bones
Rumble with the heavy bass beats
Tonight, the mayor of Palermo honors gay families
Peace and celebration, red lipsticked mouths
Blow smoke rings up to black sky clouds

Cani randagi—stray dogs, don't circle the tables
Know better than to beg for pasta *tubetti*
Stray dogs lay in ruins, waiting
As if for the civilians killed in the spring of '43
To come home. Sicilian dogs are resigned
Begging and moaning is not the way to roasted steak slabs
After humans eat, some will leave
Pizza and grilled swordfish in tin dishes against the wall
Where stray dogs wait

Chapter Fourteen. "My Map of Sicily is Wounded"

"*SICILIA MAI FINITA.*" In just a few short weeks in Sicily, I'd already heard it said many times. Sicily never ends. What never ends is one's knowing Sicily. Sicily's landscape attests to massive death tolls to volcanoes, earthquakes, floods, and conquest by foreign invaders. "Can you feel it?" a psychic in Messina asked me. "The 80,000 underneath us from the earthquake of 1908? The bodies were never cleared. They were just bulldozed over. They are under every building. You can feel them trembling." I can't say I felt Sicilian souls trembling, but what I did feel was me trembling. I was brought to tears repeatedly and couldn't tell you why. I drove by Mount Etna and shouted Timothea's name. Etna looms over the landscape, a life-threatening and life-giving parent. This is where you want your tomatoes from, this lava fertilized earth, but to live with the threat that this Cyclops can hurl boiling lava and spit boulders at you, bombing your village at any time felt so threatening to me, made me want to eat, to indulge life, to celebrate the here and now. I remembered what I told Timothea—*I am going to paint lemons.*

> To cleanse my mind
> Lemon juice the years.
> My soul has been away.

I needed to clear my mind after my mother died. Like my mother used lemon polish on the maple furniture, and I drank lemon water every morning to clean my system, I needed to clear my head and redefine my mission for this phase of life. I was at a crossroads. For years, caregiving had been my mission, and now that was over. Caregiving was like mothering but knowing your child will die.

I drove through the center of Sicily to get a lay of the land. Sicily spirals inward from seacoasts to mountains to the lush lava fortified earth skirt around the looming Etna and the vast arid lands around the village Enna—known as the *ombelico* or bellybutton of Sicily— pretty much dead center on the island. To get to the top of Enna, a steep vertical rise, I drove up a rickety approach that jutted out from the mountain, a mid-air skinny track held up by concrete stilts. On the hair-pin curve I felt like I was on the Cyclone at Coney Island. Never again, I thought. If I'm in a car, I prefer to drive over land. Not air. On the way down, I was determined to find an alternate route on the other side of the mountain and rode my brakes down an alley that I realized too late was really a staircase cut into the hill through an arch in a building. But during my hours in the village on the very top of the mountain, I had an overwhelming experience and I didn't know why. Other forces were at work. I climbed the steps into the cathedral, and just beyond the nave found the most curious ladder. It was impossibly tall, reaching all the way up to the top vaults. The ladder was wooden, handmade, each rung a rounded knotted tree branch fitted tongue and groove into the vertical legs made from trunks of the tallest trees, perhaps cypress. The ladder had a natural bend to it like a spine gradually narrowing to the top. Of all the exquisite art and statuary and marble and fresco and gilt mosaic and carved wood ceilings and even a hand-made zimbelstern made of a wheel of brass bells pulled by a rope on a lever, out of all of it—the ladder captivated me most. I caught myself staring at it. I sat in the pews and cried. Why was I captivated by this ladder? What was it about this ladder? I cried looking at it. The thought came to me—that's what the girls needed in the Triangle factory fire of 1911 in New York—an endless spine of ladder reaching up and up and up and up, high enough, high enough, high enough. This handmade ladder was the height the workers had needed to survive. At the time, the New York City Fire Department ladders only reached the sixth floor. Workers were trapped on the eighth, ninth, and tenth floors. 146 died. Many jumped trying to catch the ladder. This ladder of Enna would have been the perfect extension at the top.

I didn't realize until years later that one of the girls who died in the fire was born in Enna, Giuseppina Cammarata, and was likely baptized and confirmed in the church where I sat crying, at the altar next to the ladder. She might have known this ladder. Four years after my visit to Enna, artist Ruth Sergel assigned Giuseppina's name to me as part of her project *Chalk*, where every year we chalk the names of the Triangle workers outside the places they lived in New York City. I researched Giuseppina's death certificate and an archival photo showing her beautiful countenance, cleft chin, direct eyes. As I looked at her, I felt she was looking back at me. I felt great sadness. One word on her death certificate seared me. "Charred." Devastating to even write. When I found out through author Ester Rizzo's research, that Giuseppina was born in Enna, I had a wake of trembling, as if it was Giuseppina pointing the ladder out to me in the exquisite cathedral in her mountaintop town, Enna. Young Giuseppina lived at 18 Cornelia Street in the West Village and walked the five or six blocks to work through Washington Square Park to the corner of Washington Place and Greene Street. She died at seventeen years old in the Triangle factory fire, three weeks shy of her wedding which she'd planned for Easter Sunday, 1911. I don't know what forces are at work, or how life and death work, but Giuseppina's face stays with me, the knowing look in her eyes, her readiness for her future, the brave journey she made from her mountaintop town to the streets of New York to land a job at a modern factory, and that simple handmade ladder from her hometown, that wasn't in New York to save her.

I didn't go to Sicily with the intention of trekking to the towns where the seamstresses who died in the fire were born, but Triangle is always there calling.

From Stefania's house, I contacted author Edvige Giunta, my beloved friend, who was born in Gela, Sicily, and living in New Jersey. "Can you put me in touch with that Sicilian woman who is getting Triangle plaques installed in the girls' hometowns?" As it turned out, Ester Rizzo was about to unveil the latest plaque in Avola.

As I drove down the east coast from Messina to Avola, I had Edvige Giunta's writing in my mind. I'd recently read her memoir, *No Confetti for the Dead*, and wanted to see the places she wrote about, breathe the air, feel the sun. I contemplated her hometown of Gela, where her parents lived through the American amphibious assault in WWII of over 600 ships taking over the Bay of Gela as part of the Allied invasion. I thought about Edvige's girlhood and her coming to consciousness as a feminist. I wanted to drive the road she described between Gela and Catania with her narrative voice inside me, thinking of her aspirations as she left Gela as a teenager to go to university, and her vivid return journeys home, looking out the window of the bus, carrying food her mother cooked and wrapped for her, crying, as she looked forward to her new life, the bus bouncing through the arid heart of Sicily. Giunta profoundly rendered the simultaneous lives of being an immigrant, the endless acts of cultural integration.

Life seemed to me, a permanent immigration, birth—an immigration, death—an immigration, my search for the elusive Eden—an immigration. A forward movement with a perpetual spinning back. A river flowing in both directions at once, a strong top current over an undercurrent of returning and returning, even as one latches onto new realities. The earth itself, spins in a magical pirouette, suspended, while the rest of us try to find our footing.

When I drove into Avola, it was raining hard, raindrops thick and cool as if from a faucet. Two villagers stood in the deluge outside their front doors pushing palmyra stalk brooms to sweep away the rain from their doorsteps. The last time I'd seen someone sweeping away the rain with a broom was in the Bronx when I was a child on a street of Italian immigrants and their descendants. This is who we are. In a thunderstorm we don't stay inside, we cover our heads with plastic and take our brooms into the street and sweep away the rain as it rushes around our ankles. A Sisyphean task and yet essential to keep the house from flooding. This is the type of act that makes me hunger to be in southern Italy. It resides in the heart, where Triangle resonates. In Avola, in piazza Trieste, an elegant and simple memorial stood waiting to be unveiled: a white shirt with a waist-belt stretched over a free-standing plaque, a ring of a dozen perennial flowers planted around the base, not yet in bloom.

A funeral was going on in San Giovanni Battista, at the head of the piazza. Men smoked on the church steps, looking down over the piazza as if standing on the bow of a ship, examining the rough sea. They took note of my presence. Mourners with black umbrellas made their way up the marble steps and into the church. Black stilettos and high heels rapidly pedaled the marble in the downpour. I waited under an awning across the street. The rain stopped and cars pulled up. Down the street, two women and one man got out of a car—a purple umbrella, long flowing bell-bottom pants, and a flowered shirt. My heart opened just at the sight of them. Their energy. Their purpose. I knew instantly these were my people—people who are called, who honor the seamstresses, who speak these names to the next generation, who are the guardians of memory of a handful of young lives. We were linked by a mission to keep their names alive as well as to continue the work for equity, workplace safety and justice. We were brought together by the workers who had been sacrificed to violent greed. We contemplated: Whose lives get sacrificed and why? What are the rest of us to do about it? We saw how in the larger context, the workplace problems that the Triangle fire illuminated were exported to factories in developing nations where thousands of workers died each year. It's too much. These 26 Sicilian women and girls, we could hold in our hearts and minds. The 146, we could know all their names. Triangle felt very personal.

We walked toward each other, into big hugs, and introduced ourselves. Ester Rizzo and her husband Giovanni "Vanni" Salvio from Licata, and Vera Parisi from Avola. Without knowing it, we had been working in tandem on opposite sides of the ocean. On the other side of the Atlantic, the Remember the Triangle Fire Coalition in New York City had honored these same girls. Through *Chalk* we marked their names outside the apartment houses where they lived after immigrating to New York. At the intersection of the streets of their deaths, we called their names and rang bells, while Toponomastica Femminile honored the places of their births.

Forty or so people gathered and circled around the *camicetta bianca,* white blouse. The mayor of Avola, Luca Cannata wore a ceremonial red-white-and-green sash. The plaque listed the names of the twenty-six Sicilian girls and women who died in the fire and read:

> "They left their land with little money in their
> pockets but a suitcase full of hopes and dreams.
> This space is dedicated to them and to all the
> women who have fought with tenacity to better
> the world. Because memory is a warning to the
> present." [translation from the Italian]

Ester Rizzo, Mayor Cannata and others said a few words. Then they clamored for me to speak. I was the New Yorker, the Italian American, from four thousand miles away and, it seemed from another point in time. I was from the epicenter of the hopes of these young immigrant girls. I was a returning granddaughter of southern Italian teenagers, peasants who had immigrated to New York. I was a founding board member of the Remember the Triangle Fire Coalition. In that moment, at that shirtwaist flag post, I represented the trust that, in America, the seamstresses were remembered and would be properly memorialized. That America didn't forget. That despite our New York fast lifestyles and the constantly changing topography of the city, these young lives would be remembered and honored. I looked around the circle of Sicilians and felt the pressure of the import of the moment. My mother always told me, "Once you open your mouth, you're fine." So, I opened my mouth, and riffed about the abject poverty that had driven the girls away from this *paradiso*, in search of work, only work; how they had become New Yorkers in short time—and with courage staunched the heartbreak of leaving their families and homeland, and staked their fate on the unknown. How they walked the downtown New York City streets, the Village, how in New York we knew each building where they'd lived, and the paths they'd walked to work each day. I spoke of some of the girls like little Rosie Grasso who left the hill town of Cerami, who most likely never saw much of Sicily beyond the port from which she left, only to move to a tenement at 174 Thompson Street and to be locked in a factory on Washington Place. Her sixteen years of life and all her potential—ripped away from her.

"We mourn these girls as our children," I said. "These are our daughters."

The word *paradiso* came across my lips a few times, and the word for girls: *ragazze*. I could never get out of my head how very young most of the seamstresses were. When I finished, a classy woman came up to me and said she had goose bumps from my speech. She held out her bare forearm for me to touch. Then she reached into her pocketbook to give me an offering; a *caramella di mandorle d'Avola*, hard candy made from the almonds of the town. I was very moved. I explained to her that I was on a book tour for *Hard Candy*, a memoir I'd written about the last years of my mother's life. The central metaphor of the book was how hard candy helps Italian ladies cope with the bitterness of life. At the book readings, I told her, I'd pass around my mother's favorite pocketbook, filled with hard candy for audience members to reach in and take. So when she, filled with emotion, pulled a bag of hard candy out of her pocketbook and handed it to me, it was as if the goddesses had granted me a golden shield and sword. A Sicilian lady giving me hard candy out of her pocketbook for my journey—the most potent of gestures. I felt blessed and knighted. I cried on the spot.

Ester Rizzo invited me to Licata, where she brought me to piazza Giacomo Matteotti, to see the marble plaque for seamstress Clotilde Terranova, engraved in classic lettering:

> To Clotilde Terranova, our fellow citizen, who died in 1911 at 23 years old at the Triangle Shirtwaist Factory Fire in New York. In memory of a broken life, a historical memory of a heroine who crossed the ocean for a better future, to pass on to the young generation, a memory of a tragedy that gave life to the women's labor movement. [translation from the Italian]

From there we walked to piazzetta 8 Marzo, where a walkway is named for Clotilde: vialetto Clotilde Terranova, and other markers for women who lost their lives to all forms of violence. The peaceful garden and fountain provided a healing place for contemplating the tragic and violent endings of far too many women's lives.

I spread my map of Sicily out over Ester Rizzo's dining room table and asked her to mark the birthplaces of the twenty-six seamstresses who died in the fire. Ester underlined each town name with a black marker, then circled all of them in red. She wrote the girls' and women's names in the sea and connected them to the towns with lines.

My map of Sicily is wounded. Red pox mark the towns where the seamstresses were born, and now marble plaques, reliefs, and street signs bear their names. When I look at my map, I don't see the names of cities and towns. I don't see Palermo, Cerami, Licata, Enna. I see: Caterina, Rosie, Clotilde, Giuseppina, Maria, Michela, Provvidenza,

Vincenza, Concetta, Caterina, Lucia, Rosaria, Vincenza, Gaetana, Francesca, Elisabetta, Maria, Grazie, Giuseppina, Giovanna, Vincenza, Caterina, Giuseppa, Francesca, Rosa, Rosina, Gaspare.

This map I can fold neatly and tuck into my tote bag, but the lives the map marks I can never contain neatly inside. My map is a topography of loss and a songline of salient effort. It folds accordion-style into a neat rectangle with a lacquered cover, but once open, presents the skin of the terrain where twenty-six seamstresses and one elevator operator were born, how close to one another, and the contour of the earth around them—the earth that didn't hold up beneath them.

Ester had diligently researched the Italian Triangle workers, traced their birth certificates, authenticated the spellings of their names, and tracked down their birthplaces one by one. She had binders of all their documents. Like a detective, she'd figured out who were siblings with whom and contacted descendants. Ester and the group Toponomastica Femminile saw to it that plaques were installed in their honor in the towns of their births. She got on the phone with the mayor of each town, informed them of the history and significance of the fire, and urged them to take the necessary action to honor these workers. My map's red wounds looked stitched by her hand-drawn black dashes. Ester Rizzo stitched wounds. Twenty-six Sicilian women and girls left this triangular puzzle piece of earth and died at the Triangle factory. In the early 1900's for them, Sicily held no promise. The 1908 Messina earthquake killed eighty thousand, with incalculably devastating effects on the area. 1911 New York lifted these twenty-six women impossibly high. Rescue ladders were not yet tall enough. When I walk the streets of New York, I can't help but call their names when I pass the buildings where they lived. Rosie! at 174 Thompson. Gaetana! at 143 Commerce. Giuseppina! at 18 Cornelia Street.

Ester and Vanni drove me a couple of hours northwest from Licata to Villafranca Sicula, where Triangle Factory elevator operator Gaspare Mortillaro was born. Were it not for the heroic efforts of the elevator operators that day, the death count of the fire would have been double. Elevator operator Giuseppe "Joe" Alessandro Zito from Sere in the province of Salerno, and Gaspare brought their elevators up into the fire to rescue workers. Joe Zito was later found injured at the bottom of the elevator shaft, after making as many trips as possible until the elevator broke. One hundred and fifty workers were rescued by the elevator operators. Joe suffered injuries from workers diving into the small elevator car still clutching fabric shears. The moment Joe and Gaspare locked eyes and pulled their elevator cars up into the fire, they transformed into first responders, into heroes. That's who those men were. I thought of my father and grandfathers. That's who they were. Risking your life for someone else and not thinking twice about it, those were the stories I grew up hearing around the dining room table. The acts of the elevator operators that day, March 25, 1911, aligned with those values. This is the true Italian American spirit. I thought about all of them as we drove up and down and around hills of fertile fields of grapevines and olive and almond and fig trees. I wished Clotilde and Gaspare could see Sicily now, that their paths could have crossed here instead of at Washington Place and Greene Street. I was jarred by the paradise from which they came. Driving through the verdant fields of Sicilian hills made the sting of Triangle that much more severe for me. We were all grapes from these vines in this rocky rich soil.

Ester arranged a visit with Mayor Mimmo Balsamo of Villafranca Sicula inside the town hall. On the wall just inside the entrance is a terracotta bas-relief by *villafranchese* artist Giovanni Smeraldi, dedicated to Gaspare Mortillaro. Featured in the sculpture are hands outstretched reaching for help away from flames; faces with mouths open in calls for help, fields of grapes beneath the workers; a tall building on the corner where girls sit at sewing machines; and on top of the building, out of the flames, a dove with wings wide in the sky. I was impressed by the depth of honor with which Mayor Balsamo spoke of Gaspare. Sitting in his office, I felt the gravitas of the moment, that as a New Yorker and as an American—we remember and honor our young immigrants.

"A Ladder of *Fiori*"

I have built
in my mind
for all the workers
of The Triangle Factory
those who escaped and those who
ran and those who
flew and those who
sang fifteen minutes
earlier and those who whistled
who tucked wages into their socks
who saved and saved and saved
but were not saved
and for those who didn't come to work that day
and those who worked just the day before
and those who pushed others toward a way out
and those who through walls jumped
heads wrapped in fabric
and for those who lifted cotton
to cover each other's mouths
a simple white ladder
bone white rungs
enough rungs
enough flowers
enough water
to climb ten stories
climb ten stories flowers
climb ten stories water
climb ten stories rungs
inconceivably high for those from hovels and barns and shtetls
rose and jasmine lilac and lavender
basil and sage and parsley daisies and lilies
purple and purple and purple and yellow and white and Baby
Breaths

climbing the sharp corner of Washington and Greene
for here, who
took, her last
jagged breath
of sky

"Deep South Italians"

We are the people
who sweep
away the rain

chh chh
chh chh
push push
push push

Heads covered under plastic caps
in thunderstorms streets stream

around our ankles, rain
we punch with short strong strokes

push push
push push
chh chh
chh chh

Push back
punch back
gods from doorsteps

with a coarse Palmyra stalk broom

chh chh
chh chh
push push
push push

Avola, 2018

Chapter Fifteen. *"Sciroccazzo"*

BACK IN MESSINA, STEFANIA THREW HER CAR into park
and issued me a warning, *"Attenzione, con la porta!"* Attention, with
the door!

"Whaddya' talkin' about?"

"Il Sirocco!"

I laughed, opened the door, and the wind blew the door right out
of my hand. *O madonnamia!* The door swung all the way open on its
hinges, slamming open against the car. I got out and pushed the car
door closed with the force of my whole body. The wind pushed back.
It took all my might, until the car door was shut.

"Me ho detto!" she said, I told you! She hurried out of the wind
and into the building.

I'd never stood in the *Sirocco* before. Stefania's street was a howling
wind tunnel. The configurations of tall buildings around the curve
of the street, became for the *Sirocco*, a canyon to race through, up
from Africa, over the Strait of Messina, whirling up the mountain,
flying through her street making a jet stream accelerating between the
buildings. The *Sirocco* can make you *Sciroccazzo* as the wind spins
sand in the tunnels of your ears and drives you out of your mind.
On Stefania's balcony, the *Sirocco* danced my shirts and pants on
the clothesline in a wild wet tango. Every day I delighted in washing
clothes and hanging them to dry on Stefania's magic clothesline, four
ropes out from the window. In the daily ablution of washing and
hanging clothes over the bay, I experienced *momenti di luce.* I washed
something every day for the sheer pleasure of seeing the dance. I rinsed
t-shirts even when they didn't need to be, clothes-pinning them to
the line. As I watched my clothes I thought, "My laundry hangs over
the Strait of Messina, one of the most complex tsunamigenic zones in
the world." I pictured the map in my mind as if I was floating above
the earth, the Siculo-Calabrian Rift Zone—a seismically complicated
set of faults and tectonic plates, subduction zones and tsunamigenic
slides. Everything is stirring underneath this ground.

I thought back to 1908 when the earthquake flattened Messina. Just a few hours before the earthquake struck, my favorite Verdi opera had played, *Aida*. Life imitated art. In the final scene, the tenor and soprano are buried alive. I'd seen *Aida* twice in my life, both times in New York, uptown and downtown, at the Metropolitan Opera house and the Amato Opera house on the Bowery. Both performances made lasting impressions on me. What amazed me about The Amato was the mission of the impresarios, Anthony and Sally Amato, who created the tiniest mightiest opera. Big productions on a very small stage, maybe twenty feet across. Every seat in the house felt like the front row. New York City is full of opera singers, and not many get to sing at The Met. The Amato gave opera-tunities to many classically trained phenomenal singers. In their production of *Aida*, animals walked up the red carpeted center aisle. It was mine and Oggi's first anniversary. I had an aisle seat. A camel walked by. Could that be possible? Did Tony and Sally bring a camel down the Bowery? In my memory, yes, the camel walked right by me, though it might have been an illusion. It's possible that the grandeur of the production conjured the camel in my imagination. At The Met, of course, *Aida* was over-the-top magnificent, just the chorus alone, upwards of fifty singers, made it a grand spectacle. I remember the tomb slowly rising from under the stage as one scene slid into another, and Radamès paced the tomb walls like a caged lion, launching his final aria into the rafters. In Messina, on Stefania's balcony, I replayed this last scene in my mind; the tenor and soprano, buried alive together. Radamès was condemned to death, and Aida hid in the tomb to have their last moments alive together and to be buried for eternity. True eternal love. On December 28th, 1908, just hours after that scene, when *Aida* played at *Teatro Vittorio Emmanuele II,* both the heroic tenor and the soprano were staying at Hotel Trinacria. In a twist of fate, soprano Paola Koralek couldn't sleep, so when the earthquake struck, she was able to save herself by immediately jumping out of the window before the hotel collapsed. The heroic tenor was asleep; Angelo Gamba was buried alive with his family. It is said that he sang while he was trapped until the screams of his family went silent. I imagine him singing, "*O Terra Addio,*" his final aria to comfort them as they cried, opening his tenor lungs with all his might in the face of unutterable powerlessness.

Soprano Paola Koralek did not run to the sea. If she had, she would have been swept away by the tsunami that followed, leveling the port. She survived.

On Stefania's balcony I didn't dream of being anywhere else. I didn't long for "home." I didn't miss anywhere. I saw the almost full moon vanish. Lightning breached the sky over the Strait of Messina. The lighthouse pulsed every couple of seconds. A white cat ran across the top of the stone wall. Ancient stones. A cat. Lightning. *Un momento di luce.* The wildly brief wet dance of my shirts in the wind, swallows circling, *le rondini girano,* dogs barking through the night, the *Scirocco* whipping the awning as I slept. The wind visited my dream.

Wind snapping sails of a great boat. I sit by the dock. The wind feels like a hello. Someone is touching me, pushing me. I feel the ocean beneath me, beneath the dock. I boil tea in a pewter kettle over an open fire. A purple and blue scarf is wrapped around my head. A pipe in my mouth. Just a couple of teeth. White beads around my fist. The sky is swirling. A silver crow stomps around my feet. The blue wind talks to me in one ear. A sailor stands there asking my advice. He wants to leave the port. He's worried about the sky. The sky is a loud rollercoaster. I am one of the witches of the winds. A windseller. I hand the sailor a rope. My voice is hoarse. He nods. "You think I can leave tomorrow?"

"The Windseller / *La Ventovendola*"

YOU'RE HERE BECAUSE THE WINDS brought you here. The winds left you here. The winds will keep you here longer than you want. *Ahh,* but when the next good wind comes, you'll be outta here, and on your way. You're waiting for a good wind so you can leave. But what you need is the right progression of winds to bring you safely to your destination, to the harbors of your choice. Tell ya what I'm gonna do. I'll offer you three winds. *Tre venti.* I got three good winds for you, so you can go wherever you want to go, when you want to go and safe arrival will be yours.

> *Teng tre venti! Tre venti! Da tre paese!*
> *La Tramontana! Il Scirocco! Il Maestrale!*
> *La forza cresce. Il primo, calma, costate.*
> *Il secondo, più forte, in quale direzione che vuoi.*
> *Il terzo, tumultuosa, una tempesta, ma attenziòne, questa tempesta*
> *non puoi controllarlo! Senti! Non puoi controllarlo!*
> *Sciroccazzo! Sciroccazzo! Sciroccazzo!*

Listen, without wind you ain't goin' nowhere. I know. You got one ear on the horizon. You're itchin' to go. You're waiting for that one good wind, that once in a lifetime wind. She's gonna come, you can feel it. The sky is gilded. She's comin' to lift you. She's goin' your way. She'll bring you to the port of your dreams. Listen, I know winds. If there's one thing I know, it's the wind. I know winds like you know wines. You can think of me like a connoisseur of the winds. I can call all kinds. I got Zephyrs. I got *Aquilo.* I got the Black Roller. I got Meltemi. Gregale, I got, *Scorciacrape.* I got a Ghilbli. I got the *Favonio.* I got *Khamsin.* I got the *Buriana.* I got the *Ponentino.* I got The Waltzing Jinn. The Borasco, Chinooks, I got, Zondas, Shams, *The Watakushi, Il Maestrale, Il Tramontano, Il Scirocco, La Gianna.* A Haboob. *Faget it.* I got ancient winds. I got newborn winds. I got winds that trick you and I got winds that got your back. I got a Zephyr so sweet and calm she caresses you. She lowers your heart rate right down. You can go to sleep and let the boat sail herself.

I got a *Refoli* so swift she gives you Mercury's wings. And I got this cranky old *Scirocco*. She'll make you crazy. She'll jam your ball bearings with sand, blow the sails off your ship. She'll sandblast your teeth and spin in the tunnels of your ears and make you *Sciroccazzo, Sciroccazzo, Sciroccazzo!* She'll blow your doors off their hinges. And sometimes she brings her cousin from the southeast.

What you need isn't one good wind—what you think you need, that's not what you need. What you need is a progression of winds. You need three good winds. You need wind after wind after wind. To work hand in hand. Winds that build and winds that weave. Winds in the right combination. You need that right combination of winds. You need one wind to hand you off to the next wind. One gets you going, the next one amps you up and the third brings you to shore. And you gotta be kept on tack. Otherwise, you're gonna drift. And you don't wanna drift, here, there, this way, that way. And at night, then you lose your way, 'cause at night stars look like the points of light on boats. The sky is the mirror of the sea, so you don't know which way's up and which way's down, or where you are or if and when you might get where you think you're goin', so you could end up anywhere. What you need is three winds workin' in concert.

Tell ya' what I'm gonna do. I'm gonna give you the right three winds. *Tre venti.* For a good price, *un buon prezzo*, don't worry. I'll give you a *Hawa Shimali* that breathes in like champagne. Her perfume elevates your imagination when you're on the open sea. And she'll get you safely and swiftly toward your destination to the harbor of *your* choice. I'll give you—well, first you gotta decide exactly where you wanna go, so I can be precise, and you gotta tell me exactly when you gotta get there. This way I can set the progression, I'll set the combination. I whisper precise incantations into the knots. In each knot, I tie an incantation. A call to that particular wind.

I'm thinkin', for you, *tre venti delle sorgente*, three winds from the source. We're not gonna fool around here. We're not takin' chances. I'll give you the best I got. The best of the best. To fill all your sails, so they ain't workin' at cross purposes.

La forza cresce. Il primo, calma, costate, una Brisa, a trade wind,
Il secondo, The Bullseye, più forte, in quale direzione che vuoi,
Il terzo, una Chubasco, tumultuosa, una tempesta, ma veloce.
Attenziòne, questa tempesta, mi raccomando
non puoi controllarlo!
Hai capito? Senti! Non puoi controllarlo! Mi raccomando!

You can't control her. You just gotta go where she takes you. Now, all you gotta do is take this rope and whenever you need the wind, it's simple. You undo the first knot. That's all you gotta do, is undo the knot. I whisper the call into the knot and when you undo the knot, the wind is called. *Eccola!* This first wind gets you outta port. All you do, you listenin'? Untie the knot. That's all you gotta do and the wind will be called.

The second, she sets you on tack. *Più forte.* A little stronger. This, this, *questa qua,* you know, when you need to set pace—you undo the second knot. She's swift. She'll take you in the direction you want. You still gotta be alert, you gotta stay awake for her, you gotta keep your hands on the wheel 'cause this one comes from the stars. She's a solar wind, this wind comes all from above and you know, there are beings, there's aeroplankton that live on this wind. She's transporting millions of beings across the earth. Microbes you don't see but you know are there. So, you'll have company. Listen to the hum. There are spiders and insects that live on the wind, and all kinds of things travel by wind, mosses and microbes, pollen and spores and seeds. You can even eat the wind if you got nothin' else left. Just open your mouth and you'll survive.

Il terzo, tumultuosa, è una tempesta vera. Remember, you can't control this one. Only untie the third knot if you absolutely cannot get where you're goin'. If you hit that wall in the sea. Otherwise, take my advice, leave it tied. *Mi raccomando! Capeesh?* This wind you cannot control. This wind you only call when the ocean is stopping you, each wave like a linebacker blocking your every move, when you gotta push through, when you gotta find a way through.

Alright, now you're all set. You can go where you want to go when you want. You're all set to go on your way.

"At Sea At Sea"

The lighthouse in Messina pulses every couple of seconds
as a signal for safety to shore,
But tonight, there are those at sea at sea.
The ports of *Italia* are closed by a government decree.

629 refugees, stranded on the search and rescue ship Aquarius,
low on water and food, await an open port,
While activists around the world shout
at the Prime Minister: *Stai Umano!* Stay Human!

Is this what we have a government for?
Just a week ago, we had no functioning government.
Perhaps the world would be better off . . .

My friend Angela Colonna says:
"I made a promise to take my five-year-old son to the beach
and focus on him for a few days.
He is the love of my life. This is my promise.
But after a while of looking at the sea, I walk away.
How can I enjoy the beach knowing
there are those in peril in this water?"

The world was always this way
divided into those who dissociate
from the earth and all beings
and those of us who can't
not even for one glorious moment

wind on waves

"Wild Caught"

I can't eat fish
with all those people
lost at sea

Nets of Sicilian fishermen haul dead bodies
out of the sea, up into light
or roll bodies back under wave swell
to avoid red tape interrogation impounding boats
Who can afford not to fish?

Nets are still mended by hand.
Live cod live squid fresh
live shrimp live swordfish
nasello, sardina, sogliola, cefalo,
cernia, vongola, spada, sgombro, alice,
mazzancolle, orata, vongola, ombrina,
tonno rosso, spigola, polpo, triglia, pagello
Live! Live! Live!
tuna live bass dead human whole and in parts
from Libya, Syria, and sub-Saharan points

The world is worse than anyone imagines
the sea more vast and fishermen
are now fishers of people

back some go, to anonymity
no one will ever know what became of them
those who fled shores in desperation for a better life
in *questi tempi,* when fish eat flesh
and the catch of the day on the tourist menu
boasts *catturati in mare aperto,*
caught in the open sea
pesce selvaggio, wild caught

"I Can't Take Pictures of Bones"

Pelvis with a gold crown
Tibias crossed like swords
On faded red velvet
in a lit glass altar case

How can it be
I just saw the bone
of Saint Lucy's left arm?

How can it be
her body is in *Venezia*
her left arm in *Siracusa*, the city of her birth, short life, death?

What of her head?
Who divides the bodies of saints?

These poor young girls, *Agata* and *Lucia*
Dismembered they have traveled the world

"Veils of Smoke"

women push out of their mouths
like they're loosening their hair
curls cascade upon curls

Etna inside them, each little fire rolled licked
lit throughout the hours
of their lives, fire curls

I am not of the volcano
burnt rocks I find unsettling, all along the shore
boulders of charcoal and ashtrays full everywhere

we walk inside this cooled-off tray of ash
but imagine Etna firing on all cylinders
hurling burning boulders into the sea

Can you see the bay filled with smoke?
Etna Cyclops
hurling rocks from her one eye

I can hear the hissing
of burning boulders
hitting the waters of the bay

Aci Castello, 201

"Church Bells and Fishermen Yells"

but it was the pom-poms of *Catania*
that brought me to my knees

the girl hand-painting fans in the alley
caressing brushstrokes, the colors—all the colors
together on everything from ceramics to straw bags, hats
yellow red black green blue—*carrozza* colors
whacked me behind the knees
the same colors we crocheted blankets with
three generations of us.

I never realized 'til this moment how *Mezzogiornese* it was
what we were doing: embellishing, Italianitàifying
our gray and green and black Bronx world
with the *carrozza* color palate.
I wondered as a kid why we used all those colors at once:
orange, even lime green, light and dark and royal blues.
My mother and grandmother gave me a total freedom
I was rarely offered:
what color to follow what on the tip of my little hook.

Like the *Catanese* girl painting fans
Mom painted designs on milk pails
how she embellished our world
so we overcame our own volcano dust
that settles after internal explosions.
She made purple pom-poms for everything.
Purple pom-pom for the antennae of our car
so we could spot it in big parking lots
Purple pom-pom for my black suitcase
so I could distinguish it coming down the airport belt
pom-poms for the tops of hats
pom-poms for the bottom fringe of ponchos and blankets,

pom-poms for bootie ties, pom-poms of all sizes
a world of pom-poms,
and one thing about a pom-pom is—it makes you smile.
A pom-pom is a praise song.
This is what I came all this way for, then.
To sit and down an *espresso con panna* in piazza *degli Elefanti*
listen to the accordion fade across the square and cry
for my mother all over again
And vow
to make purple pom-poms of my own
for everyone

"*via Crociferi camminerò*"

Avanti e indietro per sempre

Cento paio di scarpe
consumeranno, queste pietre

Cammino nei miei pensieri
queste pietre mi abbracciaono

Stretta, vicino, saldo
Come una trottola rosa

Il mondo girava
un ragazzo, capelli in nodi,

Concentrava la sua mente in tutta ciò che gira
il corpo gira

Ubriachezza
caduto in una risata

Metà sulla sedia, seduto
metà fuori, quasi caduta

Girava più veloce il mondo
in questi giorni

È diventato necessario
che tutte le gente si corichi prostrato,

Faccia in giù, a terra
Fermare questa rotazione incessante

Deve girare nella direzione opposta, il mondo
È il tempo. È l'ora.

"*Pistacchio* Ecstasy"

Catania, Sicily, June 2018

ON VIA CROCIFERI I AM HAPPY, typing at an outdoor table at *Buatta,* a pub on the corner of a hill of flowered trees, pink, white, red, peach. My fingers are tapping the keys of an aluminum fold-up travel keyboard that magically connects to my iPhone. Ever since the nuns taught me to type in fifth grade during lunch hour, I cannot stop. The speed of my fingers almost matches my thoughts—I tap just behind the wake of the thought, my thoughts throttle down to the speed of the tapping.

A butch/femme couple walk over and choose to sit at the table next to me. They are comfortable with me, the way my black t-shirt rolls up over my shoulders, biceps to the sun. The femme's hair waves all the way down her back like a mahogany mane on white lace, *scollatura* overflowing. The butch is easy in dungarees, dark spiky hair inviting a hand to run through it. No socks. Who needs socks?

A guy sitting on the curb smoking, runs to a white Vespa when it pulls up to deliver vodka for the night crowd. He hauls the case of BiVi Sicilian Vodka off the back of the Vespa and into the bar. He is running, hustling, sweating, smiling all the way. He runs as he walks, blowing smoke wherever he wants, a cigarette carefree under his moustache. He enjoys this day of his role in the world, setting up the bar for the night crowd. I am happy typing.

The butch turns with a cigarette and asks me, "*Accendi?*" No, I don't, but how I wish I had a light for this moment. She has sharp clear eyes, looks directly at me. I should carry matches or a lighter for moments like this. A match is a way to say hello. A match snapping into flame is an introduction. An exchange of fire. She sits back down. The femme jumps up to get a light at the next table for her butch's cigarette. She leans into the flame to inhale. The femme has skintight white pants and no underwear, or a thong, and long orange fingernails the color of traffic cones. I never understood thongs until this moment. It's a revelation. No lines. Two scoops fill white cotton pants.

I spill my *granita*. A fly lands in the spill. The fly seems to be dancing. Nose bobbing up and down in the *pistacchio*. The fly clearly knows it's the best *granita pistacchio* in all *Italia*, in all the world. I bite the brioche which is necessary to soak up the *granita* inside you. Otherwise, the sugar is overpowering, dizzying. The fly shares my euphoria. Legs and hands moving. The fly is dizzy. I don't slap the fly away. We are enjoying this dance. I push a little crumb of brioche toward the fly. My fingers are tapping. I stay for two hours, maybe more, drinking *acqua minerale* to wash it all down and fill me with the effervescence of all the life inside and around me. The butch and femme finish their cigarette and drinks and walk away, back up via Crociferi. I think of the Italian words I've learned for butch and none of them fit this sharp woman: *camionista*, no, *maschia*, no, *cozza*, no. There's gotta be more words.

"*i Cartocci* Revelation"

There's a woman named Giuseppina
she saves me *cartocci* seven thirty every morning
asks me if I want, "*Ricotta o crema?*"
      "*La ricotta oggi, la crema domani.*"
      Ricotta today, cream tomorrow.
Giuseppina sits with me
while I open my mouth to the warm *ricotta*
I'll never have another breakfast
like this in all my life
Complete satisfaction that makes me grateful
I have lived to this mouthful
I want to live to the next morning
knowing when I wake up
Giuseppina will sit with me
she'll have saved one for me on the side
and all I have to do is open
my mouth for the warm cream
to flow into, the soft dough
too big for my mouth
so that I don't have to talk
and if I don't have to talk
I don't have to think
and if I don't have to think
I can just be with the sensation of the fresh cream
as it swirls around my mouth
transporting me to a Bronx basement
with naked light bulbs and red vinyl banquette seats
and the slap of cards on the Formica table
my mother enters the light
bending her head as she passes the light bulb
carrying a tray under her bosom
and above her apron
fried dough lightly sugared

and a mound of *ricotta*
walking right toward me
she is
now

"*L'Indifferenziata Lazzi*"

They say you can judge a culture by how trash is dealt with.
We'll make a satellite of *spazzatura* soon enough
to circle the sun a planet of trash
but for now, we separate what we can.

You have to concentrate to make sense of the instructions.
You have to know what day it is.
Days are hard enough to keep track of
Agreed divisions of time.
You have to remember that the day listed on the trash ordinance
really means the day before
so if you're wondering what trash to put out at night
you have to look on the list for the name of the day after.
For Saturday you look on the list for Sunday
and that's what you put out Saturday night,
Monday means Sunday night
and Sunday means Saturday night
and you have to keep this straight
when you're throwing something out
you need to know what day
comes after what day it is

Every time you throw something out
you have to determine what it is
or if it's a combination of elements
in which case you're in trouble.
You will find yourself standing over the trash
wondering what bin to toss the thing into,
or if you can take it apart
to divide it into two or three proper bins?

Vetro—Sabato
  (Glass—Saturday)
Indifferenziata—Martedi
  (Undifferentiated—Tuesday)
Plastico/Alumnio—Giovedi
  (Plastic/Aluminum—Thursday)
Humido—Lunedi/Mercoledi/Venerdi/Sabato
  (Humid—Monday/Wednesday/Friday/Saturday)
Carta—Mercoledi
  (Paper—Wednesday)

It's hard not feeling like a failure tossing a thing
into *Indifferenziata*.
You can't make sense of it,
How can it be that we, people,
make things that we don't know how to classify? Recycle? Trash?
There is something backwards.
Recycling should be built into manufacturing.
Like God planned it with our bodies
returning our bones to the earth
breath to wind
H_2O and our whole inner periodic table
to tree roots to sky to clouds
to rain upon the face of oceans
steam
feeding life cycles

"Coast Guard Around the *Madonnina*"

"Strange fruit"
not from antebellum oaks
but Mediterranean tides,

Who is being protected?
Who is being blessed?
La Madonnina has her back to the sea.

No one climbs up into a boat
with the intention of never getting off.
The hope of stepping on land again

is what brings one foot
forward to the sea.
Beseech the bronze goddess

You will hear your answer.
She faces the city
not the sea

"The Veiled Christ / *Il Cristo Velato*"

The Christs are more bloody in *Italia*
true murder victims, wounds barely congealed
six pints of red visible and open layers of fascia.
Makes you wonder who cleaned up the scene
of the crime in American churches.

The Veiled Christ in *Napoli* I can't even peek at,
he suffered too much like my mother.
One look at him and I am back at her bedside
the wrinkles of her final white cotton sheet smoothed as I
move the air over her skin as little as possible.

You'd think with marble blood wouldn't be visible,
but this Christ, you can see where his pulse
once plumped veins and arteries, vital with sap.
You look at him you want to stitch his wounds,
life's heat you can feel leave his *corpus.*
Step softly around his body with museum-goer mourners
viewing the newly laid out dead.

He's lain like this for two-hundred-fifty years,
Skin marble cotton marble lace.
I can't look at any of the dying
or dead Christs in the *Mezzogiorno.*
I get filled with grief all over again,
Christs the exact pallor of three hours dead.

Even this morning in Messina
the Christ over the altar in *Santuario Madonna di Lourdes*
was bleeding all over us.
I didn't dare walk under him
to stand in line for communion, or look up,

Wounds dripping

"Lifesavers"

Americans weren't our enemy
they were our cousins.
In WWII, they came here
they spoke our dialects.
The northern Italians—we had no idea who they were.
They had nothing to do with us.
We didn't know them.
Every American soldier, we called Joe.
Every American was Joe.
They used to throw us candy,
the hard candy with the hole in the middle.
Sometimes gum, cigarettes.
So, when we saw American soldiers
all us kids would yell,
Joe! Candy! Joe! Candy!
Joe Candy!

"In the muscular hills"

of Sonoma County I looked for *Sicilia*
in Bronx alleyways under tin lids
of dented trashcans that had been kicked in their sides, I looked
in tart green shadows of Uncle Frank's grapevine
under the blankets over the Friday night focaccia
rising in Zia Lucia's basement, she called "the corpse,"
in Grandpop Carmine's driveway in Morris Park
in the teal iron chairs on Grandma Anna's porch
that bobbed with our weight behind white lace curtains
of Grandma Rose's windowsill in clay pots
of her fire-escape tomatoes in the echoes
of Spaldeen ricochets in the canyon
courtyard of brick apartment buildings
in Zio Gaetano's pigeon coops in Throggs Neck
across from Saint Raymond's cemetery, I looked
for *Sicilia* in Grandpa Giuseppe's hands
scooping a *Scopa!* on the card table on the sidewalk
outside Zio Franco's shoemaker shop on White Plains Road in the Bronx,
I looked for *Sicilia* in the Hunts Point Terminal Market
when the sun rose pink through chain link fence I looked
in the slant of light in Mamma Rachele's kitchen window
that rose in the well of flour dusting the sun
spilled on her countertop as she pulled dough into the well
two fingers at a time egg yolk volcano the last fringe
of light she and Grandma Rose sewed
I looked for *Sicilia* under the El in broken light on Jerome Avenue
on the asphalt I looked for *Sicilia* in oil slick rainbows
on St. Raymond's Avenue in the brown lace-up shoe
Rosemarie found another century inside her bathroom wall
when they remodeled the house
I looked for *Sicilia* most everywhere
but I never knew it was *Sicilia* I was looking for
until I drove up the mountain to *San Gregorio*

where the cliff curve never heard
of guard rails, a nameless road where
your whole life can be gone
if you falter
or blink

"*Nerina*"

Nerina slid right up to my leg
a little black cat, up the part of the mountain
known as *San Gregorio* between Messina and Palermo.
Nerina lived on a dirt road without a name
houses built right into the mountainside
olive trees growing up the steep rise.

When *Nerina* was born,
they thought he was a girl,
so they named him the feminine *Nerina*, Little Black.
In time they saw he was a boy
but by then the name stuck.

Nerina visits neighbors and *paesani*
across the road and up the hill.
He lives with Felicia and Zeus the dog
and Felicia's son's family.
Felicia I met for one hour in life.
She was ninety-four and it took me half my life
to get to *Sicilia* and up her side of the mountain.
Life is one brief visit
and we both knew it.
We greeted each other that way
and said goodbye that way.
Felicia winked with her one good eye
and in that wink, we shared all this:
　　　　"Enjoy life my friend. How blessed I feel
　　　　to have met you for this one hour, how lucky.
　　　　You are so beautiful, and I will treasure this visit.
　　　　This is an hour never to be forgotten.
　　　　You smile, in my heart now."

She handed me a giant zucchini from her *giardino*
and I went on my way, back down the mountain,

although I would have loved to stay forever,
for her to take me in, like *Nerina.*

Nerina visits Stefania the neighbor, who says:
>"*Fuori! Fuori!*" when he climbs the fence.
>"Outside! Outside!"
>"*Si vieni dentro, vuoi il latte,*
>*si offro il latte, vuoi cibo,*
>*si offro cibo, sempre ritornerà!*"

"If you come inside, you want milk,
if I give milk, you want food,
if I give food, you will return forever."

How much I feel like *Nerina!*
Strangers call me "Sir" though I am a girl.
Children refer to me as "he."
So quickly they are conditioned
as to what a girl should present like,
and I do not look to them this way.
But when the word "he" is spoken in a child's voice,
I can't help but feel they perceive my true nature.

I am not feral.
I am not stray.
Like *Nerina*, I too have a name.
I used to live in a house with a family
but that is all in the past
Now
the people have died or moved on
and I walk alone in this world.

I have keys to a door.
The windows I leave open so a wind can enter
and shake me loose.
From place to place I wander
into friends' houses, where I sit at tables

and visit with their families.
My species organizes themselves
into these tiny groupings called families.
Perhaps I need to change species.
Find one that organizes more broadly.

An unlocked door, warmth inside emanating from the hearth,
a woman who waves me in, saying:
       "Come in. Take off your shoes.
       We've been waiting for you.
       The kettle's on. Stay as long as you like.
       There's a job you can do.
       You are one of us now. This is your hive."
This is what I dream of. To belong. To have a role.
Friends welcome me, but the clock too
is always there and the calendar tallying goodbyes.
I sleep on couches and floors, on porches and in beds
in spare rooms. I am offered basements and attics.
But something always gives.

Like *Nerina*, I sidle up to places and people
hoping someone someplace sticks.

PART IV
COM US CE'MA E VENT?

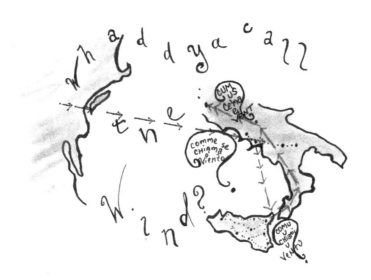

I

love

Fountains   in   the   Rain

w   t   r
a   e

g   o   i   n   g

u   p

w   t   r   o   i   g
a   e   c   m   n

d   o   w   n

"An Overpopulation of Angels"

In *Roma* angels are everywhere,
like in my mother's apartment.
She had a collection of angels.
Her apartment was overpopulated.
Angels in rose glass, porcelain, ceramic,
gold-plated pins over her heart
on her deepest purple suit and navy pea coat,

Angels

in drawers ready to come to our aid at any moment,
on shelves in position, on bureau plateaus,
around the TV, on the table, elevating candles
on their backs between wings.
Every flat surface was an extension
of my mother's very own piazza.

Angels

look at you, tilt their heads
play lutes, tambourines, bells,
kneel on clouds.
Point.
Point to Mary, point to Jesus, point to things you cannot see.
Cock their ears toward something you cannot hear.
Hold sprigs of acacia, wheat, stalks of lilies,
garlands of flowers, *fleurs-de-lys*, palettes of paint, books.
Two angels lift the crown over Mary's head,
Four raise the altar overhead of *La Madonna Nera di Tindari*
without any effort at all, as if levitating the entire chamber.

Angels

come from every direction,
hold out their hands, reach down
from the heavens with feathers.
One hands the longest feather
to a bleeding Saint Matthew at his death.
Another witnesses the Devil slayed
by a spike in the throat from the Archangel's hand.
One angel bends his index finger in an unnatural backbend,
to make a specific point to Saint Matthew.
What is he saying?

Some are babies, others in their prime.
Some stay in pairs and hold each other close
support the wings of bigger angels,
whisper to one another, wrestle
as they fly in the Holy Spirit
swiftly going where they need to be
crowded around the *Madonna*,
push fabric aside to see, hold chalices, sleep,
lower their wings one at a time, smile
blow kisses, bow, pray forehead to knee
look away, bless
make way for the light
fly fly tumble and fly

"7/13/18—Two years today"

i am
missing
my mother's hands today
wet from cookin' and cleanin'
i am
missing
my mother's hands today
sprinkling raisins like magic
in everything—even meatloaf
i am
missing
my mother's light touch
aerating her knitting, focaccia dough, biscott'
adding life and "give" to everything she touched
i am
missing
my mother's pink rose manicured nails
gold bracelets, delicate leather wristwatch
i am
missing
holding my mother's soft as rose petals hands
i am
missing
how we intertwined our pinkies
pinkies that have been crooked for generations
the emptiness can swallow me whole
today
i am
missing
my mother's hands

i can only take one step at a time this morning
i am up and out for coffee

the waitress in Bar del Fico, in *Roma*
adds raisins in my granola
and for this i am grateful
she greets me with insistent exuberance:
      "*Ciao! Tutto bene!*"
the way my mother used to:
      "Hi Darling, how's everything, good!"
these waitresses walk fast as nurses
wear sneakers with tennis socks
tight black pants and black short sleeves
with the rapt attention of Forest Hills ball girls
who run to the net on every missed serve or volley.
That was the job i dreamt of when i was twelve,
all sharp attention and quick reflexes.
Now my reflexes serve to save me
from falling to the ground after tripping
on an overhanging bed sheet or uneven ground
or the gap between two *Sanpietrini*
or when my knee buckles
under the strain of it all
i am
missing
my mother today
who gave everything
she never would have for herself
because even this she gave
the promise of her own future

i walk up to the bar to get a second cappuccino.
The barista sees my mother's scapular around my neck
and reveals his, says he too celebrates with devotion on 7/16
as he was born on 7/17. He tells me his name is Carmelo,
for *La Madonna di Monte Carmelo.*
He makes me an artful cappuccino
chocolate leaf embellishment in the cream.

i tell him how *La Madonna* saved my mother's life
on 7/16/28 when she fell out the window.

An iceman walks by shouldering ice.
A chimera of a visitation by my father and grandfathers
who shouldered ice,
a reminder of ancestral strength
the iceman is the strongest man in view
sure and steady with shoulders
you can land on.

"Ladder of Time"

Our schedules, Italians are very consistent
and systematic about. A *sistemazione*, an order
to the way you do things. Everything. There's no deviation.
It's still an agrarian survivalist clock.
A rigid sense of time and how to organize your day.
This *l'orario* makes it easy to make plans with friends.
You never need to ask what time.
If you're having lunch, you know what time,
If you're having dinner you know what time,
A walk in the piazza you know what time.
There's no leeway.
You get up—everybody—you get up
before the sun, before the heat
Let's say 07:00. You down a cappuccino and a *dolce*
If you're lucky a *cornetto di crema*
That's the *prima colazione*, the first breakfast.
There's something about a mouthful of warm cream
when you're just waking up. It makes you go to bed happy.
You wanna go to sleep to wake up the next morning
'cause you know as soon as you wake up you go downstairs,
"*Buongiorno Signora!*"
The *cornetto*, the hot cream, fresh overflowing
comes right toward you. All you gotta do
is open your mouth . . . This is why Italy's
got the lowest suicide rates.
It's because of these *cornetti di crema!*
You want to live to the next morning!
It's a miracle. A lactating goddess.
You can't even believe how you feel
when it comes in your mouth first
thing in the morning. It is breastfeeding.

So you're up by 07:00 you have the mouth full of cream
08:00 you're on your way to the market, or work,
or wherever you gotta go, shopping, whatever you gotta do.
Then the *colazione* you grab if you can
a *pannino*, something to hold you over
'cause 13:00, you gotta eat again!
Yes, Italians are on military time. No. This is serious.
If you're eating out, if you're grabbin' a bite
if you're early like 12:30, the food is not out yet.
if you're late like 13:30, it's all gone
there's maybe nothing left, a crust *apizz'*, that's it.
You gotta be on time, exact, *a punto,*
and if you are, it's *glorioso magnifico perfetto*
stupendo meravigliosa Che buona!
Mammamia! Madonnn! Una giornata stupefacente!
You never ate like this in all your life.
By 14:30 everyone is asleep for the *pisolino*, the afternoon nap.
16:00, you have a *caffè,* an espresso, go back to work,
or whatever you gotta do.
The whole country lifts a coffee the same moment.

The only flexible time of the day is the *aperitivo:*
a Spritz and olives, focaccia, nuts, whatever whets your appetite.
Something salty to pump your electrolytes back up
so you can function throughout the night.
The *aperitivo* can be anywhere from 17:30-19:00
and lasts 'til 19:47 or so.
It's in the piazza, or a bar by the sea, they will serve you,
a glorious glass filled with orange sparkling wonder
on a silver platter to wherever you are sitting.
The spritz matches the sunset.
That's the point of the whole thing.
The melting of the light.
So you don't sundown.
You drink the sunset.
So you don't sundown.

You take the transition of the light inside you, so it cheers you
You lift the inevitable dying of the light
in a wide, shapely big bottom glass
that rests in the palm of your hand
and you can handle it,
take your portion of it,
so you don't sundown.
The spritz takes a while to drink. It's not fast.
Savor the light. The glow.
The dip below the horizon.
The spritz lasts as long as a sunset.
Like the sunset, it's only meant to be taken in, one at a time.
It's all about the color,
drink the light, take in the brightness
The sunset you sip.
Take it inside you.
All those colors between the colors
you can't name. Let's call it orange.

You can still sense the loneliness, the abyss
that is always just an arm's reach away.
The pit of the heart. The emptiness.
You lift your Spritz like a warrior to the sunset and it's all okay.
It is a good day to die. And a day to live.
Like a hug from an old lover, who assures you:
"Yes we did okay didn't we?
You weren't such an asshole as you've imagined.
You can put down that weight you've been carrying around.
Put it down. Now."

20:00 you eat.
21:00 you take a walk.
'Na passeggiatta nella piazza.
You talk to people. Arm in arm, you walk.
Sciamaninn'!
The next day you do it all over again.

And all night long
you hear *conversazione*
in through the window of your *balcone*
from the *caffè* down the alleyway,
ricocheting off the clothesline
slipping through the slats of your shutters
into your bedroom
as you close your eyes
for dream time.

Chapter Sixteen. "*Cadere nella Madreterra* / To Fall in the Motherland"

SANPIETRINI **HAD MORE TO TEACH ME.** I took the train up to
Rome and was back walking the streets alone like in my first days in
Napoli, no one's arm to link with, so naturally, I tripped and fell again.
It might be a syndrome or a state—falling in the motherland. They
say, "kiss the ground," when you arrive. I did more than that. I fell all
the way down, face to face, *faccia a faccia,* cheek to cheek, *guancia a
guancia,* with the black cool basalt *serci,* the signature of these ancient
streets. From down on the ground, I got a good look at the meniscus
of each stone. These were the oldest stones, in use five hundred years
or more—hewn from larger stones which paved the streets of ancient
Rome two-thousand years ago. Tooth-shaped, beveled on top with facets
and narrowed toward the root, set into a base of sand, smoothed over
by time, *Sanpietrini* settle and move with the earth, with the cars and
Vespas, with the rain, with the centuries upon centuries of pounding
feet. *Sanpietrini*, little Saint Peter's, named because they began here in
Rome, in piazza San Pietro. All roads do lead here. Pulcinella of course,
was nowhere in sight. I had no one to curse or blame. He stayed back
where he belonged in *Napule*. Now it was just *Sanpietrini* and me. It
was time I bought a *bastone*, a walking stick.

I sat on a low wall on the flank of *Fontana di Acqua Paola* in the
mouth of Trastevere, where street performers took turns singing sets.
One by one they rolled up in flip-flops with small amps on wheelies,
guitars on their backs, and let their sets flow, nice and easy. The sky
broke open in thunderous applause. Cumulonimbus clouds tumbled
above the *Tevere*. A voice inside me said, "Never run on *Sanpietrini*
in the rain. Treacherous." It was a lesson I'd learned long ago when I
was young and agile enough to recover my footing. I did a slow walk
in the rain like I was walking on a tightrope over concentric arcs of
Sanpietrini, to an awning I could stand under, on a curved corner.
I stood there for hours, as night came, watching *Sanpietrini* turn
rainwater into rivulets and gloriously shining ribbons; arcs of motion.

Nightfall, like standing in the black ocean. Streetlight slapped a patina on each cheek of the *serci,* like moonlight gilds the tips of waves, the blinking lights of shops and cars flashed white, blue, red, gold, green, skittering across the facets of the wet stones, as zooming tires kicked up rainwater in spurts. Rain leaped in patterns between them, for no two *serci* ever meet, and no two are exactly alike. The spaces between form patterns, smiles, sweeping arcs, checkerboards. Rain bounced up from the black as onyx surface and ran in the inter-*serci* spaces, finally settling into the sand beneath the street, absorbing back into earth.

The next day I set out to see in person, what I'd read about in Stan Pugliese's book, *Desperate Inscriptions: Graffiti from the Nazi Prison in Rome 1943-1944.* I had to see the prison cells for myself, at *Museo Storico della Liberazione*, the headquarters of Nazi torture. Via Tasso 145 from the outside looks like any other sturdy apartment building, a classic Roman pale ochre facade, five stories tall. From the outside you'd never know what happened inside; the evidence of which, is preserved in the walls. I walked up four flights of steps to see the messages prisoners had scratched into the walls during WWII. Scratchings and etchings scar the walls, made by Italian resistance fighters who were imprisoned, tortured, and murdered by the Gestapo under the Nazi occupation of Rome. Kitchens were converted into prison cells, windows bricked over, carvings on the walls included: the image of the cross, the word "*Attenti*" with an image of a rabbit with big ears, and ladder shapes. As Stan noted, the question remains to this day: Who was the traitor known as the rabbit? Beware of Rabbit. Whose street name was "Rabbit?" Whose *soprannome?* The image that most struck me was the carving in the shape of a ladder to keep count of the days that passed, each week was counted by seven rungs. The struggle to keep track of time, to keep oriented through interrogation, torture, imminent death. To keep moored by counting *giorni e notte giorni e notte,* days and nights, days and nights. "*Condannato a morte,*" one etching reads. Condemned to death. One prisoner emphatically scratched his utterance in all caps. I could feel the rage building within him through the exhaustion.

"LA MORTE È BRUTTA PER CHI LA TEME"—Death is ugly for those who fear it.

"ITALIA RISORGI"—Italy rise again.

When I walked out of there and back into the light of day, I felt unsteady. I leaned against a building across the street. Poets take everything in. Between the emotion, the heat, the *Sanpietrini*, my unsteady left knee, I felt afraid I would fall again. I had to get a *bastone*.

I started walking and went into the first pharmacy I saw. I asked the pharmacist for a *bastone*. But the pharmacist had them put away in the back storage room and I wondered why they weren't on display. Everything else seemed to be on display. I wanted to look at a variety and choose, hold a few, see how they felt in my hand, how heavy they were, how sturdy. Maybe one with a bronze handle or something beautiful to hold. But there were no canes on display at all, so I had to stand there and describe, as best as possible, what it was I was looking for. "*Voglio un bastone. Nero. Semplice. Perché sono caduto per strada.*" I want a black cane because I fell down in the street. "*I Sanpietrini mi inciampano sempre.*" *Sanpietrini* always trip me.

The pharmacist raised an eyebrow and looked at my knees. I was wearing shorts. He could see the arthritic swelling. Then he disappeared into the back storeroom behind a door. I pictured him having to rustle through boxes. He was gone long enough so I knew I had put him through some measure of trouble. He came back with a black cane with a tripod foot, a flexible base that adjusted to the landing like a foot with an ankle joint. But I wasn't really ready for that. It looked medical and I didn't want to be reminded constantly of my brokenness. I wanted a cane with style, panache, elegance, like I was carrying it for a different purpose, a poet's purpose. I didn't want to feel more broken than I already was, more beyond repair. I wanted a little graceful help, that's all, *in lieu* of an arm to hold onto.

"*No. Grazie. Un bastone semplice. Nero. Semplice.*" No thank you. A simple cane. Black. Simple.

I pictured a classic black *bastone* with a bronze handle, something suave, like an old Italian man, like a gentleman, a *signore*, or on the other hand something powerful, a tall walking stick like a shillelagh or something with spirit, something a *cantastoria* would carry into the piazza to start the ritual. Either style, or power, or meaning, that's what I wanted. It's hard being a consumer shopping for meaning. In

New York I walked with a branch I'd carved from Grandma Peach Tree. That held ancestral power. That's what I'm talkin' about. A spirit stick. Plus, it held a story. The pharmacist went in the back and disappeared for a while longer. He came back holding a gray walker, four legs and two wheels.

"*No!*" I shook my head, "*Tttt. Tttt. Semplice. Semplice. Classico. Classico.*" With my limited Italian vocabulary, I tended to say everything twice for emphasis, to make sure I was understood. I looked at him and visualized exactly what I wanted and described it to him miming gestures for effect. I stepped by the door to see if there were any men around in the street with a classic *bastone* to bring into the pharmacy. Then, I realized that I hadn't seen any old men walking around with a proper *bastone*. Why is this? Where were they? I'd seen a couple of people nursing injuries with crutches that buckled up around their biceps, and one tourist with two ski poles as hiking sticks, but no one with an old-fashioned proper classic *bastone*. Where were all the classy old men in Rome with their suave *bastoni*?

"*Devo penso prima di decidi,*" I must think before I buy, I told the pharmacist. And as I continued on my walk, watching where I walked, it hit me: the *Sanpietrini*. They seemed to be smiling up at me. A regular *bastone* would get stuck in the space between the *serci*, a cane is a liability in *il centro*. I'd be sure to fall again and again. That's why the pharmacist was pushing the tripod foot. He knew! He figured if I was sight-seeing in the old part of town, that's the safest way. *Ahh!* He was right. But I wouldn't give in. I wasn't ready for something that looked orthopedic. I was trying to hold it together.

I kept walking until I came upon the basilica of *Santa Maria Maggiore* and entered from the top of the hill. I was tired, hot, and relieved to sit somewhere cool. I leaned my head against a marble pillar and stared up at the gold quilted ceiling, breathing in the cool frankincense. There comes a point in the day when you're traveling alone when you need to talk with somebody, anybody, it doesn't matter who, you just need a conversation. Confessional booths lined the wall on the right. Over a dozen of them, with a little red light on top that indicated "on," meaning a priest was inside. It was the confession hour. Each booth had the name of a language posted over the door. You could confess in any language you want. I said to myself, you know what, you haven't spoken much English the past couple of months, not with a native English speaker, so why not go confess in English. What the hell. I headed for the English confessional, hopeful I'd have a deep conversation. I stepped up and pulled the curtain aside. A priest sat inside the booth. He was old with a reddened pruned face and rancid expression. He spoke with a British accent. Immediately our interaction turned sour. He looked me up and down. He looked at my hand to see if I had a wedding ring on my finger.

"Are you chaste?" He asked.

Why's this old *stronzo* asking me this? Chaste? Who even uses that word? Forget English. Who needs to speak English? This is the kind of word in English I have to hear? Who even wants to speak English? I don't care if I never hear English again as long as I live. Thank God the pharmacist didn't sell me a *bastone*, I might have cracked this old creep perverted priest over the head with it. Then I'd have a bigger problem. I'd go straight from confession to being a *prigioniera*, where I'd scratch messages into the walls. This creep priest doesn't know anything about my life and right away he inquires about my pussy. Who walks into a church to discuss my pussy? That's not why I'm here. That's my pussy. *Vaffanculo!*

At the time, I wasn't getting any action, so I answered:
"Basically."

And he said, "Well thank God for *that*."

This isn't why I came to confession. I came to confession because I wanted that clean swept feeling I used to get as a kid walking out of confession. That lift, that spiritual renewal to feel forgiven for whatever weighs on your conscience. That chewing bubble gum on the walk home feeling. I pushed on. I confided in the old creep priest what weighed on my mind. Let him do his job, let him absolve me and take it away. I wasn't really talking to him, I was talking to my ancestors, the spirit of my mother, and my grandmothers—thinking of them as impoverished girls who'd left all they knew behind, for the shaky ocean of unknown.

"Do you go to Mass every Sunday?" The priest pointed this question like a spear.

"No," I said, "I don't." I couldn't sit through a whole Mass run by a man anymore. I got panicky in situations where men were in control.

"Well, start by saying ten Hail Mary's, and start going to church every Sunday."

I ran the hell out of there, shakier than when I walked in. I felt like he bashed me in the gut, and in this gorgeous basilica dedicated to the blessed mother, how dare these men destroy her all-encompassing healing spirit, or try to. And on this spot! The ancient Roman temple to Juno, the guardian to all the Roman women! How did men ever get in charge anyway? The world is inside out.

The heel of my foot had to find a stone I could center my foot on. I made my way over the *Sanpietrini* to piazza *Navona* where the water pressure was so low, the gods were dribbling from their marble lips. An artist picked up the slack making thousands of bubbles between the fountains. He stood by Bernini's fountain of four rivers: the Nile, the Ganges, *Río de la Plata*, and the Danube, dunking a net of ropes attached to two broomsticks into a large vat of soapy water, then lifting the net up into the wind magically releasing a river of bubbles into the sky. Gleaming rainbows, thousands of bubbles airborne, children screaming, chasing the bubbles around the piazza, trying to catch one, chasing the wind.

A Roman friend set me straight. "Well, what did you expect going over there to those old conservative *pezzi di merda*?" She rocked her hand in the air. "*Ma dai. Cosa stavi pensando?*" C'mon, what were you thinking? "Church is the last place you'll find benevolence or compassion."

A few days later, I found the *bastone* of my dreams, a *bastone* full of meaning, and power, and stories. I visited Rita Passeri, a painter friend of mine who'd moved back home to Italy after living in Brooklyn for many years on a street named Verona. Rita painted a series of life-size portraits of women in oil paint on antique barn doors. The cross-slats of the old wood made it seem the women were each entering the room with you. The effect of seeing them all together in one studio was a gathering of the ancestors, all mid-action, looking, turning, lifting a lamb, buttoning a back button, holding a chicken whose neck she'd just twisted. The painting that most grabbed me was a portrait Rita painted of her grandmother holding a chicken upside down by its feet. The stern yet serene and determined look of *sopravvivenza* weighed heavy on her grandmother's dark resolute brow. A peasant who knew how to do everything, how to give life to the land and all beings on it. Rita had her women around her, surrounded by ancestors, a powerful gathering of spirit. In the corner of her studio, amidst stacks of paintings were various sticks leaning against the wall; lengths of wood that figured into the composition of her paintings. Rita had collected them from the beach, walking in the forest, and from old farms. I must have told her that I'd fallen repeatedly on *Sanpietrini*, and she pulled out a *bastone*, "*Ecco qua.* Would you like this one?" The *bastone* she handed me was an ancient carved hardwood branch filled with stories. I could feel it. It had power, it had lived a useful life. This *bastone* had been around. It looked like the tall bone of an animal, the tibia of a giraffe. The top was gnarled like an old bone at the knee, and the bottom cleaved like a hoof, thicker than the space between *serci*. Perfect. It was held together with a circle of thick wire twisted tightly. This *bastone* lived a life on a farm, I could feel it in the grip. I thanked Rita for the spirit gift and felt equipped to walk on.

At *Fiumicino* airport, it was easy to find my sister Rosina and her husband Rocco at the gate. We screamed "*Buongiorno,*" when we saw each other, and grabbed a coffee before continuing onto Bari together. Ever since I was a little kid, these two brought me on adventures around the Bronx and Manhattan, and now that they were retired, there was time for more. Rosina and Rocco were dressed smart, comfortable, and ready in summer sandals and sunhats. They had a fantastic amount of get-up-and-go energy. They'd dated since they were teenagers and still had that youthful spirit. As we walked through security, the guard stopped me to see my *bastone*. He took the *bastone*, asking in a high-pitched voice, "*Ma che cosa fai con questo in aBherrrrrie?*" And what are you going to do with this in Bari? He said "Bari" like a goat bleating vowels, as if I were going to a long-lost land where people still lived in caves and walked with tall staffs in the fields. He and another security guard laughed and laughed at me, turning the *bastone* upside down, tapping all its edges. He turned it every which way and checked to see if the hoof screwed off, in case I'd concealed something inside the shank. He made sure it wasn't hollow, hiding a rapier. The *bastone* was as long as a scabbard. Longer. Theoretically I could hide a nice sword in there. They bent back in laughter, as if I was the funniest thing they'd encountered all day. Me, in my Hawaiian shirt, cream pants with pink rose applique walking with my *terrone bastone*, headed for the *paese*. I looked like I'd lost my goat herd. Lost in time. Lost in place. I laughed too, seeing these two men in uniform examining my old peasant stick, the bottom of which resembled a hoof. It was an anachronism. You don't see things like this in the modern aesthetic of airports where there weren't even faucets anymore, you waved your hand under a white underlit counter where soap, water, then a blast of hot air triggered by motion sensors. When the security guard was done with his physical examination, he instructed me to put it on the x-ray belt, and I watched as my *bastone* moved down the conveyor belt. As expected, it was solid wood, and the guard let me board the plane with it. Off we went, Rosina and Rocco, me and my *bastone*, back to *il nostro paese*.

PART V
COM S CHIEM U VIND?

I dreamt of
               t h e
                              s
                         w
                      o
                 l   l
                   a
             w
         s

             o f
                  S a l e r n o

                    who
                talk
           back
       to
         you

                              and the
                              ants
                              of

                                   a
                                 n
                                 i
                                   s
                                   s
                                  e
                              M

                 w h o   n e v e r

                    k
                    l
                    a
               w

               i
                 n   s   h t
                      t   g
                         r   a   i
                                        l
                                         i
                                          n
                                        e
                                     s

Chapter Seventeen. "*Il Volo dell'Angelo* / Flight of the Angel"

Castelmezzano, July, 2018

ROCCO HAD AN EXCITED LOOK in his eye. Before heading to Acquaviva delle Fonti, he wanted to go to the top of the *Dolomiti Lucane* mountains to fly the highest zipline in the world, "*Il Volo dell'Angelo.*" I was the driver. We agreed to do a couple of excursions before going to see the family. We got down to Basilicata and up to Castelmezzano. The mountain peaks were sharp, steep, craggy rock, like flints cutting the sky. As we pulled into town, overhead, every few minutes, a body flew across a vast chasm of sky between two mountaintop towns, Castelmezzano and Pietrapertosa. Everyone on the ground cranked their necks looking up in wonder. The flyers were strapped in horizontally and launched head-first off the cliff, at speeds up to 75MPH. In the center of town, we could see the flyers hopping into a van to get up to the launchpad. I said, "Rocco, they all look like Olympic athletes, young Swiss blondes in Lycra body suits. I don't see anybody your age going up there." But he had the spark of adventure in his eye, a Bronx boy at heart with street bravado. I worried about his heart, his age. My sister and he were lucky and healthy enough to enjoy their retirement and their grandchildren. I could hear his daughters' voices in my head saying, "Don't let my father do that! I need him around!" I also wondered where my own sense of adventure went. I was focused on getting to Acquaviva to see Zia Annunziatine one last time and to introduce her to Rosina. It was a now or never moment. Zia Annunziatine was the last living daughter of Grandma Rose's sister Maria. Rocco looked up at the sky in awe at the bodies flying overhead. He seemed to be doing calculations in his mind, to picture himself flying off the cliff. He looked at how the flyers were strapped in, their helmets, and what kind of flight posture they had to hold. My sister and I exchanged glances of worry. We were not tempted at all by bodies zooming across the sky. Rocco's eyes held boyish wonder. He had one night to decide.

A full ice-cold moon rose over the mountain. From a restaurant terrace on the side of a cliff, I felt closer to the moon than I'd ever been before. I stood up as if to play with the moon, forming postures as if I was holding her over my head, posing for photos. Rosina and Rocco joined in, so did everyone in the restaurant. We each did a moon dance.

Early the next morning, Rocco said he'd thought the better of it and decided to keep his feet on the ground. My sister and I were relieved, saying, "Thank God," simultaneously. We decided to hike to the top of the mountain where there was a remnant of a Norman castle. They walked fast. I lagged behind, walking with my *bastone,* more interested in saying hello to locals along the way. It was a steep climb. Soon, an elder man was walking beside me. He also walked with a *bastone.* We were dressed similarly, short sleeves and caps and walking with tree branches. We both had strong calves and barrel guts. We made a funny pair, walking at the same pace, and naturally fell into a conversation. Donato compared his *bastone* to mine. He wanted to see mine and asked where I got it. He had reasons why his was better, it had a crook end on top, so that when he was resting, it could hang off his shoulder, and the crook could also hang grocery bags when he carried them up the hill. He demonstrated all the things you can do with a *bastone* with a crook on top. I knew my *bastone* was magic, it just made me a new friend. We passed a luscious fig tree growing off the side of the cliff. Donato quickly hung his *bastone* on the fence that protected us from falling off the edge, pulled himself up a few feet of fence, and pulled figs from the tree. He put six into my hands, and he pointed two fingers at Rosina and Rocco who were up the hill, indicating two for each of us. These were his trees he said proudly, and this was his house that he built himself. A miraculous yellow house built right into the rocky cliff. I wondered how Donato did it. What a feat of engineering. I broke the fig open and slid half into my mouth. The nutritious jewels inside, I knew that this was the moment, *un momento di luce.* Heaven is . . . a fresh juicy fig from a tree on a cliff on top of a mountain, given by a friend I'll know for just one hour in life.

I hollered at Rosina and Rocco to wait for a minute so I could hand them their figs and introduce them to Donato. We all were in awe of Donato's prowess building the big yellow house in the rock on the side of the cliff. We thanked him and continued our hike up the mountain. We made it to the top where there was a rocky remnant of a Norman castle around a thousand years old. The rocks remained and you could see how they'd cut steps into the rock to have the vantage of the highest lookout for enemy invaders. On the way back down, Donato was waiting for us outside his house, with a tray of shot glasses and his homemade *limoncello*. "Look at this," I said, "Donato!" We all raised our glasses and listened as he recounted stories from his life. He was king of the mountain and his *limoncello*, an ambrosia.

As we drove out of town, the GPS told us to go a different way than when we came. At the *rotatoria* we debated whether we should listen to the GPS or not. I wanted to intuit my way down the mountain. I said, "GPS isn't reliable in the south." I'd developed a decent intuition for roads years ago when cycling cross-country, learning viscerally how roads go around mountains, how train tracks follow rivers in valleys, how to find the center of a town. Rosina and Rocco wanted to follow the GPS. A thunderstorm was coming. We had to get down the mountain to go on our way. I wanted to ask a local, but it was the lunch hour, everybody was already at home for *il pranzo*. We came to a fork in the road. I wanted to go right; GPS directed us to go left. It didn't make sense. That was the inside track of the mountain, while we had come up the outside of the mountain. I figured, what's the worst that could happen? We turn around and come back? Maybe we'll find ourselves in an adventure in a different town than we set out for. I'm an improviser. We decided to follow the GPS. Big mistake. The road got smaller and smaller and took us through woods, then opened up into farmland on the side of the mountain. I saw a sign out of the right corner of my eye; I didn't know exactly what it meant but I thought it stated, 'private property.' We kept going. The GPS was sure; the line for the road was a promising bright blue. Clouds were darkening and hanging lower in the sky. We were descending. On my left was a muddy, rocky cliff. On my right, a sheer mountain wall with a vertical rise. The sky got darker and heavier and closer to us. The road was single lane, turning rockier. GPS said to keep going straight, it showed a beautiful blue stripe for a road winding down the mountain.

All of a sudden, Rocco yelled with a long operatic vowel, "Stop!" He jumped out of the car and I jammed on the breaks. The road ended. Dead ahead was just a field on the side of the mountain. There was no more road. It was mud. GPS showed a road but there was no road. The beautiful bright blue line was an illusion. With a sheer cliff to my left, where if I sneezed, the car would have rolled off the mountain, there was no room to pull a U-turn. Rocco started tossing big rocks off the road behind me to clear the road and waved for me to back up. I took a deep breath and focused. I silently coached myself. "I'm gonna back-up to get off this mountain, drive in reverse until I find a spot to pull a U-turn and turn the car around." I took a deep breath and didn't say a word. Adrenaline surged through my body; our lives were in my hands on the steering wheel. I had faith that if anyone could drive in reverse to get us off the mountain, it was me. I knew a 5th gear inside myself; an internal state, an out-of-body zone of hyper-focus which had gotten me through chemotherapy and radiation as a teenager. I can keep my cool. No doubt this developed as a trauma response in early childhood to survive the violence surrounding me. A 5th gear. I drove in reverse, the thunderstorm came, we got back to that fork in the road, took the right, and found a local who had finished his lunch and gave us directions to the highway to get off the mountain safely. At the end of the day, we each were filled with adrenaline, and had our version, even more dangerous than "*Volo dell'Angelo.*" We all would have been better off taking the zipline off the mountain.

My *bastone* got me into another deep conversation, with yet another Donato, over another shot glass of *limoncello*. The *bastone* gave me the feeling of support from the ancients. Donato Cascione, a poet, born and bred in Matera, turned his passion for collecting the tools, wares, and furniture of our ancestors into the museum, *Museo Laboratorio*

della Civiltà Contadina (Museum Workshop of Peasant Culture). He preserved a cave in Matera, in reverence, to show how our ancestors lived and the brutality of their struggle for survival. Walking through the threshold into the dark, cool cave, was walking backward through time but also into an interior chamber of the heart. Donato's collection of tools and housewares, cast iron and stone, wood and terracotta, were hand-worn, and held untold hardships and stories. He examined my *bastone* and showed me his collection. Mine fit right in. Donato showed us how some of the tools were used; he pushed a stone over a stone groove to demonstrate how grain was crushed. We each tried our hand at it and one or two thrusts of the heavy stone was enough to inject into our biceps a drop of the vast abyss of our lack of comprehension of the strain of their daily existence, what they had to do to survive and why so many died young. In Donato's cave we got a sense of what we could not fathom about our ancestors' struggles, that they worked like beasts of burden, lived with their donkey in the back of the cave, and went to great lengths to keep everyone warm and fed and dry. We had to sit down and let it sink in. Outside the mouth of the cave, Donato opened a bottle of *limoncello* and we all cried as he recited poetry about the crushing conditions under which they lived. One of his poems struck me deeply, it was called, *"Quegli Uomini,"* These Men. In his lines, he excavated the rage, what the men did *"per non morire di rabbia,"* to not be killed by rage, their own rage. Brutality was inside and out. I entered my own dark heart; I had my own rage. I realized that my father's rage and violence not only destroyed parts of us, but it destroyed him first and foremost. He was his own primary victim. His mind, his life and livelihood, his health, his marriage, his business, all suffered. In our brief hours in Donato's cave, clinking iron hammers and pincers, scraping rocks together, holding ancient hoes, and hammers and *bastoni* and baskets, it all came down upon me, generations of desolation, isolation, frustration, violence, rage, pain, despair, suffering, hopelessness and the struggle for faith, creation, and existence. It was all within my bones, my loneliness and sense of isolation was nothing new, in fact I had eons of company. I heard the rhythmic plucking of strings, I heard the silences in between. Donato might have pulled out an old stringed instrument, or maybe an ancestor did a thousand years ago in the cave and it was in my mind, a pulse, a rhythm—the plucking of strings. Drinking the sugared lemon allowed our tears to flow through centuries, swallowing the reality of the harshness of life for the ones who had come before us. In my cave of hearts I felt *capeeshed* in the shade under Donato's grapevine. It was a relief to be in a place where suffering was communally acknowledged. Donato did the job of a poet, being porous to detail, to energies, to what is unspoken. To breathe in the still life of a moment and render it in syllables. To feel and perceive everything and express it in words. To point out what is profound in life. To honor the past by weaving it into a future. He brought us inside the caves within us.

I closed my eyes and felt the cave echo with all the basement kitchens we inhabited in our Bronx childhoods. Cool, dark, cellars were the center of activity in so many of our *paesan's* households. We'd walk down steps into basement level apartments that opened up into kitchens with big tables. This is where all the serious cooking was done. Upstairs was for show, for guests. A distant echo of cave life. And all my father's years in all the basements. As a boiler repairman, basements were his refuge. In the last years of his life, he stayed in the basement of the mental home, sitting by the furnace taking things apart, and arranging things in the crawl spaces of the basement walls. With the stone walls of the cellar surrounding him, no one could penetrate or enter without him knowing it. There is only one mouth to the cave. Here you are safe.

I thought of leaving Donato my *bastone* but it kept me upright, as I walked on my way.

That night we ate dinner on a terrace overlooking the ancient city of Matera which had an amber candlelit glow. Silence echoed through the canyon and the caves and the houses carved into the rocks, layered on top of one other, connected by a network of streets made of stone steps that went up and up and up the mountain. On the menu, we saw *polpette di pane*, breadballs, our mother's signature dish which none of us had ever had outside her kitchen. I thought my mother had improvised this creation to not waste the leftover egg after she ran out of chopped meat for meatballs. A breadball is a meatball without meat: eggs, breadcrumbs, garlic, parsley, pecorino, onions, in the right proportions, always filled with air from our mother's light touch. When we ordered it, among other appetizers, we were not expecting much, though clearly, we thought it was a direct message from our blessed mother Rachele, but when we each took a bite, I looked at my sister and she looked at me and we both fell apart into tears. Clearly our mother was alive and working for the restaurant cooking these breadballs. Or somehow from the angelic sphere, she snuck breadballs onto the menu just for this night and inspired the chef's hands. We were beginning to sense the thousands of years of tradition that we came from, that what our mother created in the kitchen was rooted in the ancient past, a past of poverty where breadcrumbs were all you could muster.

Chapter Eighteen. "*Sangu Mi*"

Acquaviva delle Fonti, July 2018

ZIA ANNUNZIATINE GLIDED HER WALKER into the common room of the nursing home, a soft white knit cable sweater over her shoulders, clasped at the neck with one mother-of-pearl button. Thirty years before, I'd seen her ride her bicycle to the outdoor market in Acquaviva, and take care of her mother Maria, and now she gently, but still speedily pushed her walker. My heart melted like a wax candle, I felt the drip and the sharp icy flame inside my chest. We shared a gentle long hug and were all in instant tears. It was as if Grandma Rose left Acquaviva and then in a blink my sister and I, one hundred years later, returned. I could see Rosina's heart exposed. Zia Annunziatine looked and sounded so much like our precious Grandma Rose, sharp swift eyes taking everything in, fast talker, hands flying, a sparkle in her blue eyes. Her voice, her mannerisms, her wit, were so much like Grandma Rose. "It was like Grandma Rose was alive again," Rosina told me later. And just as we could see our grandmother in Zia Annunziatine, she could see our grandmother and her mother, in our eyes. Zia Annunziatine held each of our hands. She looked right into Rosina's eyes and grabbed the moment, knowing it would never come again. She confided in her as if they'd known each other all their lives. She squeezed our hands with all her might and said over and over, "We always thought of you every day. We love you even when we didn't see you."

We all opened up into deep-breath sobbing. Zia Annunziatine had kept track of us in her mind and her prayers. We were linked through the silence and the absence. It was like there were three groups of people who were connected for us: the dead, the living, and the relatives overseas. You knew they were there, but you didn't know who they were. Rosina shared her memories of sending packages to Acquaviva, and she remembered as a little girl, mailing her communion dress. I was relieved to land in a moment where I could cry without holding back, a moment none of us could fully understand. A moment where we all could cry together. Let it all out. All the unspoken. All the grief. All we didn't understand about life. We were each a facet of cut glass, like the crystal that hung in Aunt Grace's window, together we completed a picture that had been hidden from all of us. Growing up in the Bronx, Grandma Rose had seemed singular to us, and now, she had a context. Rosina could see clearly the people and the place Grandma Rose came from, and suddenly our little grandmother wasn't singular at all. She was part of something bigger, a culture, a language, a tradition, a town, a whole set of ways. I know Rosina imagined Grandma Rose and Annunziatine together. It was impossible not to, to enter the past as if you could lift the veil of time and be there, yourself.

Zia Annunziatine told us this story three times to make sure we got it, that we caught the nuance and could take the story away with us. Some stories are adamant to be told and bubble up in a person until they are transmitted and handed-off to someone else, to the next generation. We are the keepers of this story now. Annunziatine slowed down her speech pattern and spoke in Italian for us to understand, with a little *Acquavivese* jumping in. The language of the heart. This is my translation of what she said to us. I understood everything Zia Annunziatine said. I *capeeshed* her. I *capeeshed*, not a word for word, but deeper, the bark and bite, music, phrases, intention, whistling, calling and answering, clapping of hands, slapping the table, sounds, squeezing my hand, saying what you mean how you mean, what you want not what you think, bits and bites of words without hesitation, sounds that turn corners, syllables that cut to the chase, expression. Pure flow. *Pura Defluit,* the town motto of Acquaviva delle Fonti. She cried and held our hands as she told it over and over, speaking with the rush of a waterfall:

"When Zia Rosina and Zia Lucia arrived in America, every month they would send ten dollars. Every month we would wait for the envelope from America. They sent packages too. American clothes. When a package came from America, we would wait to open it until everyone gathered around. Neighbors, friends, everyone. Then we opened it. We passed everything around. They all marveled at the American style clothing. We never saw such style. My school friends were jealous of my American dresses. I carried my shoes to school to conserve the shoes, then I would put them on once I got inside the building. My school friends would say, "Look at her in the American dress," and they'd turn the fabric of my dress over and over in their hands. They never saw such stitching. Clothes of America. They'd look at the details, the collar, the shape, the trim. I told them, "*Sangu mi in America.*" My blood in America. They would examine the style and try to copy it by sewing their own clothes based on what they saw. Times were hard. Sometimes I would ask my mother, "When's the envelope coming from America? Will we make it until then?" We had little to eat. Maybe a piece of bread. My mother Maria would assure me, "Yes, we will make it, my love." And then a package would arrive from America. And everyone would gather around and then we would open it."

As Zia Annunziatine finished the story, she squeezed our hands harder, and told it again. She wanted to make sure it got through.

I wondered what style dresses my grandmother would have sent in 1919. Maybe a shirtwaist? Perhaps it was the first time they saw such collars and embellishments and waistlines? Clothes for the working woman, away from the farm, out of the kitchen and into the city. And in the 30's and 40's when Annunziatine was a schoolgirl? I thought of what my grandmother had to do to save ten dollars in 1919. How did she do it, working in the factories as a seamstress, then as a finisher, and taking piecework home to work on late into the night. At one point she made beaded combs. I wondered what they looked like. My imagination and memory for things I had no way to remember was on fire, sparking into dark corners with just tips of light as hints of detail.

The sparkle in Annunziatine's eyes made it easy to picture her as a little girl enamored by these magical aunts in America who she'd never met but who sent packages that enabled them to survive. Then, in 1981, at eighty-one years old, Grandma Rose returned to Acquaviva, sixty-five years after she'd emigrated. What a reunion that must have been. Her sister Maria was eighty-five. One month together after a lifetime of separation.

This is what the tears were for when I left New York. This moment. Aunt Grace's tears. Rosina's tears. Zia Annunziatine's tears. My tears. My cousins' tears. Annunziatine's children and grandchildren's tears. All the same tears. Tears of the ancestors. All the tears our grandmothers held in. Tears of being torn apart. Tears of breaking open. Tears of return. Trying to find each other's shore. Tears from birth through death with the force of rivers rushing toward oceans. Tears where words crumble in their efforts. Tears for silence. Tears for holding it all inside. Tears for the moon's howl. We cried for our mothers and grandmothers. We cried for everything we would never know about each other and everything we would never say. We cried for Grandma Rose, we cried for her sisters Maria and Lucia and Angelina and brothers Gennaro and Giacomo. We cried for a hundred years back like the snap of fingers to when little Rosa and Lucia got on the boat as teenagers and left. We cried for Annunziatine's mother Maria who was ready to get on the boat when World War I interrupted the plan and all our lives reversed. We cried for each other and the ocean that swelled in between us. We cried for the women. All the unspoken violations that pave women's lives. All the pain borne in silence. We cried. A saltwater stream backward through time, all the way back, longer than time itself, our own saltwater contribution to the ocean of time that separated us. Our tears were greater than us. Life is a set-up. Death a mystery. Our hearts were naked like those pictures of Mary and Jesus, exposed hearts throbbing, ringed with thorns, hemorrhaging light, draped with roses, skewed with swords, topped with diadems. Mary and Jesus cried for us, pointing to their exposed hearts, outside of ribs, beyond sternums. What was it they were saying? Life hurts. Bear your pain. Walk with your heart open. I am with you. That's what I heard. I felt my own heart open. I watched my sister's heart open. Ribs got out of the way. Sternums unzipped. Zia Annunziatine's heart opened. We cried for the lifetimes that separated us, we cried for things we couldn't name, we cried for the suffering, we cried for the century, we cried for the world wars, for post-war trauma and schisms, we cried for the hunger and desperation, we cried for divorce, we cried for diseases, we cried for lonesomeness, we cried for our lack of understanding of ourselves and each other, we cried for the language barrier, for all that was lost, the knowledge of hands, the language of leaves and trees, olives and grapes, we cried for our limitations, we cried for the people we had become, for our blind spots, we cried for births and deaths and miscarriages, we cried for souls who never arrived, we cried for what was never to be, we cried for violence and rage, we cried for everything each of us had suffered alone, depressions and addictions, cancers and PTSD, schizophrenia and manic depression, isolation and persistent poverty, we cried for the American dream and the desperate cries of those who went to New York for work to help the others survive, alone or with a sister, like little Rosina and Lucia, as teenagers. We cried for those who left and those who were left behind and for those in our families who would never know one another. We shed sheaths of cement off our hearts. The Bronx came off. The U.S. came off. A hundred years came off. English came off. The soil was tilled, turned over. We cried for joy. We cried for all we survived. We cried for the miracle of making it to this momentous moment. The *sorgente* rose within us.

The heart is an ocean opening. The heart is an ocean opening. The heart is an ocean opening . . .

In Acquaviva *vecchio*, the old part of town, I stared down into a *pozzo* and understood. We walked on top of water. Ever-present, life-giving water. I could see my grandmother as a young girl, retrieving water from the well, pulling the rope, filling her terracotta amphora. I could feel the grooves worn into the stone well by my ancestors' ropes. Acquaviva delle Fonti is named for the natural aquifer on which it stands, *la sorgente*, the source, of sweet water, *acqua dolce*. Acquaviva is about waters that run deep, waters that rise up, water that is ever-present. It's spiritual. Water is life. Water is the secret to life, to the *cipolla rossa*, to everything, the source of life. People came from all around, especially in times of drought, to Acquaviva to get the ever-present water. The name itself, Acquaviva delle Fonti—Living Water from the Source. I tumbled the words in my mind to let meaning open in the spaces between the words: alive water, living water, water of life from the source, the *sorgente*, that flows up from the ground, a spring, and more, the *sorgente* has power and plenitude. Over the years, I'd gotten the name wrong. The town insignia is a three-tiered fountain. *Fonti* sounded to me like fountain. I grew up thinking the town name meant Living Waters of the Fountains. But the *sorgente* is much deeper than that. Wells were dug, the *pozzi,* and the town built up around them. *Pozzi* are all over the old village. Looking down into a *pozzo* is to become part of the flow of life. It's a secret window where you can look down into the earth and know that's where we come from, this living breathing life-giving mother that birthed us all and will take us when we die.

Over the next few days, we had beautiful times with Annunziatine's children and grandchildren. One of our cousins, Agata, was Rosina's age and when they met, they ran into each other's arms and held hands like two little girls about to do cartwheels. They had memories of the same family and world events over the course of their lives. They each remembered the wailing sadness over the death of Grandma Rose's sister Lucia. Agata remembered her grandmother Maria being inconsolable that she'd never see her sister again. As long as they were alive, they held the hope of reuniting. Rosina remembered Grandma Rose crying endlessly over her dear sister who she journeyed to America with and raised daughters in tandem. As they talked, and I interpreted, they each put the puzzle pieces of their lives together, and the grand picture of life began to fill out.

In the *paese,* our inner *paesans* came out. At night we bought lemon ice in the piazza. Rocco was very social and would have loved piazza life, walking in the square at night talking with the other men, wearing pressed pants, polished shoes and a button-down shirt. I asked the lemon ice vendor to lend his uniform vest to Rocco so he could try it on. He fit right in. In a way, it seemed we all had parallel lives unlived in the *paese.*

Rosina and Rocco went back home, and I stayed on in Acquaviva. I wanted to have more time with Zia Annunziatine, and I was determined to get to Bitetto and search for the cousins who I'd never tracked down on our father's side of the family. My hours walking with Zia Annunziatine around the nursing home halls were my most joyous. She'd squeeze my hand and say, "*Stai nu pic,*" stay a while. We ventured outside to the garden and sat with the statue of Jesus. Annunziatine taught me a beautiful song in praise of Mary. "*O Maria, quanto sei bella, sei la gioia e se l'amore.*" We sang loud together and paraded through the halls of the nursing home belting the song over and over, day after day. I learned the words as we repeated it. Her voice was resonant, and the song filled both our hearts. These moments felt miraculous and had to last forever in our hearts. As we walked, people waved to us from their rooms through open doorways. We were a two-person parade. Twice, someone asked her who I was. One time, Annunziatine looked up at me and answered, "*L'American*,'" with a sparkle in her eyes. Another time a nun asked, and Annunziatine looked up at me and said, "*Boh,*" which basically means, *I don't have the faintest clue.* We all had a good laugh over that. It didn't matter who I was. What mattered was our hearts sang this song together, a praise song to the feminine power of the universe, the eternal mother. And as we said goodbye, and I hesitated to leave, she repeated a local expression which always brought a smile to me because I couldn't say the whole phrase, "*Ci n'ge na ma sci, sciamaninn, ce non ge na ma sci, non ge ne sim scenn.*" It roughly means, if we're gonna go, let's go, if we're not gonna go, let's not go.

Chapter Nineteen. "The Wallmakers / *I Muraturi*"

Bitetto, August 2018

I DROVE TO BITETTO ALONE. I didn't know anybody, but I had a couple of clues. First: the name, phone number, and address, of one of my father's living cousins: Pasqualeen. Second: the name of the town saint, *Beato Giacomo,* who my father's sisters prayed novenas to on my behalf especially every time I had cancer. Third: an old street address where my grandmother was born, the grandmother for whom I am named. Fourth: the nickname, *il soprannom'* of my great-grandfather, *Mangiasard,* / Eats sardines. I also had *il soprannom'* of the father of one of my uncles through marriage, but I knew the rules. I was not to invoke this nickname under any circumstances unless I was in grave danger and needed the use of special powers and privileges, because the way my uncle described it, the mention of his father's *soprannom'* in the *paese,* had the power of God. I kept this name secret.

I telephoned my father's cousin Pasqualeen a couple of times, but nobody answered. Maybe she was at *al mare*? It was August. In August everyone is at the sea. I knew I had as many cousins in the heel of the boot as I did in New York. Some left the *paese* for cities up north, but many were still in town. The four branches of the family tree didn't know one another, although they were all *paesans,* and many of them, neighbors. I felt like an errant puzzle piece to a giant jigsaw puzzle. Whenever I completed a big puzzle, there were always a couple of pieces missing, odd-shaped holes in the overall picture. As an American who didn't know the dialect or the ways of the town, who only knew bits of the standardized language, and who had lost the knowledge of the land that my grandparents knew so well, I felt like one of those missing pieces, under a rug, stuck on the bottom of a shoe and taken outside, somewhere never to be found, never to be put into place.

I drove from *Strada Provinciale* 48 to 236 to 90, to get from Acquaviva delle Fonti to Cassano delle Murge to Bitetto—the three towns in the heel of the boot that formed a trinity of olive and fig trees and grapevines—where all my ancestors were born for hundreds of years, and many cousins still lived. I wanted to drive the whole circuit from town to town to town to get a sense of the land and how close they all were to one another. All my family, all the lineages, all my bloodlines, came from this small triangle of fertile earth. Each of the towns are connected by county roads, *Strada Provinciale,* between millions of olive trees and hundreds of thousands of acres of grapes. The olives and grapes and almonds and figs are as much my *paesani* as the people. In the province of Bari, outside the city of Bari, the names of the towns read like a poem: Acquaviva delle Fonti, Bitetto, Bitritto, Bitonto, Binetto, Altamura, Modugno, Gioia del Colle, Cassano delle Murge, Sammichele di Bari, Toritto, Turi, Triggiano, Locorotondo, Alberobello, and more. We descend from the ancient Apulians, the people of the spur and the heel of the boot. I imagine them as diviners of water who walked the *murge* with V-shaped branches to find underground springs of water. The *murge* is a limestone plateau west of Bari. My ancestors were from the *Bassa Murgia*, the lower *murge*, a fertile land whose gift was to make fruit, *fruttificare. La terra di fruttificazione.* The land that bears fruit. A rich reddened earth.

To get from my grandmother's town Acquaviva delle Fonti to my grandfather's town, Cassano delle Murge, there's one way in and one way out. One thread of a road through olive groves connected two peasants from two families, and the destinies of so many lives to follow. At every intersection of the county roads are roundabouts. You gotta read fast to go in the right direction, round and round before you get it right: My head spun with all the different names: *Binetto, Bitetto, Bitonto, Bitritto. Binetto, Bitetto, Bitonto, Bitritto.* You get dizzy before you even try to find your relatives.

Endless stone walls line these roads. Miles of walls. I thought of the men in my family. On their immigration papers, for *occupazione*—occupation, it either says: *contadino*—farmer, or *muratore*—wall maker. I'd always pictured my grandfathers building walls the way my father put up walls in the Bronx. He'd hold three nails in his mouth sharp ends sticking out his lips, lay a frame of two-by-four studs sixteen inches apart with cross-struts, hammer vast clean sheets of plasterboard to the frame, and as a finishing touch, sink each nail just below flush by tapping another nail onto its head with one shot. But on *Strada Provinciale* 236, it struck me. These are the walls my ancestors built. I'm looking at them. These walls. These stones. These fields. These endless walls. My grandfathers and great-grandfathers and great-great-grandfathers built these walls, uprooted these stones with their hands, carried these stones across these fields, this sun stepping on their backs, simmering their spines. They built these walls.

My Grandpop Carmine, my father's father, came to *L'America* when he was twelve years old from Bitetto and like many *Barese* in New York City, carried three-hundred-pound block ice to earn a living. This was work available to immigrants who were strong as oxen and willing to beat out the sun to work. The *Barese* in New York dominated this trade. At eighteen Carmine joined the U.S. Army, which, according to my father, he perceived as a vacation from the ice business. The Army fed you, issued you two good pairs of socks and leather boots—that was something. Grandpop fought in the 1918 Battle of the Argonne Forest in The Great War. My father told me this story many times: "When Grandpop was in the Army, there was a rock pile the Sergeant wanted moved. So, he ordered a private, a southerner, to move the rocks. "Private, move that rock pile. I want it moved over there," and he pointed to another spot twenty yards away. The southerner balked at the order. The Civil War was always being fought amongst the ranks, so the Sergeant looked for a Yankee next. "Watch this," the Sergeant says, "the Dago will do it. He won't even think twice." He eyeballs Grandpop. "Charlie," he says, "Move that rock pile over there." Grandpop, they call him Charlie in America, thinkin' nothin' of it, carries all the rocks, a bunch at a time, to where the Sergeant pointed, with the whole platoon watching. When he was done, Grandpop says to the Sergeant, "Sir, where do you want them moved to next?" The Sergeant says, "Put 'em back." "Yes Sir." And Grandpop carries all the rocks back without even thinkin' about it. Rocks to him were child's play."

Perhaps it sounds like bravado, but after carrying hundreds of pounds of block ice every day, a rock must have felt light as a feather. Imagine my grandfather, a boy, seven, eight years old in Bitetto. Imagine taking him out to a field and telling him, "*Uè guagliò!*—Yo boy! Clear these fields of rocks. That's your job, your career, your *occupazione.* Your post. Your *stazione,* your station. You're a *cavamonti,* a rock digger. Unbury the rocks. Pull them up outta the earth with your bare hands. Your hands are shovels now. Your hands are spades. Your fingernails are blades in the earth. Unbury all the different size rocks: *quadrelle, pedache e catene.* Use the *piccone.* Pry up the *pezzetto lungo.* Carry the rocks. Arrange 'em into walls. Make 'em fit tight. Get all the rocks. Clear the fields of rocks. Make one long wall here, along this donkey path we're gonna turn into a road to connect the towns. When you're done with that, make a row over there. See the edge of those olive trees? Make one over there. And when you're done with that go a kilometer down and continue the wall. We need walls everywhere. *A pète a pète se fàsce u parète.* Rock upon rock makes a wall. Do a good job. These walls will last forever. One day your grandchildren will look at these walls and say, "My grandfather built this with his bare hands."

Imagine being that boy. Imagine a world without walls. You look at endless fields in the hot open sun. You're looking at nothing and you have to make something. And you know this job will never be done. One day you won't be able to move your back is all or close your hands ever again because your hands cast into shovels somewhere in the hot hard earth. Shovels like starfish, five thick muscular open fingers. And when you get to Ellis Island and you're twelve years old and built like an ox, and they ask you your occupation and you have to give the guy in the hat and shiny silver badge a word to write on his paper, what are you gonna say? "I pull rocks outta the fields all day barehanded?" No! You give an indication of pride in creation. *"Sono un muratore."* I am a wall maker.

Chapter Twenty. "Certainly We Are Cousins"

ON *STRADA PROVINCIALE* 236, DRIVING by these endless stone walls, through fields of olive trees, I saw something red coming up on the left. A woman. Right there in the middle of two olive trees a woman was walking. She wore a fire-engine red bra, red thong, and red stilettos, had long black hair and walked impossibly slow around a big cream-colored cushy divan. So slow as if she was under water. She held a red umbrella with a rippled edge, silky, that undulated in waves like a giant jellyfish when she pumped it up and down. Up up! Up up! She pumped it up to me twice inviting me over. This was her calling card. Up up! Up up! She saw me as a *signore* in my baseball hat, sunglasses, short hair, left arm hanging out the window, and sleeve rolled up over the shoulder revealing a muscular bicep. As soon as I noticed her, I whizzed past and continued meeting her eyes in my rear-view mirror. Her skin stood out from the olive trees, sun-worn, not young, she'd been out here for a while. Bare arms, belly, long strong legs. She was of this terracotta land that she walked, stilettos on soil. She watched as I went, pumped the umbrella—up up—twice more, knowing I'd be coming back this way because there's only one road between these towns; my grandfathers' towns: Cassano delle Murge and Bitetto.

I drove down from *la murgia*, the limestone plateau that characterizes this land. Cassano delle Murge, where my mother's father was born, is a thousand feet up. I drove down into Bitetto. At the roundabout, I read as quickly as I can, the names of the towns and the arrows. I drove in circles twice around, aiming to get off in the right direction on the first try. I don't know how any American or Argentinian or Australian or Canadian or any descendant of the diaspora finds their right ancestral town on the first try, especially if going by the way your grandparents pronounced the town name in your ear. Syllables get cut off in mouths. The names of towns look different in lettering on signs than how the truncated syllables flew off our grandparents' tongues. My grandparents were always working. I never saw them sitting except when they ate. Peasants carry heavy things. When you're carrying a hundred-pound sack of sand or cement or a thirty-pound lasagna, or sweeping the driveway or hosing down the sidewalk, you pronounce things differently. I'd ask a question on the fly and they'd shout an answer.

"Grandpop, what's the name of the town where you were born?"

"*Bah! Vetétte.*"

"Hah? Pitett'? Piteet'? Beetet'?

"*Vetetta.*"

"I don't see that on the map."

I worked hard to make the syllables stick in my head. Memorized what they'd said. Classic Italian comes from the North, maybe they weren't heaving such heavy things around all day long up north, maybe they worked sitting down, maybe that's how you get a language that sounds like violins. *Olio d'Oliva! Lalala lalalala.* Try talkin' like that when you're lugging a three-hundred-pound block of ice or hundred-pound bags of sand or cement on each shoulder.

At the roundabout, arrows pointed in different directions toward several towns. The names swirled in my mind. I had to read fast. What did the sign say? Did I see the right one? Go around again. Get it right. If I went to a few towns before I found the right town, that would be okay, all part of the journey. Some town names were differentiated by just a consonant or a twist of a vowel. I got lucky. Like a homing pigeon.

I pulled into Bitetto and parked on the side of a road, relieving the car from the engine's heavy breathing. A thousand years whirled inside me. Driving is the wrong pace for ancestral land; I needed to walk. My grandparents walked. My grandmother spoke of hitching a ride on a donkey cart, a basket of figs balanced on her head, coming home from the fields. My grandfathers might have gotten a chance to mount a horse or a bicycle here though they never owned one. I walk. My legs have to do this. Meet the earth. My thighs need to pump memories through my brain. Walking orders my thoughts. I wanted to breathe this air my grandparents breathed before coming to the Bronx, the olive infused air swirled in through my skull. To my New York nose, *Bitettese* air was champagne. I paused at the memorial to *Padre Pio*, nodded a prayer to the bronze statue, and made eye contact with him. My mother always loved him because he was a hairdresser like her.

The first cross-street I came to was via Maddalena where my grandmother was born, the grandmother I was named after. I had the address written on a scrap of paper in my pocket. As a girl she was Anna Cianciotta in Bitetto, then after marriage Anna Lanzillotto in the Bronx. I walked down her street and found her house. I walked around the outside, touched the sandstone, closed my eyes, and imagined the sounds and scents from one hundred years ago when she was a girl; donkeys and goats and chickens, a soft breeze in from the sea, in from the fields, the same breeze greeted me, whispering silk around our necks and off into the trees. What happened in the hundred years and two world wars in between? I stood there in the mid-morning August heat. It was dead quiet, and hot. Nobody was out. I was being watched, and I knew it.

I walked back to the piazza, found an open *caffè*, stepped inside and felt a jolt of coolness from ducking out of the direct sun. The *caffè* was charged with espresso and music and conversation. I loved the instant wake-up energy. "*Un espresso con panna per favore.*" In *Napoli*, I'd learned to order my espresso with a topcoat of thick fresh cream. A tall, vivacious blonde like a beauty queen behind the counter took one look at me and asked, "*Hai parient' Bitettese?*" Do you have relatives in Bitetto? Maybe she recognized my cheeks as wide as *la murgia* and my eyes the Constantinople blue. Maybe she saw under this layer of butch *Americanismo* to my inner little old *Bittetese* lady. It's not hard to see if you know what to look for. *What it is, what it is, what it is, what it is.*

"*Sì ma non conosce'. Sto cercando.*" Yeah, but I don't know them, I'm looking for them. I told her my name with pride and announced it loudly to the whole *caffè*: "*Io sono Lanzillotta, e Cianciotta.*"

The blonde responded: "*Uè! Uagnone Bitettese!*" Hey! *Bitettese* names!

A voice behind me, stated firmly: "*Io sono Lanzillotta e Cianciotta.*" I am Lanzillotta and Cianciotta. A woman with a healthy head of white hair sat upright, formal, in a crisp navy dress dotted with tiny white daisies. She drank her espresso like a queen. She epitomized *la bella figura* for an elder *signora*. I stepped toward her:

"*Certamente siamo cugini!*" Certainly we are cousins!

I opened my arms, but no hug came. I sensed her reticence but took a step further, proudly stating the names of my grandparents and great-grandparents as credentials, all of whom were children in Bitetto. "*I miei nonne erano Cianciotta Anna, e Lanzillotta Carmine. I miei bisnonni erano Scigliuto Apollonia, e Cianciotta Saverio, anche Soranno Arcangela, e Lanzillotta Giuseppe.*"

She squinted tight. A door shut. I had touched a nerve, struck something. I could feel the pressure. *O!* We were related. She didn't want nothin' to do with me. Yet there was something in her eyes I wished I could break through. I asked her if she knew Pasqualina, the cousin I was looking for, and she winced her eyes tighter, with a firm, "*No!*"

Wow, I struck something. Of course, she knew Pasqualina. I remembered my father telling me about family feuds from long ago and I knew I'd just fallen into a hole in that jungle camouflaged with underbrush. I stepped back and looked down at my black cargo shorts, dusty running sneakers, unshaven legs, belly, in my black t-shirt of Our Lady of Mount Carmel, lime green bandana around my head, and fanny pack. What must I have looked like to this *La Signora Bella Figura?* Some middle-aged, hungry, bulky butch, *'Mericán,* no ring on my finger, no watch, no *pockabook.* Here, how you dress is a big mark of respect. It means you made it up from the fields. You got the earth out of your fingernails and could sit in a *caffè*—a human being handling the tiniest of cups in all the world with ease, with your peasant tool-hands. Who drinks out of cups smaller than espresso cups with such tiny handles? Nobody. It's tinier than a child's tea set. I backed off. Who walks into Bitetto in the dead heat of August, alone, when you're supposed to be at *al mare*—the sea? Alone, a woman traveling alone, that's suspicious enough, no man, no child, no mother, no father, no nobody, a stranger, no lipstick, not even a combed hair. I strode into town, all open and available, like in the movies, that's where the story begins, a stranger comes to town. Paul Newman jumps off the train and fords the river by foot in *The Long, Hot Summer,* asks around, "Who needs a hired hand?" Gets a job in the hardware store, falls in love with Joanne Woodward. *Dio Mio! My God!* And wreaks havoc on the town. I walked into Bitetto like that, all open, a casual stray cat sidling up to things to see what sticks. Maybe I'd move back and start an art colony? Who knows? Just sidle up, see what sticks. Since my mother died, I had no reason to be in any one place in the world. No mother, no child, no vestige of an umbilicus spirit rope in either direction. The past decade had been a slow parade to the graveyard: Dad, Grandma, Mom, a lost relationship, my dogs. I had no tether. It was time to reinvent my life. But how? I felt alone in the world. Did *La Signora Bella Figura* sense this in me? This wanting? I expected it to be easy to waltz into my father's ancestral town and find my living cousins. To walk in, announce my name and immediately bump into a cousin. And I did. Just the wrong cousin. Riffs can last for generations. I've heard of people cursing seven generations of their enemies.

Here, strangers are met with caution. Strangers are threats. The province of Bari has known invasion after invasion, changing hands over a dozen times. Italy's unification was an invasion and exploitation from the north. And WWII held no reason for southern Italians to fight their American cousins. Why fight your blood when you have zero ties to the north? Regional allegiance was everything and national pride nothing. Strangers are interruptions. Strangers beckon suspicion. Strangers want your land. Want something. In her eyes I saw she wondered what I wanted.

ANNIE RACHELE LANZILLOTTO

Chapter Twenty-One. "The Heart Too Has Oceans to Cross"

I BOOKED A ROOM FOR A COUPLE OF NIGHTS in a B&B, a mustard color compound with an interior rectangular courtyard. It was an old nobleman's estate, a Bourbon invader from the sixteenth century. I wondered—Who comes to stay in all these rooms? I could bring eighty people here. One day, I'll come back with my New York cousins, and we'll fill this joint! The front door tripped a bell and a kid about thirteen moseyed through an arch from the back room to work the front desk. I took one look at his face, all cheeks big as *la murgia*, big brown eyes, full lips and I knew he was my cousin. I said to him: *"Certamente siamo cugini!"* Certainly we are cousins! But, nothin', no response. I press him. *"Come ti chiami?"* What's your name? And he tells me his name, and I say, "I knew it! We're related through marriage. We're *procugini*, like third cousins or whatever." Nothin'. The kid wants to get back to whatever video game he's been playing in the back room. I think everybody must be everybody's cousin down here, so it's nothing special. At this point, I start asking myself, why are you so interested in finding long lost family? You got enough problems with family you already know. There are feuds and schisms on both sides of the ocean. But I was curious. And I'd cultivated curiosity, studied opera *libretti* and taught myself as much of the language as I could. As a child, I'd paid rapt attention to my grandparents' stories, asked questions, dug for connection, and asked for words in the language they spoke. I felt the quest deeply. And cousins, I always got along with, cousins were just distant enough.

I closed the door to my room in the nobleman's house and all the air got sucked out the little window at the top of the room. *Wshhhrrrrrrrurrrpp!* Time inverted. Flipped. Time is infinity and like the symbol flips back on itself. Nothin' comes before or after nothin'. I can't tell you if I was there for a moment, a day, an hour, a month, a year, a lifetime, if my grandparents even ever left the *paese* in the first place, or if I ever came back a hundred years later. I walked backward through centuries of consciousness. I had the sense I'd watered my grandmother's peach tree before she even spit the peach pit into the ground.

I took a cool shower and let the water run down my body, rasping off the heat. It was time for the *pisolino*—the afternoon nap. I conked out. The effect of sleeping twice in one day took a weird hold on me. Sleeping twice. Dreaming twice. August in the *Mezzogiorno* leaves you no choice. When I awoke it was afternoon but felt like morning. I needed an espresso to snap me back from dream time. 16:00—I climbed back onto the rungs of the clock. I began to grasp that rigid system of time, *la sistemazione*, the order to your day. As my mother used to say, "There were rules for how you did everything from the time you opened your eyes in the morning to the time you shut your eyes at night." I gripped rungs on the ladder of time to climb back into the present moment, to orient myself, to catch up with everyone in the country, to eat when they ate, sleep when they slept, down coffee when they downed coffee, dream when they dreamed. I began to feed time. *La prima colazione. La colazione. Il pranzo. Il pisolino. Un'caffè. L'aperitivo. La cena. La passeggiata. Dormire.* First breakfast. Breakfast. Lunch. Nap. Coffee. Appetizer. Dinner. Stroll in the piazza. Sleep. I climb back to a number on a clock. The letters of the name of a day of the week. The numbers of the years we count. I feed time. This is serious. The whole country drinks an espresso at exactly the same time, 16:00. This is what unites north and south. This is why Grandma Rose always wanted me to wear a watch. To stay in sync.

Early the next morning I sat in the common area for *la prima colazione*. On my first cappuccino I saw a tough girl like me in the music video on the TV overhead. She did pushups, ran, threw punches, dressed like a twelve-year old boy, bright t-shirt and shorts, like me. She didn't dress in *la bella figura*. Intercut with scenes of her sparring in the gym, were images of her father beating up her mother. I was stunned to watch a music video that was a page out of my own upbringing. It was the first time I ever saw something like this in Italy. I had to find out what song this was. I asked the *ragazzo*, my third cousin who says he's not my cousin, her name and to please write it for me. He says,

"*Va bbène*," and scribbles on a napkin: *Fiorella Mannoia, "Nessuna Conseguenza.*" "No Consequence."

On my second cappuccino a woman smashes a car windshield with a baseball bat, dumps a man's clothes onto the street then waves to a guy up on a balcony as she drives off, satisfied, with a friend in a convertible. The *ragazzo* wrote on another napkin: *Nina Zilli, "Ti Amo Mi Uccidi.*" "I Love You Kill Me." How many songs are there in Italian about strong women surviving domestic violence? I felt seen, suddenly, recognized—if only by these artists whose songs and music videos emboldened and fortified me. Otherwise, I was an androgynous woman walking around alone in the *paese*, asking too many questions. These songs made me feel my childhood was *capeeshed*, these Italian songwriters understood. My quest had grown a new tributary. Now I wanted to better understand the roots of the domestic violence I grew up with, the cave of rage, and all the mental illness and maladjustment within my family of origin in America. Some of the roots were here. Deep human misery roots. As I sipped my second cappuccino, I wrote in my notebook, getting lost in my thoughts, exploring these questions with ink on paper. The songs triggered me. My pulse was racing as I thought back, back to the lives that came before mine, back to the lives that made me. My father's violence was born from war on top of a brutal childhood and something else hundreds and thousands of years old. Pent up rage. I don't want to simplify it with the word patriarchy or the culture of male dominance, or the church, or anything. I want to keep hunting, thinking back to the caves, painting questions in my mind. My father was a U.S. Marine, First Division, Fifth Regiment, who fought in Operation Iceberg on the island of Okinawa in WWII. He came home with severe PTSD. My mother bore the brunt of his rage. Violence against women—how many roots, how deep, how far back, how intertwined? My mind swirled like a Chagall painting: intergenerational trauma, genetic memory, the degradation of poverty, generations of poverty and despair, the cave walls telling our stories, the fraying of families by lifelong separation through immigration, the uncounted casualties of war. Over the years, I'd felt I was hemorrhaging, seeking help, and all well-wishers offered were jelly beans, sweet offerings. The psychiatrist who specialized in cancer survivors had told me to lose weight, the career counselor told me to change the font on my resume, the art patron urged me to seek Shambhala Buddhism training, the yogi suggested a silent retreat. Silence was the opposite of what I needed. Silence was the problem. If I began to scream, if I let myself continue to cry, I might never stop. So, I held the reins. There have been women in my family who have lost their voices altogether. Years ago, they'd say, "There's a frog in my throat." But the frog is these screams. There are screams in my throat. And my body grew tumors. A ton of cement had fallen on all of us, all our hearts, our earth. Hearts have their own oceans to cross. All earth, all life, busts up through cement. The lifeforce finds its way through cracks in walls, up through Etna and Vesuvius, through the crust of the earth. Was this part of why everyone was crying when I left New York? An immigration of the heart? Aunt Grace facing her final stretch of time on earth, Faroukh faltering before the decisive charge forward to start a life from scratch and to become American. As long as he stayed in the safe cage of the gas station, his heart did not yet cross over. Once he let New York City inside of him, he would fundamentally change. The heart too has oceans to cross.

And me. Once I crack open that door to the heart, it will be an avalanche of tears. The heart will capsize. Like a fig, I break open. The separation of self is no longer necessary. In the *paese*, I picked up some pieces of myself that have long eluded me, found some errant puzzle pieces, and realized that the picture is complete as it is, with pieces missing. My *Barese* cousins have always acknowledged that America existed, New York existed as a possibility for hope and change, but few Americans acknowledged the *paese*. Was it easy for Americans to forget? Necessary? Whenever I asked my grandmother to teach me Italian words, she indulged me, but urged me to learn something new, as if Italy was in the past. Going to Italy felt like a journey to the past until I got here the first time. Once I met the cousins, I realized I was in the present, a whole different present. It was an immigration of consciousness. Something in me wanted to remember my great-grandmothers' lives, wanted to build this bridge, wanted to learn enough of the language to communicate with my cousins and reabsorb the culture that is in my blood. It's a bridge to build, a bridge of hearts. I have revived that part of myself that feels most alive back in the *paese*, in the sounds and foods and air of my grandmothers' lands. My spirit finds effervescence here as I drink the water, as the sun hits me, and yet a part of me is lost forever, lost in the split of immigration, a part of me, I can spend all my whole life searching to retrieve. When I float in the ocean, ears underwater, I can hear my own heartbeat while I face the sun, and the sun too has a heartbeat. The beating heart of the sun.

I down the last slug of my second cappuccino with the sugar grains that have settled in the bottom of the cup and head outside for *l'aria fresca*—a breath of fresh air. There is no wind. The air is as still as heavy drapes. I can't breathe. Mosquitoes are out early. I need a wind to come swiftly and push my thoughts around, refresh my mind. All I can do is get in the car and drive with the window down, pick up speed and find the wind.

Chapter Twenty-Two. "Donated to *La Madonna*"

IN THE *MUNICIPIO*, THE TOWN HALL, A CLERK escorted me
into the back room, where we stood looking through shelves of books
of handwritten records from the 1800's. He turned pages to find my
great-great-great-great grandparents. I noticed that every birth certificate
of every baby born in town had the same name, some variation of
Donata Maria in their name. Page after page, every baby, on the line
where it says *il nome*—name, is handwritten *Maria Donata,* or *Donata
Maria* plus another name. I ask him why the birth certificates all have
the same name. It feels like a stupid question, because in my American
mind, it can't be true. Can it? Am I reading wrong? I'm looking at
my great-grandfather Saverio's birth certificate. It says he was born
in 1843, and named Saverio Maria Donato. The clerk tells me that
indeed every baby had to be donated or offered to *La Madonna*, the
mother of Jesus. *Donata a Maria*—donated to Maria. I'm sure it was a
blessing and in the days of high infant mortality, a spiritual necessity.
The clerk says, "*Masche, femminile, lo stesso: Maria Donata.*" Boy, girl,
the same: donated to Mary. If I understood him correctly, up until
a certain year, all babies born in Bitetto were named some form of
Donata Maria, or Donato, or Maria Donata, and every baby also was
given an additional middle name that was the identifier. I might have
been named: *Donata Maria AnnaRachele.* I wonder if the rules for
baby naming changed after 1861, after the unification, when most of
the peninsula was called one country under one flag in one kingdom,
The House of Savoy. At some point, it was no longer mandatory to
dedicate babies to the *Madonna*, but still traditional. I thought about
the two men named Donato that I'd recently met in Castelmezzano
and Matera. I didn't know that their names meant "Donated." Even
in my family in New York, this tradition has carried through to some
degree. Every baby, all my cousins of my generation, were dedicated to
a saint. Mandatory. We were all named in honor of a saint and relied
on their protection and intercession, their blessings. My father's saints
were Joseph and Rocco, my mother's saints were Rachel and Claire.
Plus he had *Beato Giacomo*, from his town, and she had Our Lady of

Mount Carmel who saved her life when she fell out a window at two years old on the saint's day. Find an Italian American and you'll find a Mary or Joseph or Ann or Anthony or Francesco or some saint in their name somewhere. In my family, there's dozens of variations of Mary and Ann, the mother and grandmother of Jesus amongst my cousins: JoAnn, AnneMarie, MaryAnn, Ann, Nina, Marie, Annette, BethAnn, Roseanne, Rosemarie, and on and on. And in Italy, in the south, people call me by my middle name: Rachele. The first name goes to the saint and the middle name is the signifier, the identifier. Plus, with the system of being named after your grandparents, many cousins all have the same name. If there's one Lanzillotta, Anna— there's fifty. This went on for hundreds of years. So, everybody needs a nickname, a street name—*u soprannom'*. Even in the Bronx in the 60's and 70's it was your street name you were known by. I knew my great-grandfather's *soprannom'*, *"Mangiasard"*—Eats sardines. But I didn't know my cousin Pasqualina's *soprannom'*. How would I ever find her?

I wandered around Bitetto, the old town's labyrinthine streets, and I ended up on my cousin's street. It was abandoned. House after house, *abbandonato*. All the buildings, empty. I double checked the address on my folded piece of paper, and I felt devastated. Could it be I was a few years too late? I walked back to *il centro* and up the marble staircase into the cathedral. It was afternoon. Was it afternoon? No. It was before lunch. I didn't eat yet. A wedding was taking place. My cells were buzzing. I wanted to open my arms. I could sense in my body that I had cousins in that crowd. I wanted to hug somebody and shout my ancestral names. This was the only time in my life I was ever in my father's ancestral town: *Lanzillotta! Cianciotta! Silecchia! Rossano! Rutigliano! Squicciarini! Sgiliuto! Signorile! Soranno! Pilolla! Rizzi! Monti!* If only I had the right intro, or an App that could tell me who in the room shared DNA with me, it would've been lighting up, buzzing. I wanted to yell: *"Certamente siamo cugini!"* I wanted someone's arms to open and wrap around me tight as a vine. I had the strong sense I was related to almost everybody in Bitetto.

I remembered the activist sign in *Napoli* offering a coffee in exchange for solidarity, and thought maybe I could do something like that, sit in the piazza with a coffee pot over a flame and a sign that read: "*Ti offro un caffè, se può dimostrare che non siamo cugini.*" I offer you a coffee, if you can prove we're not cousins. I'd draw my family tree and we'd see whose great-grandfather is whose great-grandfather and whose grandmother is the sister to whose grandmother. At the same time, I held the opposite feeling inside myself, that bloodline is the last thing that matters in life. What truly matters are the spirit bonds of common purpose, the rarest connection that has to do with recognizing that we are alive in this moment, and only briefly, and walking one tightrope—What is worth dedicating your lifeforce to?

At the end of the church service, the wedding party exited the cathedral and posed on the marble staircase. The bride called her bulldog and instructed him, "*Sedutto!*" to sit for the photo. He didn't sit but he faced the camera. The groom bent down and coaxed the bulldog to sit. A drone buzzed overhead taking aerial photos of the wedding party. I bent back and opened my arms up to the blue sky and spun around and around. I thought of the whole loop of all my ancestors from Bitetto to Cassano delle Murge to Acquaviva delle Fonti, spiraling out to the Bronx. Even if my grandparents never immigrated from *la murgia* to the Bronx, my parents might still have met and married anyway, right here in this *Cattedrale di San Michele Arcangelo*—the cathedral of Saint Michael the Archangel. The drone buzzed over us. Right now, somewhere in Bitetto, in some photo album on someone's coffee table, in an aerial photo of a wedding party outside the steps of *la Cattedrale,* I am in those wedding photos: a blue and white blur. That blue and white whirling blur is your cousin from *L'America.*

The wedding party vanished. I walked around looking to get lunch, but everything was closed, shut, shuttered. All the gates down. Locked. *Chiuso.* I missed my chance. Everyone was inside by now for *il pranzo* and *il pisolino*—lunch and a nap. Even the street cats. I didn't want to nap. I felt squeezed in. I had to get outta town. Once you get out of sync with the people, it's like you're on a bicycle and your chain falls off the crankshaft. I jumped in the car, ate some grapes and almonds stashed there, and roared onto *Strada Provinciale* 236. The Lady in Red was there, pumping her red umbrella to me. Up Up! Up Up! There's nothing more ancient than this—old stone walls, olive trees, and a big red hot *hhhlrrrrrpppp* open cunt ready to suck you in. Suction is the primal force of the universe, not protrusion as the patriarchy would have you believe. I beeped my horn, rolled down my window and yelled:

"*Certamente siamo cugini!*"

Chapter Twenty-Three. "Grave Sweeping"

THE NEXT MORNING, I GOT UP, downed a cappuccino made for me by my cousin who says he's not my cousin, and headed for the cemetery on the edge of town. If I couldn't find my living cousins, I figured I'd go find my dead. I drove through olive and grape and fig fields up to the cemetery's white wall and locked wrought iron gate through which I saw two women polishing a gravestone. I asked them how I could get in. They motioned for me to go around to the other side. I drove around and around the walls until I saw other cars parked. I walked up four steps through an arch, in through the one open gate by a small office with a sign on the door: *Il Custode*—The Caretaker. "*Buongiorno*," I said as I stepped forward.

Three aisles of graves. Ladies in dresses walked around with buckets of water, rags, and straw brooms. These were the elders wiping, sweeping, washing the gravestones of their dead. I walked straight down the central row of graves. The first grave was a *Silecchia*. That's one of my great-grandparent's names, surely a relative. The next grave, a *Squicciarini*, also an ancestral name. Stone after stone, all the names on the headstones were my family names: *Lanzillotta, Cianciotta, Silecchia, Rossano, Rutigliano, Gatti, Squicciarini, Sgiliuto*. It felt like a private graveyard of all my ancestors. Could I be related to everybody in here? I walked slowly, step by step, and stayed in all the shade I could. Tall pine trees showered long green needles on the marble slabs that lay flat on the ground. The women mourners swept pine needles away. The sound of sweeping accompanied the breeze through the pine trees raining green needles down onto the marble slabs. I stepped carefully to keep my footing. The graveyard was on a downward slope. The air was thick with pine. Nina Simone's voice: "Lilac wine I feel heady . . . Lilac wine, I feel unsteady," ran through my mind. Mosquitoes on my neck, legs, arms, offered pokes and hellos like ancestors. Pricked blood. Mosquitoes flew with *Bitettese* blood all around the graveyard, landed on everyone standing. One grave stopped me: Lanzillotta, Anna. My name. I looked at her face on the oval porcelain cameo portrait. She looked exactly like my Grandpop Carmine. If you put an iceman cap on her, they'd be identical. The same dark straight eyebrows, thin line of lips and blunt Lanzillotta nose. I wiped away the pine needles, smacked my neck where a mosquito landed, drank water and stood affixed to the spot. Was she my grandfather's sister? Cousin? To see my own name on a gravestone—was a spiritual vertigo. A disorientation. What realm was I in?

Il Custode walked by me: "Perché sei qui? Dovrest' andar' al mar'! Vai al mare! Al mare! Al mare!"—Why are you here? You should be at the sea! Go to the sea! To the sea! He motioned with his hand. The hand was stiff. It was a mannequin hand, just like a hand in a Macy's store window. Long and stiff, with tan-colored fused fingers, blackened with dirt. The Hand motioned east toward the sea, where the sun was coming up. I asked him if he could help me find the graves of my great-grandparents. The Hand motioned down the hill over the far wall. I didn't know what he meant. I jotted down a list of names and gave him the paper. He raised an eyebrow as if to say I gave him too many names and told me dismissively to come back tomorrow as if tomorrow will never come. "Vai al mare," he told me again, insisting I am in the wrong place at the wrong time.

In August, Italians go to the sea. You rent a chair and umbrella and they set them up in rows. I didn't want to look at water. I wanted to look into the faces of cousins who I'd never met. I didn't want to look at cliffs. I wanted to see the lines on their hands, the contours of their noses. I wanted gli abbracci forti—strong hugs, from those who knew a lifetime had passed between us. I didn't want to be out in the hot sun. I wanted to be in the shade of my cousins' voices, those sonorous Lanzillotta vocal tones, resonant with a patina of hoarseness.

As the heat rose, I walked out of the cemetery. This was a good time to drive to the church dedicated to the town's patron saint, Beato Giacomo, our family saint, our hometown saint, our private saint. Chances are, if someone knows about him, either they're from Bitetto or they're related to me. The whole Lanzillotta clan is devoted to him. To cure me of the cancers, my godmother and aunts and uncles prayed novenas to him for me. That's stints of nine days straight! This was my chance to thank Beato Giacomo directly.

Chapter Twenty-Four. "Our Hometown Saint"

BEATO GIACOMO. ALL MY LIFE I'd heard his name but didn't know anything specific about him. My aunts and uncles gave me his holy cards, where he held his big *bastone* or was on his knees staring up in adoration at *La Madonna.* I parked close to the church entrance, and as I stepped out of the car found a shiny gold coin at my foot. That's my father talking to me, telling me I'm on the right path. My father always spun quarters with me since I was a baby. Quarters he flicked into fast shiny silver pirouettes across the maple dining room table, hypnotizing me. He could get six going at once. And now as a spirit he tosses coins at my feet. It's metallurgy. Somehow the dead move coins.

I walked into the church feeling lucky with my gold coin, and stepped up to the altar, and there, above the altar, in a glass coffin, was *Beato Giacomo* himself! He was right there! I wasn't prepared for this. Nobody told me. His whole body, wearing his Franciscan robe. He was *"incorrotto,"*—uncorrupted. *Rigor mortis* never set in. His hands, folded. Barefoot. He looks like my father. He's got a brow like a Lanzillotta, a blunt nose, full lips, and a kind expression. I talk out loud to him: "Thanks a lot for curing me of the cancers. I'm so startled to see you. No one told me you were here. You look like my father. *Certamente siamo cugini!* I gotta walk around and clear my head. I'll be back."

I stepped away from the glass coffin and walked around the church and came upon a reliquary, a carved gold pedestal with glass windows. Inside was a bone. A sign next to it read: *il dito di Beato Giacomo.* His finger. A big finger. Long. With three joints. A finger encased in glass and gold. An old man came and stood face to face and worshipped in a whisper, the finger. He leaned on his *bastone,* and told me, *"Beato Giacomo aiuta tutti."*—Blessed Giacomo helps everybody. The man's face lit up as he told me stories. He had a sweet countenance, flushed, round and ripe with full-blooded soft skin, the combination of faith and daily doses of homemade *vino* and *olio d'oliva.* His name, like my father, was Giuseppe. There's always a Joseph to guide me. It's always been this way. Wherever I go, a Joseph shows up and helps. Giuseppe told me that before *Beato Giacomo* was beatified, receiving the honorific

"*Beato,*" he was known as *Fratello Giacomo* or *Fra' Giacomo*, a Franciscan brother. In the last years of his life, he took care of victims of the plague of 1482. Born on the century, in 1400, *Fra' Giacomo* was eighty-two himself, yet he served everyone. He lived in a state of uninterrupted prayer, tending the garden, growing vegetables and cooking for all the brothers and anyone else who was hungry. He fell into ecstatic states of rapture while cooking and gardening. The Franciscan brothers in Bitetto loved fava beans. Beans were expressions of both humility and interior richness. Lives could be saved with nutrient rich beans. Meat was a luxury the poor could not afford. Once, as *Fra' Giacomo* stirred a big cast iron pot of fava beans, he stared off into the fire underneath the cast iron pot and entered a state of rapture. He saw an apparition of *La Madonna* in the flames. As Giuseppe recounted this story, I pictured angels helping *Beato Giacomo* with the stirring rhythm of the tall wooden spoon around the cast iron cauldron over the fire, the wooden spoon carved from a branch of an olive tree. Giuseppe went on to tell me that while *Fra' Giacomo* stirred the fava beans around and around in his ecstatic state, he wept in spiritual rapture and his tears fell into the pot of fava. In this way, he salted the beans with his tears. The *Fave alle Lacrime*—fava salted with tears were considered blessed. When the Archduke of Conversano came to eat, he could have had anything he wanted. There were offerings of goat and lamb, but the Archduke asked for the *Fave alle Lacrime di Fra' Giacomo*. He insisted on eating the fava beans salted with Giacomo's tears. To this day it's said to be a blessing. I marveled at the idea of reaching a state of spiritual ecstasy while stirring beans, while performing a mundane task. He wasn't meditating in seclusion on a mountaintop, he was just stirring beans. I gotta hand it to my ancestors. This is in line with who we are. You're on a spiritual quest? You wanna reach Nirvana? Find inner peace? Stir a pot of *fazool*. Sweep the sidewalk. Therein lies your ecstasy.

Giuseppe told me another story. *Fra' Giacomo* was in the garden with one of the *Bitettese* girls who is remembered as being disobedient. *Fra' Giacomo* threatened to beat the girl to discipline her. He raised his *bastone* overhead, but instead of striking her, threw the stick into the ground on a downward thrust like a javelin, and it speared the earth.

The stick began to grow in place. It took root in the garden. The stick is still there to this day, six hundred years later. Every year the stick grows an incremental bit. Now, it's about ten feet tall. At the top, it's shaped like a divining rod, a V-shape crook.

As Giuseppe told me this story, his face became enamored, his eyes and forehead opened, in love as he was with the saint, yet I felt more and more uncomfortable, my face squinched, pinched between my eyes. My walls went up. This is what passes for a miracle in my grandparents' town? To *not* beat a girl! Given how I was brought up, this made sense in the basest of ways. Women were subjugated every step of the way every day. No wonder I never wanted to be a girl. In my childhood, violence was *la vita quotidiana*—daily life: yelling, rage, smacks, servitude, domination. I rebelled at an early age. *You want me to serve the men coffee? If this is what being female means, I want no part of it. Let the men clear my dishes. I'm gonna lean back on my chair and put my feet up on the table.* Something was always raised overhead, a belt, a rolled-up newspaper, an open hand. Men were ready to strike women. I'll never forget the threat of the open hand of my father above my mother, above me, above the dog. It's common for Italian American men to be raised to believe they should be served by their sisters, and that they have dominion over their sisters, and their mothers, as they age. I know Italian Americans do not corner the market on this behavior, but I'm writing from what I've experienced and witnessed. In the absence of my father, my mother would threaten me with the words: "I'm gonna call your brother!" I thought back to the *femminicidio* walls I came across in *Napoli* and *Roma,* hundreds of posters of women who were all killed by men, mostly men they knew or were related to. And the garden in Sicily, dedicated to women who died in violent ways. And the priest in the confessional in Rome asking me if I was chaste. Femicide—I didn't hear this word being used much in America, but we should've been using it. In Italy it's recognized as endemic, the history of honor killings in a culture where men are groomed to feel the right to beat and kill *their* women: husbands to wives, fathers to daughters, boyfriends to girlfriends, brothers to sisters. And what am I to think of this miracle of *Beato Giacomo?* What message is this to *Bitettese* boys? *You wanna be a saint? Drop it! Drop it!* This is where I come from. This is where my father comes from, and his father and his father and his father. This stick in the garden that is venerated. This stick at all. And this is the stick on the holy cards I was given as a child. And this is the stick on the cards I was given the two times I had life-threatening cancers in my teen and young adult years. This stick. This stick. I feel it sticking inside me right now. And it hurts.

All these thoughts jolted through me in a flash as I next asked Giuseppe, who now seemed like an apparition to me, about the finger. What of the finger? Why was the finger encased in gold? Why wasn't it kept with the rest of *Beato Giacomo's* body? Why do they pull saints' bones apart? What's special about the finger? Why is it over here away from him? Tell me about the finger. Giuseppe recounted that four hundred years ago, a duchess, *La Duchessa di Gravina*, came to worship the body of *Beato Giacomo* and asked the Franciscan brothers if they could open the glass crypt so she could kiss his hand. Her name was Donna Felicia Di Sanseverino. The year was 1619. *Baciare la mano* was a supreme honor. Since she was a duchess, the friars nodded and unlocked the glass crypt, and as Felicia bent down to kiss his hand, instead of kissing the hand, she opened her mouth and bit off his finger! She hid the finger. I imagined she tucked it inside her brassiere, where else do Italian women tuck things? There are all kinds of nicknames for this special hiding place, including *il banco*—the bank, where I've seen women tuck money, holy medals and a variety of objects. Where else would a *Barese* woman hide a finger she just bit off a dead saint? Felicia stepped down, thanked the monks, and headed for the door. As the brothers opened the church doors to escort her out, the sky turned black. Winds came. Furious winds and rain and thunder took hold of the chapel doors and blew them open like sails. The monks wrestled the tempest so the doors wouldn't blow off their hinges. They couldn't get the doors closed again. *Il Scirocco* raced up from the Sahara, over the Mediterranean, hot, humid, and low, spiraling sand into Felicia's mouth and ears, making her *sciroccazza*—from the sand whirling in her ears. *Il Maestrale* came across the Adriatic, swirling and fickle and lifted her gown and snapped her cape and ripped the *mantiglia* off her head. Sweeping down from the mountains, down the spine of the boot, *La Tramontana* whipped an ice-cold slap across her face and whacked her from behind! Felicia fell to her knees and cried. She revealed the finger to the brothers and confessed that she'd coveted it for her private collection of saints' bones, but apparently *Beato Giacomo* fiercely protested. On the spot, on her knees, she declared two vows. The skies quieted and became blue again, blue as the gown of *La Madonna*. First, she pledged a commission of a carved silver and gold reliquary to house *Beato Giacomo's* blessed finger for eternity. Second, she pledged to construct a straight thoroughfare, the straightest street anyone ever saw in this labyrinthine town, a street linking the crypt of *Beato Giacomo* directly to *il centro*—the center of town. A straight uninterrupted street, a sign of honor and for pageantry. All who stood in the town center would forever see a direct path to *Beato Giacomo*. There would be no chance for wrong turns. No one would get lost in alleyways trying to find him ever again. *Sempre dritto!*—Always straight! *Bitetto* would be oriented toward *Beato Giacomo* every moment, every day, an open boulevard to the venerated patron saint.

And every year, for the past four hundred years, on April 27th, marking his death date, male devotees dress in powder blue capes, white veils, skirts, white gloves, and carry on a bier of white roses, the finger of *Beato Giacomo* up the straight street via Beato Giacomo from his crypt to the center of town and around the labyrinthine streets. Centuries later *Roma* followed suit, constructing via della Conciliazione connecting the body of Saint Paul at The Vatican to Hadrian's ashes in *Castel Sant'Angelo,* the heart of the ancient empire.

I thanked Giuseppe for telling me the history, and went outside to drive with the window open, and just breathe, letting the wind sweep my thoughts.

Chapter Twenty-Five. "How I Found the Living through the Dead"

TO THE CEMETERY I RETURNED every morning for the better part of a week and sat on the bench talking with the ladies with their brooms and rags and buckets. I wiped pine needles off the graves with my ancestral names, not knowing how we were related. It was an ad-hoc sunrise club, a secret community of elders all at the cemetery at the top of dawn, sweeping marble slabs, buffing headstones with wet rags, arranging amulets, flowers, and candles, praying and caregiving the spirit world. Caregiving didn't end at death. Nor did conversations. My parents answered me quicker now that they were dead. I walked through different sections of the graveyard. One morning I happened to come upon my great-grandparents' graves: Arcangela Scigliuti and Saverio Cianciotta. Arcangela means a high-ranking angel. I loved that name. That was my godmother's name, my father's sister, named after this Arcangela. One high-ranking angel named for another. I felt protected by these angels of rank and power. I wiped the pine needles away with my yellow bandana and stood there praying. Then I aimed my cell phone and clicked a photo.

The Hand, saw me, approached, and shouted, "*No foto! No foto!*" Then he resumed his barrage: "*Vai al mare! Al mare! Al mare!*" Go to the sea! To the sea! To the sea! The Hand motioned east, then west, then south toward the seas. We were surrounded by seas in three directions. I'm wasn't interested in vacation. I asked him again about the names on the list I'd given him. On my fourth or fifth morning, after realizing I wasn't going away until I fulfilled my quest, The Hand made a pole-vault gesture, a motion that signaled to me that the bodies had been thrown over the far cemetery wall. I didn't know what he was talking about. He couldn't have thrown the bones over the wall. He waved for me to follow him. The Hand motioned toward him, as if to pull me. We walked down the slope to the far end of the graveyard to an open area the size of a basketball court. We went around the side, and he bent down, guiding me to peer through a little window covered by an iron grate in the side wall. I bent down beside him and looked inside and saw a vast underground cave with stacks of boxes lining the walls.

"*L'ossario!*" he said. The bone place. He went on to explain that after some years, he recycles the graves, washes the bones, and puts them in these boxes. Every All-Souls' Day, November 1st, the priest says mass on top of the cave of bones for all the ancestors of the town. "*Quattr'ossa!*" he summarized the human condition. We all boil down to four long bones.

This is where my great-great-grandparents are? The Hand himself washed the bones of my ancestors? I felt as hollow as that big open cave. I thought of my great-great-grandparents. Bones in a box in a cave. I can't stand beside them or pray to a porcelain portrait of their beautiful faces, or sweep pine needles off their graves, or wash the grooves of the lettering of the longest spellings of their names carved on their gravestones. This was as close as I was going to get. Another layer of my naiveté was peeled back. I had to learn my culture and history one shock at a time.

The next morning, I sat and talked with the elder ladies of what I came to think of as The Cemetery Sunrise Club. They'd accepted me on their bench and invited me to pray at the graves of their beloveds. One woman kept a glass altar for her son who died at twenty-seven in a motorcycle accident. She arranged talismans inside the glass case: photos, a motorcycle statuette, a red candle, and the red and black leather jacket he wore when he rode.

Another woman, Preciosa, befriended me. She was interested in my quest to find both the graves of my ancestors and my living cousins. Preciosa told me to follow her. She walked with her cane over the uneven ground. I followed her down the third aisle of graves, turned right by a more modern tall wall of names on crypts, then turned left to another lot of the cemetery where her husband's grave was set in the ground. She wiped the stone with her rag, turned on a red battery-op candle, and I joined her as she quietly recited the *Ave Maria* ending by making the sign of the cross. Mosquitoes and blades of sun pricked my neck from different angles. I veered into a swath of shade and snapped my bandana to keep the mosquitoes away. Preciosa walked on and waved me to follow her. She stepped up through the arch to leave the cemetery and told me to drive behind her. I figured we might go for *colazione*. I didn't realize she'd taken on my mission now, to find my living cousins.

Preciosa drove a gray Fiat Panda. I drove behind her. She drove swiftly and adeptly through the streets by the olive tree fields on the outskirts of Bitetto taking turns fast and confidently toward the center of town. She pulled her Panda into an alley near the cathedral and left the car blocking the alley. She walked me to the street of my cousin's address, the same abandoned street I'd found a few days before. But she didn't stop there. Preciosa stepped a few doors down and rang the bell of the first occupied house. A woman appeared on a balcony three flights up. Preciosa yelled up to her in *Bitettese*. This is how my Bronx ear heard what she said:

"*Mmo! Uè! Teng sta na Merrican', chiann Lanz-il-lot-ta, Jànna.
Eeyosh stamme va dende, c'è cos iè u fatte.
Ma terrestr' yeh a ken ye sacce.
Ca dijsce a mme va vol' achianne pperr parient'
na cggin' uagnone Lanz-il-lot-ta Pasqualeen.
U marritt' a Vincenz. Tu i canush?*"

Roughly, I understood her to say: "Hey I have here this American named Anna Lanzillotta who doesn't know her cousins, but says she has some. She's looking for her relative named Pasqualina Lanzillotta, who has a husband, Vincenzo. Do you know them?

The lady on the roof threw up her hands. Preciosa walked on. I followed. She instructed me to take her folding chair out of the back of her car. She sat on an abandoned corner outside the cathedral. I leaned against the stone wall. Preciosa employed her second strategy to help me on my quest, namely, shouting to passersby. We were cut from the same cloth.

"Hey that guy's related to a Cianciotta!" She called him over, an old man on his bicycle, and began the conversation. Then she'd go to the next, "I think this lady's related to a Lanzillotta." In this way we talked with a bunch of people, all who denied being related to me or knowing my cousins. The sun was directly overhead, and I was ready to give up for the afternoon. Wasn't it time for an espresso? One by one the people came to talk with us, but no one seemed interested. Only Preciosa dedicated herself to my cause. A man shouted from the alleyway. I walked over to identify the source of the commotion. He was in a wheelchair and couldn't get through, the way Preciosa had parked her Panda. She had to back out to let him through. Then she resumed her post on the chair in the shade.

A lady approached us, a little fancier than the others, and because of the approaching lunch hour, interrogated Preciosa about me. It was almost the hour of *il pranzo.* Her questioning took a thematic turn. "*Ma dove che si mangge'? Caza du?*"—Where will she eat lunch? Your house? Maybe if you can find the cousin, they can feed her. That's the right way.

Preciosa waved me on, to her third strategy. We drove through the streets to a newer part of town. She knocked on a door. A young energetic lady came out and after a brief exchange, nodded her head and ran back inside. Then she came out with an iPad. She looked at the local directory of people, and streets. *Ahh*, she figured it out! There were three streets in town with the same name because the streets were named after soldiers killed in WWI. The three streets with the same name were for three brothers who were killed in action. The streets were differentiated with the initial of the first name. Further complicating our search, there were streets in *Bitetto vecchio*—the old section of town—whose names were replicated in the new part of town. We drove to the second street on our list and found the house number. Preciosa rang the bell three times. A woman popped out on a rooftop. Preciosa yelled up:

"*Mmo! Uè! Teng sta na Merrican', chiann Lanz-il-lot-ta, Jànna. Eeyosh stamme va dende, c'è cos iè u fatte.*

Ma terrestr' yeh a ken ye sacce.
Ca dijsce a mme va vol' achianne pperr parient'
na cggin' uagnone Lanz-il-lot-ta Pasqualeen.
U marritt' a Vincenz. Tu i canush?"

The woman hollered down that she had no idea who the people were. I was ready to pass out in the heat. I didn't know how Preciosa kept going. I thanked her and said—that's enough for today. I was ready for an espresso. I was getting that Mediterranean/Middle Eastern mentality, *domani, domani*—tomorrow, tomorrow; *bukra in sha'Allah*—tomorrow if Allah wills. Preciosa waved me on. She was driven. We drove to the third street. Again, the routine. Ring the bell. This time, I stepped back. A man called down the stairs. Preciosa yelled up:

"*Mmo! Uè! Teng sta na Merrican', chiann Lanz-il-lot-ta, Jànna.*
Eeyosh stamme va dende, c'è cos iè u fatte.
Ma terrestr' yeh a ken ye sacce.
Ca dijsce a mme va vol' achianne pperr parient'
na cggin' uagnone Lanz-il-lot-ta Pasqualeen.
U marritt' a Vincenz. Tu i canush?"

"*Aspetta nu pic*" the man said—wait a sec—and he went and got his wife, and there at the top of the stairs was this beautiful face with big brown sweet eyes and cheeks as vast as *la murgia*.

And I yelled: "*Io sono la nipot' di Carmine Lanzillotto, figlio di –* *Mangiasard'.*"

And at the mention of my great-grandfather's *soprannom'*, she grabbed her face, and her eyes filled with tears: "*Mangiasard'!*" she cried, "*Assomiglianze!*" You have a resemblance! She recognized my cheeks as vast as *la murgia* and opened her arms to pull me in. I climbed the stairs and fell into her hug, the hug I'd craved for so long. The circle was complete in the only way it could be.

Preciosa waved goodbye with a big smile and got back in her Panda. My cousins invited her in, but she said she had to go. We all yelled profuse thanks as she sped away.

I went inside Pasqualina's house, and the story begins. The story of getting to know my beautiful cousins. We talked of the century and our lives, of our parents and our grandparents, we stared at each other and cried as we broke open black figs, *i clummm*, with our thumbs. Pasqualina stepped into her kitchen and like a magician, came back out carrying a giant bowl, white *mappine* slung over her shoulder. She carried the world in that bowl, the red and lavender flowers of her housedress bouncing off the greens and pasta in the bowl. I don't remember what exactly she whipped up, but that it was soul food, spiritual nourishment, and how she held the bowl with absolute strength and a delicate touch as if she were offering a life itself, and she was—The Garden of Eden walking. A purposeful and magical look in her eye. The effect on me was a complete balm, a healing, an integration. We looked at photographs of ancestors and cousins, and I was so full, overflowing, I had to lay my head down. Her husband found a *ventilatore*, a fan, to point at me, *L'Americana* who couldn't take the *Mezzogiornese* heat. I dove down deep and dreamt of all of them, and the expression on Pasqualina's face when she came to the door and looked out, how she grabbed her face and tears streamed down her cheeks when I spoke our great-grandfather's nickname. The nickname was the key to opening the lock of her heart. I could feel myself smiling while I slept. I'd walked out of a different time and place, a different reality. I slept with a smile and dreamt of the fields and the blinding white light of the afternoon bouncing off the stones, and the miles of stone walls and all the stones pulled out of the land by the hands of Grandpop and *Mangiasard,* and all the hands and all the stones and all the walls.

Pasqualina cooked feast after feast through the August heat. Her hands held the wisdom of generations of women's hands. We ate to catch up on a century. She cooked all the miraculous delicacies I would have had at her house over the years if I'd grown up down the street. She knew how to draw the juices and natural flavor out of the foods of the land: *melanzane ripiene con ouva, formaggio, pomodoro*—stuffed eggplant with egg, cheese, tomato; *melanzane a pezzettini*—chopped eggplant; *peperoni piccoli fritti*—small hot fried peppers; *fiori di zucchini fritti*—fried zucchini flowers; *fiori di zucchini fatti in padella con agli'olio e menta*—zucchini flowers in the pan with garlic, oil and mint; *funghi fatti in padella agli'olio*—mushrooms in the pan with garlic and oil; and in honor of *Mangiasard'*, *sarde fritti*—sardines sautéed with the touch of the ancients. The freshest of greens, salads, desserts, pasta, fava and *ceci*; we ate, took naps, sat on her terrace at night, the gentle *Maestrale* brushing our napes and shoulders.

Pasqualina spoke with the sonorous Lanzillotta vocal tones that were so familiar to me. I wondered how it was that vocal tones got passed down through the generations, what part of it was innate and what were learned patterns. I could still hear the voices of my parents, grandparents, aunts, uncles, and cousins, inside me. My father's four sisters were called, "the four roses," by their father Carmine. Together they made a gorgeous bouquet: one brunette, one redhead, one jet black and one blonde, each stunning, and together magnificent, but it was their soothing vocal tones that struck chords in my soul. What I felt most deeply with my aunts was the link of voice; I could hear who was related to me. My aunts' voices still call my name inside me, and I do, I do hear their tones, even now that they're on the other side, especially now, after the final immigration of soul that we all must one day do. I hear the call of the ancestors. Maybe Heaven's as bustling and confusing as Ellis Island and all our names will be changed one last time, vowels and syllables chopped and dropped—who knows, certainly there are as many tears for the eternal embarkment.

Chapter Twenty-Six. "As Grapes on That Vine"

I BOUGHT A PIECE OF SKY-BLUE oak tag and a box of colored pencils, brand name Giotto, and over the weeks drew details of the family tree with notes, who crossed the ocean, who returned, who stayed. I jotted down stories cousins told me, it was the stories that interested me, more than the who-married-who. I studied all the gaps in the tree. Where were my gay ancestors? Where were the poets? What stories are missing? All the missing stories. All the spaces in between the branches. How did some of the women die young? Women's stories. Babies who died young. Unburied washed bones. All the washed bones, ancestral and *paesani*, in the *ossario*.

The family tree seemed more to me like a grapevine with inter-tangled roots, cousins marrying cousins, names repeated over and over. Both sides had names that repeated. There's twists and turns as Cianciotta appears on both sides of the tree, somewhere the cousins intermarried, but I couldn't yet tell where. It seems my father's parents were most likely *pro-cugini*.

On my vine, I am the last grape at the bottom of the page, never marrying, never having children, wishing my books and songs and poems could count somehow in the family. We are all as grapes on that vine.

I went for long walks through the town. Life felt like circles, circles, circles and spirals and lemniscates. One hundred years after my grandparents immigrated as teenagers I was back in their villages, while in New York in my mother's old apartment, I'd taken in a young immigrant who had left his village and was just starting out in America. Time itself seemed something to be folded over and hemmed. I remembered my mother, pins in her mouth, hemming my pants so they fell precisely over my shoes and never touched the ground.

I sat in the local bar. They call it a bar but to me it was a coffee shop, it's where I drank my first cappuccino every morning and my last *camomilla* at night. I sat at my favorite back table, a banquette, and in walks this butch. I never felt a hundred percent completely myself in the *paese* before, as a woman. If you don't embellish yourself as a woman, sometimes people get confused. In walks this butch. She walks in with a Border Collie on a short black leash, dungarees loose and boxy up top and cuffed at the boot, spiky blonde hair shaved up the back of the neck, heavy footed walk like she's on the night watch, keys dangling from her belt loop on a thick silver chain that hangs around her hip, thick black leather belt, brown eyes that land on everything with Peter Lorre heavy lids, and a sensuality that says she can undress a woman and lift her right now against the bathroom wall, just after her espresso, *per favore.* Her t-shirt fit tight, the band, a dark blue rim hugged her biceps. Her forearm was tattooed with sexy legs in high heels coming out of an espresso pot. I laughed loud. I had to talk to her. She walked directly up to the counter, jutted out her chin and bottom lip in an *Italiana* gesture to the women baristas. Chin mannerisms say it all. One of the sweet young femme baristas with long curly hair and creampuff intonations in her voice walked up to her at the glass counter. I was jumping out of my seat. We clearly could be friends. I'd never met a true out butch in the *paese* before. It takes courage to live your gay life right where you are, to integrate into the life of the town, to not have to move to some hip enclave, just be part of the mix where everybody respects everybody at least enough to leave them alone. A butch is unmistakable to a butch. It's in the walk, the eyes, the greeting that says, "I'm not in the male gaze. I have my own gaze." A good half of the women around here have butch characteristics. I'm not talking tough. Some of the women will stare you down and slice you to shreds with a stare and without even a syllable. I'm talking about an out soft lesbian butch who looks tough but will melt around you like a bulldog belly-up on the sidewalk for a rub. I've met tough ladies here over the years. I remember one in particular, decades ago, who lived alone in a second floor flat filled with her original paintings, canaries in cages, flowers, yellow walls, rooms filled with sunlight. I remember when I met her, thinking, this will be me when I'm older, intensely independent, not serving any man, an artist living alone, making myself happy, *faccia contenta,* surrounded by my art, open windows and birds chirping.

When the butch turned to scan the *caffè* on the hypervigilant rounds of her eyes, I waved giddily and said, "*Ciao! Ciao! Ciao!*"

until she understood I was waving to her, and then she gave me the lip, squinted, jutted her chin out, bottom lip forward. She rocked her closed hand toward her and away, thumb propping index finger up above the others.

"*Ma no ti conosc'!*" But I don't know you! Her eyebrows squinched with skepticism.

"*No! Sono Americana!*" No! I am American!

She laughed when I said, "American," a big smile broke open. She walked over to my table with her dog, and we started talking. The dog bonded with me right away, licking the palm of my hand and barking enthusiastically. I asked her how the life was here and got the low down. Her name was Dom, and her dog's name was Sole. Dom slid into a chair and said she came to the bar most nights after work as she was dating one of the baristas. She told me about a monthly dyke bar night in Bari called, "*Pala Ghiaccio,*" Ice Palace, where women gathered to dance and meet. That sounded exciting but I was even more relieved to realize that Dom could hang out with her girlfriend in the neighborhood bar living her life along with absolutely everybody else. The bar was open around the clock, and everyone was there, old men, old women, kids, young gay couples, teens, you name it. I never had that before in my life, a *caffè* that never closed with tables inside and outside, my favorite banquette in the corner where I could spread out my notebooks and the newspaper and write, where I could meet my ninety-year-old cousin in the morning to learn how to crochet lace over a cappuccino, and my butch friend at night to play *Scopa.* The *caffè* only closed an hour a day for cleaning, and I don't think they'd kick you out even then if you needed company. I was proud of the *paese.* There was a humanity to the place. I wished my grandparents could see their towns now. Every day when I was done writing and ready to take a break, I never had to be all alone. The *caffè* was always open and there's always someone who will say *Buongiorno* or *Buonasera.*

"For Those Who Came with Nothing"

Today, we honor the lives that came before us
Those who crossed the ocean looking for work
Who read the Atlantic waves like want-ads
Who left everything
Who left everyone they ever knew
Who never got to see the immense beauty of *Italia*
The many countries in one
The big cities, mountains, lakes, statues, sculptures, vistas,
And the remembered beauty
Of caves in the *murge*.

Who never got to hear the gold church clock towers or read Dante.
Who came to the sea in their one pair of good shoes
as if the ocean they would walk across and perhaps they did.
Pacing in steerage, rinsing and sewing and cutting and tying
Fixing always fixing.

Those who remembered, as the years went on,
more and more details of where they came from,
the goat of their childhood
and how to balance a basket of figs
on the crown of their heads.

Our grandmothers, we salute
And how they lived for all
the lives to come.

"A job is easy"

A job you get up
put on a nice dress and shoes
go to work.
Everyone is a manager today.
Try staying home and taking care of everything.
Fixing everything.
Cooking, shopping, cleaning, gardening, sewing,
taking care of everybody.
That's work!

Chapter Twenty-Seven. "Serpentine Alleys"

WALKING THE SERPENTINE ALLEYS of Acquaviva delle Fonti, looking for the chapel of *San Rocco,* I thought about his life. It was August 16th, 2018, the annual outdoor rosary for his feast day, and I was lost in the ancient alleyways where Grandma Rose was born. The doors of the houses opened directly into the stone street. The cobblestones were flat, not like *Sanpietrini.* I never tripped in Acquaviva delle Fonti. I was walking in circles, I'd walked down this same street just a few minutes before, via Amapani, Street of One Who Loves Loaves of Bread. Where was the church? I didn't know if it would be a big church or a little church, just that I would know it when I saw it by the painting of Saint Rocco on the facade. In all the statues and paintings depicting him, Saint Rocco points to a lesion on his knee, the way we all point out our bloodied wounds to those who will listen and to share in the awe of a spiritual healing of an ordeal of the flesh. Saint Rocco's wound is not yet healed. A dog is always beside him, looking up at him, with a big hunk of Italian bread in his mouth. For years I thought Saint Rocco must have been a lover of animals like Saint Francis. Francis is depicted with sparrows, and Rocco with a dog. But Rocco's story was quite different. As I walked through the small winding streets, hoping I would find the church on time, or find someone else walking to the recital of the rosary, I turned on via Squicciarini, one of my ancestral names. Probably generations ago, this street was named after my great-great-great somebody. Everything was super quiet, so much so that I was aware of my lumbering footsteps. All of a sudden from a second story balcony, Aretha's voice was blasting, and my shoulders automatically bopped into a dance rhythm. Aretha's voice, her song, reached this ancient alleyway and my bones responded. She broke open the silence. Who was playing "Think" on via Squicciarini in Acquaviva delle Fonti *vecchio?* I wanted to go inside that house. The buildings lined the alleyway, all attached, two and three stories tall, peach and white and sandstone. The volume was blasting so high her voice took over the alley and I couldn't tell exactly which balcony was playing her song. I looked along the railings, balcony to balcony, expecting to see someone dancing. I pictured a man in a white tank shirt grooving around his kitchen, pouring himself espresso, a *mappine* slung over his shoulder. Maybe I can find a new friend in Acquaviva delle Fonti. Aretha's voice reached through time and space to this tiny stone road in the old city. I felt outed as an American. I felt America calling me in her chorus: "*Freedom freedom freedom freedom! Yeah! Think. Think.*" I couldn't help but sing along and do a twirl in the street, it might as well have been my national anthem playing. It was a spirit anthem. Aretha's falcon soprano may be the single greatest achievement of the whole American experiment. And she is singing of love, love for self and love for the beloved.

I walked on, to find the chapel. Saint Rocco had been a healer who helped victims of the plague until he eventually got sick himself and was banished from Piacenza as the sick were isolated for fear of contagion. He retreated alone into the woods, taking shelter under boughs in a cave. As the days went on, Saint Rocco was dying. Then one day a dog found him, and the dog dedicated himself to Rocco's recovery by taking an Italian bread from his master's house every day and bringing it to Rocco. Day after day the devoted dog fed Rocco and licked his wounds. Some days the dog refused to eat, instead he ran with his bread through the woods to Rocco. The dog kept Rocco alive. A nobleman named Count Gothard Pallastrelli was the owner of the dog, and he wanted to know why his dog grabbed a loaf of bread every day and ran off into the woods. So, one day he followed the dog, and the dog led him to Rocco. The Count was inspired by Rocco's spirituality, brought him home and saw to it that Rocco was nursed back to health. The Count became a devoted follower of Saint Rocco. He treated his dog as good as a saint too.

The streets were completely silent. There wasn't a soul around. I was the only one out walking. I turned on via Nicola Abrusci. Then from a window, Aretha again, booming, "Rock Steady," with her soaring "*Ohhhhhh*," and the chorus: "*What it is, what it is, what it is.*" Aretha's deep well of voice flooded the stone street. Aretha amplified. It was jarring, almost shocking to walk these ancient stone streets as the alley swelled with her voice, as if this street was her throat. Aretha strips me bare. It's as if she is saying to me, "How can you walk so austere and quiet while you are alive? Why do you match the quiet reverence of these streets? What voice is inside you? Let me hear that voice. Bare your soul. Show what's inside you. I am outed. I don't want to be quiet or contained. I want to yell, "Whatever!" I don't want to be in a set of *sistemazione* where there's a "right" way to do everything and I by default do everything wrong. I don't want to try to achieve *la bella figura* and fail miserably. What I love about life is the messy improv, the artistry of making things by hand, and creating Bohemian uses for old things. The rulelessness. I missed ripped dungarees and dreadlocks and every kind of person walking in every kind of style, and the New York way there is no one way or time to do anything, all the rule breaking for every aspect of life. The glorious anonymity of New York City and knowing that so much is going on every day you'll never know what's going on, but you get in on what you can. "*What it is, what it is, what it is.*" It's impossible to hear Aretha and not break into a dance step and open my throat to sing. All the suffering, through all of history to forge this voice. This one. This Aretha. The radio station announcer cuts in. "*Aretha Franklin è morta.*" Aretha died? On the feast of *San Rocco?*

I found the chapel, a one room church, like an open cave. Saint Rocco and the dog were painted over the door. There was the big hunk of Italian bread in the mouth of the little heroic dog, holding it up to Saint Rocco who points at the open wound over his knee. I'll call the dog, *Amapani,* One Who Loves Loaves of Bread. I stepped up inside the cool dark stone room. The women were already gathered and in the middle of saying the rosary. Their eyes noted my presence as I entered. I sat on a bench against the stone wall. I didn't have rosary beads in my pocket. How could I not have a rosary in my pocket? I fingered the beads of my bracelet: blue amethyst and tiger eye. "*What it is, what it is, what it is.*"

One woman asked if I knew how to say the rosary. "*Sì!*" I answered, proud that I could recite the *Ave Maria* in Italian. I memorized it as an adult. The *Ave Maria* in Latin and in Italian is among the most beautiful meditations I've ever heard. When it came to the rosary, these women were professional. I long forgot what to pray on the middle beads, and what mysteries to name and all that micro-rosary business. So, when the lady who seemed to be in charge asked me to lead the rosary, I panicked and begged her, *"No, per favore,"* and the others chimed in, *"Saacce,"* she doesn't know, raising their eyebrows. And it was true, I am the one who doesn't know, but I am trying to find out, I am the one who asks questions, one who listens. I leaned my head back on the cool stone wall, as the *Ave Maria* commenced in rounds of call and response.

Don Mimmo walked in, and the ladies stood right up and aside. The rosary abruptly paused. Don Mimmo said the rosary would start in half an hour. He pointed to the benches and a few guys lifted the benches and carried them out into the street. Don Mimmo set up his altar then decided to move it so that the congregation would not be in the way of the occasional car. He set the wooden altar table behind a car in a small alcove of houses. He pointed to the men to set the benches along the walls and the chairs in front of him. We all grabbed the end of a bench or a chair and moved them outside. The women sat down, one resumed the recitation of the rosary and we all followed. A man came out onto his balcony to join in the recitation. Pigeons flew through. After a full rosary the woman recited a litany of the attributes of Mary, the *Litanie Lauretane:*

Maria Santa Maria, prega per noi. Santa Madre di Dio, prega per noi. Santa Vergine delle vergini, prega per noi. Madre di Cristo, prega per noi. Madre della Chiesa, prega per noi. Madre della divina grazia, prega per noi. Madre purissima, prega per noi. Madre castissima, prega per noi. Madre immacolata, prega per noi . . .

Aretha echoed in the background from another balcony, *"Daydreamin' and I'm thinkin' of you. Daydreamin' and I'm thinkin' of you."* Aretha's voice was in my head on repeat like the rosary: *"Hey baby let's get away let's go somewhere far, baby can we, where I don't care."* The alleyway swelled with her voice. Aretha's voice is the *sorgente* welling up from the deepest earth.

As we prayed to *La Madonna*, Aretha answered.

Chapter Twenty-Eight.
"The *Affamaith l'Americana*"

CHURCH BELLS RING IN ACQUAVIVA delle Fonti through the night and through the day. The message is clear, time flows on. Bells mark time. 15:00.

I jumped up from the *pisolino*, the midday nap, hearing a voice clearly: "Call Aunt Grace." I was excited to report back to her, all about Acquaviva and her cousins. I rolled over in bed, grabbed the phone. Her son answered:

"*Oh*, did your sister just call you?"

"No. What happened?"

"She's in a deep coma. From which she won't revive."

I felt punched in the gut. All August she'd stayed alive through the stifling heat. And now she's dying? Now? Only a couple of days before I return? Days. Days tricked me into thinking I would see her again and get to share with her all about Acquaviva and sit at her kitchen table with the wicker basket of plastic fruit and show her photos and videos and drink tea as rainbows slid on the wallpaper around the kitchen. I thought I could be Marco Polo for one of our afternoon cups of tea, but no, our goodbye on her steps where she cried, was, goodbye for life. Our last moment. We never know what cup of tea will be our last cup of tea. I was so looking forward to seeing her, showing her photos of the cousins, and sharing this with her. I knew three months could be an eternity in the life of a ninety-six-year-old, but now only days away from coming home, I had regained faith I would see her.

I stepped out onto the balcony to hang my pants to dry and saw the elders walking down below, pushing little shopping bags on wheels. I wished Aunt Grace could have had this in America, a community of elders who spoke her language, a fresh vegetable store to walk to just down the street in a pedestrian piazza where it was safe to walk, for farm fresh peaches, plums and apricots, green olives off the trees, *cipolle rosse*, a doctor to walk to two doors down. I remembered her telling me, "You only see half of people's bodies these days. They step out of their house. Maybe you get a wave hello. They get in their cars. *Zooooom*. That's it. You never see them."

I walked into the *caffè* at about five o'clock. I could see there were still some croissants behind the glass counter. A cup of tea I needed, a cup of tea. There were still three hours until the dinner hour, but I was hungry. The *affamaith* American. Couldn't wait until dinner. I had to shove something life affirming into my mouth. I stepped to the counter and ordered a cup of tea with milk and a croissant. The barista looked at me like I made a completely inappropriate request and refused to serve it to me. "*Signora, ma dai*," Lady, gimme a break. Her eyes widened and her head turned down and to the side as if to say—*You know better. We've trained you. It's not the hour for that.* "*Puoi bere una Spritz o una soda.*" You can drink a Spritz or a soda. She had a look of disappointment on her face, like I had just failed my final exam. *How dare you ask for a cup of tea and croissant at this hour, when you know better.* I'd been coming into this *caffè* for weeks. We knew each other to say hello to and have casual conversation, but her raised eyebrows told me that I was a lost cause, I didn't understand anything about life, and this was a line she wouldn't cross, a rule she wouldn't break. It was how Grandma Rose used to look at me for not carrying a pocketbook, not wearing a watch, not combing my hair, and sitting with my legs wide open like a man. The barista's counteroffer was this: "*Do'mattin', puoi mangiare il tuo cornetto e 'na tazza di tè. Do'mattin'. Non adesso.*" In the morning you can have your croissant and cup of tea, in the morning. Not now. I made it worse. I pointed out the croissants in the case that were left over from the morning. But I knew I'd gone too far. I'd broken a cardinal rule. So, I backed off, thanked her, and told her I'd see her in the morning, and went and had a bowl of cereal in my room.

It was time to go back to New York. Sometimes a New Yorker needs breakfast at midnight. I wanted my New York—anything you want anytime you want it. I wanted to have a cup of tea anytime at all. I didn't care what time it was. I didn't want to know what time it was. I didn't even want to wear a watch. Ever. It was time to go back to the land of the punk rock renegade rule breakers of which I was one.

PART VI
WHADDYACALL THE WIND?

A   t i m e l e s s -
n e s s   a b o u t   a   l e m o n . . .
L i g h t   b u r s t i n g   c o m p l e x i o n.
S h a d o w   l i c k i n g   e d g e s .
How yellow is   Light rounding the bell.
SEE   born   **HOW YELLOW**
THE   of green.   **IS A MIRACLE**
EYE of the lemon. How the lemon grows to its full self. **OF SUN SIFTING**
Where it held its connection to the tree. THR**OUGH BRANCHES**
Is it turning toward you?   Squeeze the s**kin. Let its scent**
Let light throw the sphere into shadow.   **transport you . . .**
Sunrays hot earth into roots   o**ut through tips**
This moment flowers   **in spacetime.**
Paint the   **dark triangular cave**
'tween **a trio of lemons**

Chapter Twenty-Nine. "A Tangle of Threads"

August 2018, Yonkers, New York

FAROUKH DECORATED THE HALLWAY and apartment with "Welcome Home" signs, balloons, and teal starbursts hanging from the ceiling. He saw the *bastone* I carried and said, "You look like *fellahin.*" I grabbed my keychain from the hook by the door and clipped it back on my belt loop.

The day of Aunt Grace's funeral, I counted seven baby peach tree sprouts outside my window. Aunt Grace was right when she'd consoled me after the landlord chopped down Grandma Peach Tree. "Just wait 'til next year," she'd said with utter confidence in the face of my despair. "Things will shoot up again, I promise you. It always does. You'll see." I wanted to remember her as she was. I couldn't bear walking into the interior room of the funeral home, exactly where my mother's funeral had been just a few years before—so I sat in the lobby and talked with my sister and cousins. I told them a story about how one day I went over to Aunt Grace's to ask if she had turquoise thread so I could sew a hole in my sweater:

"Of course, she had every color thread imaginable. Aunt Grace said to me, "Look in my sewing box," and pointed to a cabinet. It was a beautiful handmade box with little gold handles, three drawers and was covered with contact paper of white with pink roses. She told me that her father had made the box for her when she graduated Jane Addams High School. She went on about how she majored in dressmaking, while my mother picked cosmetology. She was proud that they were academic diplomas, where you learned both a trade and got an education. She explained how in cosmetology you had to take first aid, and how they all studied home economics, and got a well-rounded education. She said, "Today kids don't even learn how to balance a checkbook. I don't know how they survive."

Inside the sewing box were hundreds of old wooden spools in every color ever invented. The wooden spools were stamped with company names, Lily's, American Thread Company, Star. The threads were all tangled in a mess. Seventy-eight years of spools of thread.

"Mind if I straighten this out for you?" I asked her.

She said, "Go right ahead, and take all the thread you want."

I told her, "No, I'm not gonna take your threads. You're a seamstress. Just the turquoise for my sweater. That'd be great, so I don't have to buy it."

"Take more thread," she'd said. "To go out and buy it today, God knows what a spool of thread costs. It used to be fifteen cents for five hundred yards. All cotton."

Her box of threads showed the story of the world through the colors of thread. A treasure of spools with colors through the eras, colors you don't see so much anymore. Muted olive, pale pink, silver-gray, champagne, mustard gold, from the Depression years, dark reds and mint green of the post-WWII years, 1960's green-aqua, bright lemon, turquoise, 1970's Day-Glo orange, pink, lemon yellow, and lime. Every other color was mixed in, every shade of purple, lavender, many shades of pink. I sat at her dining room table for more than an hour untangling, cutting, winding, tucking the tails in the notches of each old wooden spool, thousands of yards of thread. I stood them all up like chess pieces in formation by color; eighteen shades of blue, everything from baby blue to royal blue, denim, navy, midnight, then greens, golds, purples, pinks, so many shades you could find whatever color you needed to sew the whole universe. I thought about what other clothes I had holes in, and I told her I'd take a couple of the colors of which she had duplicates. It seemed to me that over her lifetime, with her sewing machine, she'd sewn the whole world together.

She looked at the box and said, "Take all the thread, I'm never going to use it."

Seven baby peach trees, plus the one in the white enamel pot in the kitchen now three feet tall, were all ready to be adopted. I asked friends who owned property, "Who wants to adopt one of Grandma Rose's

peach tree babies?" I told them each to dig a two-foot hole and fill it
with water. One by one I gently dug up the baby trees, wrapped their
roots in wet newspaper and drove them to their destinations in Jersey
and upstate New York.

August had taken her toll. The ensuing weeks brought a string of
deaths and funerals, parents of friends, one after the other after the
other. Every other week I went to an Italian funeral home and saw
one crew or another of Italian American women friends. We were
mourners, and like a good Italian lady, I wrote out mass cards with
pictures of Saint Theresa or *La Madonna*. We sat in Greek diners
talking for hours after each wake, where I ordered the most American
things I could think of, just for the Americanness of it: cheeseburger
deluxe with French fries and ketchup, apple pie à la mode with vanilla
ice cream, and coffee. American coffee. I wanted all of it. In Italy,
espresso was served with a glass of water chaser, in America, the glass
of water was built in, the pleasure being to sip hot coffee for a good
long while over conversation, hold the hot cup in the joined palms of
your hands, then get a refill. Warm palms led to good conversation. In
theory. I relished the fact that in New York I could have a cup of tea
and croissant anytime I wanted, round the clock. There was a strange
freedom in that simple act; tea and croissant anytime at all, without
order to the day. Anarchy.

Mornings felt empty. Breakfast in America confounded me. I craved
that feeling of waking up knowing I would start each day with full
satisfaction, two or three bites filled with fresh *crema*, the life affirming,
"*Buongiorno Signora!*" seven-thirty every morning when I had barely
opened my eyes and was brought a warm crusty *cornetto alla crema*.

Faroukh and I listened to impassioned patriotic speeches about
America during the week of Senator John McCain's funeral. We talked
about what it means to live in a country where tribe and bloodline,
sect and religion, language and culture, are not the unifying forces.
We talked about how New York's strength is diversity. Diversity of
mindset and whatever we all bring to the table, down to the genome
and diversity of bacteria. New York City gains strength from exposure
to all of it. I told him, the word *paesan'* had expanded meaning for
me, not just townspeople or neighbors or people cut from the same

cloth, but a vast sense of relatedness, by no blood at all, all beings, as is said, by stardust. "We're all *paesans*," I told him.

Faroukh got distressing phone calls from a closeted gay friend back home who was suicidal and wanted to know if I could help get him out of his country and to America. We tried to connect him with organizations to see where he could seek refuge. There were incidents of beatings of gay men, and he was terrified of being outed. At the same time, Faroukh showed me photos of a boy he met online. He said they talked every night, were in love and he was planning to take a bus to Alabama where the boy lived with his family. "Just one problem," he said, "unfortunately, his family, they don't know he is gay. The father is very religious."

"Forget it," I told him. "You're not going to the south to out some boy to his mother and father. You're liable to get beat up or shot. Not gonna happen. You're in New York City. Find guys in New York. I'm going to take you to the place that saved me."

I drove him to The Gay Center on West 14th Street in Manhattan and when we got there we stood outside for a moment. "Look up at the bricks," I told him. "When I was your age, I held onto this building like a life raft in a storm-tossed ocean." We walked in through the door and saw a sign for a queer immigration fair coming up. Upstairs I left him to contemplate in the gay Sistine Chapel—what was once the men's bathroom, now turned into an exhibit room, where Keith Haring had painted hundreds of penises all over the ceiling and walls. Faroukh was in a safe zone, and on his way.

Chapter Thirty. "As a Mist"

I BEGAN TO WALK EARLY MORNINGS with my neighbors, the three prayerful ladies of The Angel Squad. I walked with my *bastone*. One man sitting on his porch looked at me with my stick and said, "Whaddayou Moses?" In the (odd) court, I was one of the few with a computer and a printer, so I became somewhat of a neighborhood scribe when an elder needed me to write a letter, or print something, or look up a fact on the internet. One night there was a knock on my door. *La Baronessa* stood there, in a wide brim royal blue floppy hat which matched her button-down silky shirt, knee length cream colored skirt and bejeweled slip-on flats.

"*Baronessa!*" I said. "*Avanti.*"

"*Ciao. Ciao,*" she hammered words into place. Speaking even just a greeting in Italian was an infusion of iron—built us up from the marrow.

"Come in, come in. To what do I owe this surprise?"

"I got a favor to ask ya'."

Before she was even in the door, she unsnapped her white leather pocketbook, pulled a scrap of paper out and handed it to me, a torn-off piece of an envelope that she'd held onto for many years. She shuffled inside and sat down. When I say shuffled, *La Baronessa* couldn't lift her legs unless she held onto a banister. Whenever she walked down the sidewalk to get out of the court, if the hose was out across the path, I'd run outside to move it for her. She couldn't lift a leg two inches to clear the hose. I'm sure if she had a cane or a walker she could have managed, but she wouldn't be caught dead with any of that, too much pride. *La Baronessa* grew up in the South Bronx, in Soundview, a tomboy who'd climbed down into the sewer with a bucket on a rope whenever the boys on the block jimmied the sewer cap off, so she could fish out their lost Spaldeens. She was one of the only neighbors who lived in the (odd) court before my mother and I. We'd known each other from the time I was twelve. She lived alone by choice, an old school Bronx broad who never skipped a beat in life, never was anybody's fool, never had a regular doctor, never got a flu shot, never cooked or cleaned for any man, was married a short time until he told her, "I'm hungry," then she said, "yeah, what does that have to do with me?" She'd punctuate this story with a stern look, and say, "I got rid of him." *La Baronessa* didn't take any medication and still worked at the same flower seed company where she got a job sixty years ago when she was twenty-five. She was satisfied with life as it was, on her own terms.

Scrawled on her piece of paper were several syllables, and a number. "What's this?" I asked.

"This is where my father was born. I want you to find the house for me. I know you know the compute."

"What's the name of the town?"

"Cima. My father left me the house. I want you to find it."

"Have you seen the house?"

"No."

"Never been to the town?"

"No. Never."

"Do you know what the house looks like?"

"I saw a picture once. It's got a balcony. It's in *la provincia di Palermo*. I'll know it when I see it. I want to know what condition the house is in and if anybody is living in it. When I hit the LOTTO, I'm gonna go, and you'll come with me as my interpreter. I don't know what if anything I want to do with the house, but I don't want to abandon it either. I want to honor my father. Plus, I have fields of olive trees. Someone is making oil with those trees and by rights, it's my oil. That's right. It's my oil."

"*Baronessa*, probably some cousin is living in the house, and the last thing they want is you waltzing into town with me in tow."

"Pro'bly."

"Okay, lemme open up my computer. Do you want coffee or tea or something?"

"No thanks. You sure you have time now?"

"There's a saying my Grandma Rose used to tell me. "*Prima il dovere, dopo il piacere.*" That means, first do what you must do, then do what gives you pleasure. This we gotta do. Plus, it'll give me pleasure. Let's do it." I took one look at the scrap of paper and saw two syllables and what amounted to half of a street address, a number with the name *Giovanni*.

"Is Giovanni the name of a cousin? Or the street?"

"I don't know."

I knew it was half of half of what we needed to find the house. It was missing syllables, but it was a clue. It was a start. Half a name, half the name of a town, half the name of a street perhaps, a phonetic spelling of how she remembered her father pronouncing the name of the town. "You know, even if you hit the LOTTO, even if you make the pilgrimage, fly to Palermo tomorrow and start driving around, even if I go with you and we get to the basic vicinity, even if we get close in the mountains, chances are we'll hit a *rotatoria* with arrows pointing in four directions with similar sounding town names and we'll have to drive in circles to guess which way to go and what the missing syllables are in the name of the town. Plus, who knows if streets are named the same, or if the town still exists. Sicily's had earthquakes and volcano blows over the century and was bombed in WWII. Maybe towns tumbled down mountains, got wiped off the map. Who knows?"

"You'll find it. I know you. You're smart."

"You've got a lot of faith."

"No, you're smart. I know you."

I pulled up a map of Sicily from 1900 and began to look at town names. "So," I said, "let me ask you some questions about the town." I opened the Google Earth App. "How do you remember your father saying the town name?"

"Cima."

"Say it again."

"Cima."

"Say it slower."

"CHEE-ma."

The words were chewed. "That's not the whole name of the town."

"Yes, Cima."

"That's how you remember him saying it, but that's probably not how it will appear on a map." I repeated the sounds and extended the syllables, improvising with what the name of the town might be, *Alta*

Cima, Cima delle something *Santacima.* Who knows? *Cima* means up top, like up top of the road or top of the mountain. Whenever I drove in Italy, someone offering directions would always tell me, *Vai al cima.* Go to the top. *La Baronessa* reminded me of myself, and all the Italians I'd grown up with. Growing up in the Bronx I didn't know nuttin' 'bout nuttin' 'bout the life in Italy. I'd heard a *patois* version of the name of the towns, the name of the saints, the nicknames of our ancestors, but what did I know? Italy existed in a mist in our minds. Bari existed in a mist. I can't say Italy because we didn't really think like that. We were *Barese.* I learned early on to point to the heel of my sneaker whenever anybody said to me, "Where you from!" Questions were not really asked, rather you were ordered to give answers. "Where you from!" was an interrogation, not an inquiry. I did just like Grandma Rose did, she'd point to the heel of her black shoe. It was a way of answering without answering. That's "heel of the boot" mentality. I did know how to dig my heels in and get a job done. Dig in. Focus on the task at hand. I asked *La Baronessa* to repeat over and over how her father said the name of the town, and I listened closely to the minutiae of the syllables and where she accented syllables.

"Say it again."

"Cima."

"This isn't the whole town name, that I know."

"No?"

"No way. Words get chopped in mouths and in your ear. You know, when I went to find my cousins for the first time, if I'd only gone by the way my grandparents' voices were in my ear, I don't know how I would have found the towns. My grandfather, I don't know if he said: *Pitett' beeteett' betetta' Vetett'.* There were four towns in the same province it could've been: *Bitetto, Bitritto, Bitonto, Binetto.*"

"No kiddin'. Well, the way he said it, Cima."

"If your father was anything like my father and grandfather, he was always carrying heavy things and people talk differently when they're carrying heavy things. Let me tell you about a dream I had. The other night I dreamt of a man carrying a giant vat of olive oil on his back, a terracotta amphora, big like a barrel, and he walks by me, hunched over and he turns his head to me, and says, *"Djeel, djeel,"* in husky, hoarse, deep tones, and I knew he was telling me, "olive oil," but how he said it, was just, "*Djeel, djeel.*" He was trying to tell me something, and all that came out of his mouth were two syllables like on sandpaper, "*Djeel djeel,*" and he never stopped working. He went back and forth, shouldering this heavy barrel, back and forth, and I knew he was talking like that because of the weight he was carrying. He could barely breathe. His heart was slammin' to survive 'til the end of daylight, the end of the workday. When I woke up, I wrote the phrase down, like a secret message from beyond, "*Djeel, djeel.*" I'm still trying to figure out what it all means."

"It means you gotta come with me to Cima and make olive oil, that's what I think."

We laughed. "That sounds right. In my grandmother's town they say if you make olive oil, you're making gold. The sun's gold."

"That's right."

I zoomed in on the map around Palermo. "Alright, so tell me, *Baronessa,* how far is this town from Palermo?"

"I don't know."

I asked questions and her answer was always the same: "I don't know."

"Do you know anything about the location? Is the town up a mountain?"

"I don't know."

"Is it by the sea?"

"I don't know."

"Did he talk about fishing?"

"I don't know."

"Did he talk about going into the mountains? Did he mention going hunting?"

"I don't know."

"Did he say if he was near the volcano?"

I don't know.

"All I know is the town is in *la provincia di Palermo.* It's two stories with a balcony. Not a big balcony. When I see it, I'll know."

"Okay, so I'm looking for a two-story house in Sicily, with maybe a pocket balcony in the province of Palermo. That's a start.

I have two syllables that hint at the town name and maybe half a street name."

"Yeah." She looked at me with complete faith.

I began the detective work, scoured maps of Sicily, old and new. I'm looking for clues, for the names of towns which might include these syllables, or syllables like them. Syllables that twisted over the generations in our Bronx mouths. I narrowed my list of possibilities down to a couple of town names that were likely contenders. I narrowed that list down further by looking at street names in those towns, and who knows what street names were changed after WWII. I looked for streets that contained the syllables as she's saying them, and as is scrawled on her scrap of paper. She has the word, Giovanni. That could be part of the street name, or it could be her cousin, who knows? Eventually I figured out which town it could be, it might be and then which street in that town, it must be. I focused on a town southeast of Palermo, called Ciminna, and with these probabilities I went to Google Earth where we could look through the streets as if we were there walking. *La Baronessa* leaned in, looking into the computer and she couldn't believe her eyes. She was walking, figuratively, through the narrow streets of Ciminna. I turned the camera to look at the facades of houses. *La Baronessa* and I, courtesy of Google Earth, were on a virtual *passeggiata*. We walked down via Paolo Borsellino, via Vittime, and via Giovanni Falcone.

"Look," I showed her, "this town named streets after anti-mafia heroes. Falcone and Borsellino, I saw a plaque honoring these two in Palermo when I was there last summer. They were judges, very honorable men who fought against corruption, against the mob, and they were both assassinated. Killed by bombs. One under the car, one under the highway. They both grew up in Palermo. I walked around piazza Magione where they used to kick soccer balls around as kids."

"No kiddin'? I can't believe these pictures. I feel like we're there."

"*Cammina! Cammina! Iammo iamm!*"

La Baronessa laughed. And I laughed. We continued walking through Cimmina and came across a street named via Papa Giovanni XXIII. I was super excited. "*Baronessa*, this could be your street. Look, it has Giovanni in it. It's named after the Pope. Does that sound right?"

"I don't know."

"*Madonn'!*"

We walked to the number she had written on her scrap of paper. I swiveled the camera directly at the doorway and there was a balcony, a white pocket *balcone* on a two-story aqua-green house.

La Baronessa was amazed. "Yes! That's it! That's the house from the old pictures. There are curtains in the windows! Somebody's living there. Let me see the curtains. Can you get closer?"

There were white curtains in the windows, clear as day. She examined the curtains.

"Yes, there's curtains in the windows, somebody's definitely living there. *Oooh* the house looks like it needs work."

"Probably one of your cousins lives there, some cousin who wants you to leave him alone. *Lascia in pace.*"

"I bet he's selling my olive oil."

I handed her a clean sheet of paper, nice in an envelope, with the full address written in clear block letters.

That night, *La Baronessa* left with a big smile. I walked her across the court and watched as she went inside. She held onto the dream that one day she'd hit the LOTTO and bring me with her to Sicily so we could walk down those streets for real.

"*Lasciala*"

My cousin writes to me
Zia Annunziatine thinks of me often and says:
"*Finché la barca va, lasciala andare!*"
Once the boat goes, let her go!

That's how they healed their hearts
after immigration cleaved the family.
The ones who left and the ones who stayed.
Mantras to cheer themselves into the here and now.

Letting go is a constant practice.
Rooting into this moment, place and time.
Grandma Rose snapped *stringabeans*,
hemmed and sewed, stitched herself into

the here and the now
piercing fabric, pinning time into place
each tack each stitch says,
"You stay here now. Don't move."

"The Feast"

Down Mulberry Street I walk
as I walked in *Napoli,* foot by foot rising to a pause
before falling again to find the next *Sanpietrini.*

I walk Mulberry Street
as if I am in piazza Bellini
walking down the curved alley
to piazza Luigi Miraglia.

To duck out of the sausage and cigar smoke
I step behind the booths, onto the sidewalk.
Early evening, a few people are standing in doorways.
Someone is walking behind me, fast,
at a speed that far surpasses my own.
I can feel her coming.

I stay walking at my *Napoli* pace,
refusing to sidestep into garbage pails
to move out of her way.
This is a Neopolitan feast after all.
San Gennaro, the consummate Neopolitan saint.

She can find a way around me,
this *giovane ragazza americana.*
She can wait until we pass the garbage pails
and reach a point where there's an indentation,
more room to pass, but this she doesn't do.

She pushes past me, this *americana,* walks into me,
forcefully, hitting me from behind.
       I say to her, "Where do you think I'm going to go?
Where am I supposed to put my body?"
       "You're just walking so slow," she whines,

her long shiny blonde hair swishing, as she rushes forward and ahead of me.
    "No," I say, "I'm walking as if I'm in *Napoli.*"
This disarms her.
    "Yes, that's true," she says and laughs,
turns her head and smiles, walks on, waving.

I continue on my way, walking down Mulberry Street,
as if in *Spaccanapoli.* And this is how I aspire to walk
from now on, my foot stopping before footfall.
My foot swings up, suspends,
falls back to find
this earth.

"Cannoli and the Coriolis Effect"

"WHAT ARE YOU IN THE MOOD FOR?" she asks. She's got all the desserts lined up her arm, balanced up her forearm and bicep, and she points to each with her other hand, all the way up, as she sputters off, "Tortoni, tartufo, spumoni, cannoli, tiramisu." She flashes a winning smile. She's got a strong face like the Statue of Liberty and beautiful white teeth. "Then a couple of cheesecakes. *Fagetit,*" she says, "and these are just the perishables. We also have pasticiott', sfogliatelle, napoleons, éclaires, cream puffs, *fagetaboutit*." She's sexy and big and she owns her bigness like a Queen. And she is Queen, to this dynasty; her father's owned this Italian restaurant for years. I just want to see her smile. So, I say, "What was the second one?" And again, she rattles off the whole list 'cause she's got it memorized that way, a dessert routine, it has to come out whole: "Tortoni, tartufo, spumoni, cannoli, tiramisu," and she points with the other hand, all the way up the arm.

"We want them all of course." I bust her chops, "What's torrone? Do you have torrone?" And again, that million-dollar smile, she flashes. My friends and I order three desserts and share them around the table. I got a jolt of energy from the caffeine and sugar. I was hyped. I got up to use the bathroom and I talked with the waitress alone for a minute. I wanted to share what I learned in Sicily with everybody. I was a Sicilian cream evangelist. I say to her, "Do you know what cannoli means?" And she says, "No." And I say, "Cannoli means canal. Canals full of cream. There's two ways to eat a *cannolo.* You can bite it, or you can lick and suck it, depending on your orientation." She writes her number on a napkin. I didn't even ask. I'm just being factual. I'm just stating facts. I sit back down at my table, she's got work to do, and I'm frankly more interested in continuing my monologue about suction and cannoli. My friends indulge me and listen. "In the universe, suction is a greater force than protrusion. Suction is gravity plus magnetism. Protrusion gets too much play in the world, too much emphasis in society. Think about suction. Think of the Bermuda Triangle. The power of that energy. The core of the earth is molten iron as big as the moon. Imagine that? Inside the earth is a molten iron moon. Iron creates a magnetic field. And it's moving in waves. Everything, all of us, are being pulled to the center of the earth all the time. The magnetic currents and the Coriolis effect from the spinning of the Earth cause waves of suction. The earth spins fastest at the equator. Even cannoli suck you in. Everything is pulling toward the center. A thousand years ago, more than a thousand years ago, there was an Arab harem in *Sicilia*, in Caltanissetta, which means Castle of the Women, from the Arabic *Kalt et Nissa*. They experimented with ricotta, cinnamon, honey, almonds, chocolate, pistachio. They considered how to roll a wafer into a canal, they went out in the fields and got reeds, like bamboo, and they rolled thin sheets of dough around the stalks until they got the canal right. And they created this cream. That's a thousand years ago, more! These are our people. We came up with cannoli. We did this. What a contribution to humanity and the whole animal kingdom. Dogs eat cannoli. Wolves will eat cannoli. Nobody's refusing cannoli, ever. Did you ever see anybody refuse cannoli? Everyone thinks cannoli are phallic, but they are yonic too. Completely yonic. There's this place in Brooklyn, cannoli aren't on the menu, you gotta know to ask for it, and the boss hand rolls the wafer hot right then and there around a metal roller. The cream is hot, the canal is hot, *fagetaboutit* when this thing comes inside you. And for this, we gotta celebrate females, all female mammals. The cream is all about the breast in the mouth. If men breastfed, they'd be considered gods, and milk, milk would be gold. If men grew umbilical cords and gave birth to life, they'd be considered gods, and bellybuttons worshipped as icons. If men bled in cycles, they'd be gods, and blood revered and celebrated with moon cycles. If men bled, blood would be gold. We are the goddesses, the harbingers the givers of life itself. And we have the power of suction, the eternal spiraling vortex, to take in, to receive, to accept."

Chapter Thirty-One. "Next Year Never Comes."

IT WAS JUST OVER A YEAR AFTER our *Napoli* literary tour, when I got word that Francesco Durante died, right on his beloved island of Capri where he was born. Francesco's death sent a shockwave of grief throughout *Napoli* and our Italian American literary community and everywhere Francesco's work, books, and spirit traveled. He had brought the voices of those who'd left, back to Italy, hundreds of voices of Italian American writers back in translation. I spoke with Stan Pugliese and Peter Covino and we all expressed our grief and at the same time immense gratitude that we'd toured with Francesco when given the chance. On top of all of Durante's research covering more than a century of texts written by Italian American writers, Peter Covino and I turned out to be among the very last of a long list of Italian American writers who Francesco translated, toured with, promoted. I thought of Peter and I as two cherries on top of Francesco's cake. Two queer Italian American poet cherries. I hope we brought him some joy. He certainly brought joy to us, and I'm thankful I expressed to him how he'd ushered in a true dream come true. What a grand man, writer and performer. The pride of Capri and Napoli. *Evviva* Francesco!

That winter of 2020, something was bothering me. I was uneasy, agitated, like the guard dog at the House of the Tragic Poet in Pompeii. I could not stop crying. The floodgates of grief had opened. On March 9th, 2020, seven months after Francesco died, *Napoli* and all of Italy went on complete lockdown with COVID-19. I remembered a song my father used to sing to taunt my mother at the end of their marriage, when I was a child. "The party's over. It's time to call it a day." The line played over in my head. "The party's over. *La festa è finud.*" A state of emergency was declared in New York State and my county of Westchester was the epicenter with ninety-eight cases. My local doctor and his hospital were under immediate quarantine. I sheltered-in-place, immunocompromised and alone. I reflected on the *guglia*, the plague column we'd sat under in piazza San Domenico Maggiore, that had been built as an ex-voto for the saints who delivered *Napoli* through the plague of 1656. I wore my mother's scapula of *La Madonna di*

Carmine and went to sleep at night clutching rosary beads. I wondered how the world would change and if I would jump in the saddle and go along with it. I found out soon enough. Everyone in my world went on "Zoom." The human interaction in my life was now through a computer screen. As resistant as I was, when I could take the isolation no longer, I jumped in, creating theater and writing workshops through the portal of Zoom. Life felt further and further away.

My mother's scapular, about forty years old, was very worn out, and kept getting tangled around my holy medals. I ordered a new scapula online, a powder blue one. When it arrived in the mail, I was surprised to find that it came with a prayer from the mystic nun Suor Orsola Benincasa, for whom Francesco's university was named. After a prayerful conversation with Jesus, Suor Orsola began sewing blue scapulars and giving them away as blessings. This one, was part of the legacy of her mission. I prayed to Suor Orsola.

On April 2nd, 2020, I telephoned my most trusted oncologist. Part of our conversation went exactly like this:

"Doc, this is Annie. I'm calling you to say hello. I don't have COVID."

"If you had it, this would be a goodbye phone call. Ten or fifteen years from now it'll be discussed how the hemoglobin structure of Italians made them more susceptible. We look at Malaria now, we see how people with variant hemoglobin structures are differentially affected."

"Italy is getting hit hard. There's no room to bury bodies in Bergamo. I hear the death bells from the local church never stop ringing. They're saying fifteen million cases."

"But you, you're from Bari, your bloodline is really Constantinopolitan. You're not really Italian. I don't mean that as an insult. I mean it in terms of hemoglobin structure. That might actually be protecting you from the path of the pathogen."

After that call, I reflected on the journey of *La Madonna di Costantinopoli.* Further back than I could trace on my family tree, my hemoglobin structure had sailed from Constantinople with *La Madonna,* riding a current through the Sea of Marmara that had come from the Black Sea through the Bosporus Strait, into the Aegean and Ionian Seas and up the Strait of Otranto into the Adriatic Sea and was carried overland to Acquaviva delle Fonti.

Word came from Acquaviva, that precious Zia Annunziatine had died. I cried as I heard her voice clearly saying to me, "*Cammoine cammoine*" for us to walk together. I could hear her singing, "*Evviva Maria!*" hitting every resonant tone in D minor, and the words spun inside me: "*O Maria quanto sei bella, sei la gioia e sei l'amore.*" Every word of the lyrics was true . . . *You are joy. You are love.*

"*i Cpodde d'Acquaviv'*"

March 23, 2020, Yonkers, New York

running low on onions in New York and reminiscing
of the onions of Acquaviva delle Fonti
worthy of their own festival, onions
big as newborns, onions that were wages
for peasants building Khufu's pyramid
onions it is still, not to which we aspire—

the days of quarantine are here
groceries delivered to us privileged holed up
sheltering-in-place in apartments with everything
we need brought right to our doorstep
tap water and all glories are ours
doors to keep the contagion out
no matter how it comes, unseen as it is
every breath a threat carried on wind
landing on grass, steel, lettuce.
How to wash garlic?

"Back off" is the order of the day
Stay away from humans, sage advice
for this moment in time.
Weeks are lifetimes now.
Once we gathered, we
held hands, we
passed the *mezze* platter
around the table for all to share. Once, we
buried our dead

Now all we can do is sing.
My cousin with his microphone on his balcony in Bologna.
Every night I tune into his set.
Neighbors applaud from all the surrounding balconies.

All through the day I stare into screens.
Computers have taken over our lives.
The last of the peasants in my family has died
peasants who used their hands in ways so
different, peasants who grew vegetables
and made everything they touched.

We who tap keyboards and cannot hold hands,
we whose touch spreads viruses
keep tapping our keyboards and staring in through screens.
Will we be able to relearn togetherness
or will isolation reorient our brain cells?
I'm not sure I know how to look at another human
any longer. My face stopped responding,
the smile climbed away.
Life, life seems on another planet.

Chapter Thirty-Two. "Curtains"

LA BARONESSA SAT ON THE BENCH OUTSIDE my window for hours in the hot sun and waited for me to come out and talk. Her company closed its doors during the pandemic, and she was forced into retirement. I'd open my window and lean out old-school style, then I'd drag a chair out by the stump of the peach tree and sit at a distance. *La Baronessa* wouldn't wear a mask. I always did. I kept masked and fifteen feet upwind. With a propensity for lung infections, I knew COVID-19 could bowl me over.

La Baronessa kept saying, "It's a *cimitero* around here." It's a cemetery.

And I'd respond, "Let's make some noise." I taught myself how to play the tarantella on a melodica blow piano, and I played it outside in the grass. The macabre A-Minor key was the medicine I needed to survive this plague. *La Baronessa* smiled and tapped her foot. Loudness was medicine to us. We talked day after day about her house and olive tree grove in Ciminna, Sicily.

"One day we're gonna go there," she kept saying. We gave each other greetings and salutations in Italian. Whenever I went back inside, she always shouted the mandate: "*Statte bbuon'!*" One Saturday she brought me eggplant parmigiana from her favorite Italian American deli. We both had the kicking boot inside us. We were lost Italians in search of a piazza.

In the mornings, I began walking the paths with The Angel Squad. They lived on faith, family, friends, and good deeds. One would leave fresh bunches of broccoli rabe on my doorknob, knowing that I couldn't go into stores. What blessed neighbors. They prayed every day, and even as they walked. They'd call for me by my window so that I could join them on their rounds. We donned face masks and walked the windy sidewalks up the hill and around six different courtyards on three streets. Over the years there had been others who used to walk these paths for their daily constitutionals. Constantino from Messina used to walk with his hands behind his back, a formal antiquated posture. To walk with your hands behind your back, chest open, you gotta feel safe in the world. It's a non-threatening gesture toward the world. I walked more *en garde*, arms swinging with my stride, ready to defend an attack or to catch myself when I fell. For Constantino, the bus stop on Central Avenue became a temporary piazza, a place to say, "*Buongiorno,*" to whoever happened to be waiting. As he walked the empty paths, he sang to himself and whistled to the birds. He walked alone, a lone Italian man in search of a piazza. Now I was that man.

Every morning, The Angel Squad would stop and wave outside a first-floor window. I asked, "Who are you waving to?"

"Serafina doesn't get out anymore," they said. "She's housebound. Giuseppe sits her by the window where she waits for us to say hello."

I joined them in this devotional act. One by one we'd go up to the window and wave, "*Buongiorno Serafina.*" It was like four ladies lining up to receive communion. This became my most profound joy in the neighborhood as I sheltered-in-place. I waved and called at Serafina's window. Her husband Giuseppe would pull up the shade. As the months went on, I'd stand out there longer and longer waving my arms overhead and talking to Serafina through the window glass. "*Buongiorno Serafina.* I love you." I could see through the glare of the glass, a little hand waving, clutching a white tissue. I could hear her shout, "I love you too Annie." We called to each other from our own trapped isolations. Her inside, me outside. Seeing her through the glass was like looking at a spirit, someone in another world who I couldn't touch or see clearly. I pulled down my mask and sunglasses so she could at least see my face. This waving by the window became a daily prayer in action. I would report to Serafina how the air was that day, if the sun was out or the snow or the lilacs or the wind or the birds or the rain. At Christmas, Giuseppe ran outside with a pair of gloves wrapped for each of us. The gloves had zig-zag designs. That's what Serafina saw—our hands.

"It's the highlight of her day," Giuseppe said, "we truly appreciate you coming by every day."

"It's our highlight too." *Un momento di luce.*

Serafina waving through the window glass had become profound for me in my loneliest days. Her hand framed by the window brought me back to the reliability of my mother's hand waving to me for years and years and years, and which waves in my mind's eye.

Rosina and Rocco brought supplies and food and for the holidays some bottles of *vino* to share with the neighbors. Rocco always sat out on the bench with *La Baronessa* and listened to her stories about her life. For *La Baronessa's* eighty-fifth birthday, we opened a bottle of *vino* outside on the bench and everyone who passed by, stopped to make a toast. "I never got a vaccination in all my life," *La Baronessa* boasted, "I'm strong. Sicilian. I don't take any medication. I told God—lose my number." *La Baronessa* never hit the LOTTO, instead she went to play bingo at a local church. COVID-19 went around the elders at the bingo hall. They canceled it for a week then started right back up again; they should have been spelling C-O-V-I-D instead of B-I-N-G-O. *La Baronessa* contracted COVID-19 and was hospitalized. Nobody could say for sure where she contracted the virus, and none of the neighbors knew what hospital she was taken to or how she was feeling. I tracked her down. I called around the local hospitals until I found her. I called the nurse's station and asked the nurse to go answer the phone in her room so I could say hello.

"I want to come home," she told me, but she barely had the breath to talk.

Meanwhile, I had to go back to Sloan Kettering for another biopsy. I woke up in a Fentanyl haze in a field of orange flowers falling open in the breeze, tall translucent orange petals flapping in the breeze. My hand automatically reached up and grabbed the incentive spirometer and I started rounds of inhaling with my full might. The recovery room nurse, aglow with blinding white light from the window behind her, told me to slow down. "That's enough. Don't overdo it." I was on automatic pilot, my body knew what to do after surgery, I was well rehearsed. I breathed in to get the ball up in the plastic tower. I wanted to stay in that field of orange flowers for a little longer, but the nurse said into the phone, "A room on 19? She's almost ready to go," then she turned to me, "They have a room ready for you."

"I'm going to 19? Why am I going to 19?" I was startled.

"We're using every bed available. We send some post-op patients up there."

"When did that start happening?"

The nurse shrugged.

The last time I'd been on 19 was to visit Athena before she died. I wondered if it was a COVID-19 protocol, to give post-op patients private rooms that weren't otherwise being used. The patient escort wheeled me upstairs and right into the same room that had been Athena's. Déjà vu, except now I was in the bed where she once lay. Was I catching up to Athena so quickly?

When I got home, I called the local hospital again to talk with *La Baronessa*. She'd been released, no one knew where. I remembered she had a boyfriend named Joe who she met regularly at the diner. She'd said he worked in a car dealership. I called some local dealers and asked if they had a Joe working there. After a few calls, one said, "Yeah we have a Joe working here in sales," and put me through to a voicemail. I left a message, not knowing if this was the right Joe or not. The next day I got a call. It was him. He was heartbroken. Joe confirmed that she died of COVID-19.

La Baronessa would never have believed it, if a few months before, anyone would have told her she would die of COVID, she would've said, "You're crazy." Her apartment was emptied, and I could see clear through her living room window across to her kitchen window. Empty. I remembered her looking on Google Earth at the balcony windows of her family house in Cimmina, Sicily, and by the white curtains concluding someone was living there, not knowing that soon, it would be her windows that had no curtains.

"All She Wanted"

was a *balcone*, no
bigger than a tomb, to
sit and commune
with the sky, a neighbor
passing by, eye the
church procession,
hear the kick of a
soccer ball by
children's feet in the
street. All she wanted
was a *balcone* like
they had over in It'lee.

"I am beginning to see lemons"

April 2020, Yonkers, New York
Sheltering-in-place alone

How lemons are bellies of light
suns ready to explode
rinds to contain themselves

Imagine being a lemon from the slopes of Vesuvius or Etna
You can't have thin skin
but a rind, a rind to hold all that you are

an integument. I don't want to go out
into the world, the next time
I walk into open arms of an embrace,

I'll fall open there.
What is it like to be held?
To cry and someone answers?

To not have to cry and someone answers?
All that is all saved for another day.
Today I bleach countertops

hope the window screens keep out the breath
of my neighbors, the swallow builds her own nest
with her beak and flies joyfully, loudly

the wind moves through her as she dips and soars,
spirals up, sings. Three lemons
have been my only tactile company for weeks.

One day sitting at the table I saw the three lemons
as if for the first time, each with a dark eye
looking back at me. I drew their shapes,

three lemons on a blue clay plate.
Their rinds I painted yellow
and rolled each across the paper to capture

their thumb prints. Then one night, sautéing
Swiss chard, I had to cut into one to squeeze
the juice. Yellow paint from the rind fell

into my steaming hot greens.
Nothing I can't survive.
That's my mantra these days.

Do you call the wind?
Has the wind spoken to you?
The best way to know wind

is with wings, a rhythm of feathers.
Swallows sing or cry as they dive
in figure eights, making the sky come alive

To be on the wind, to feel their joy,
to not wait to land
to voice

sky

"What position do you want to be in for *l'eternità?*"

April 2020, Yonkers, New York
Sheltering-in-place alone

I cry everyday
and it's okay
I bake a lemon cake
lemons it's always lemons
I circle back to

lemons in *l'America* I imagine
lemons of lava plains
Vesuvius and Etna breastfed slopes
the hottest openings in all earth
Vesuvius' two warm breasts

My pillowcases I boil
in the big aluminum pot
forks, spoons, knives in the last
of my mother's white porcelain pots
five bucks on Jerome Avenue

Mom never needed an infectious disease specialist
to tell her how to disinfect the house
how many feet to stand away from people
how to catch a cough in a hanky
then bleach it in the sink.

My cough she was tuned into
rooms away. The degrees of my chest congestion
she could hear over the telephone.
The state of my sinuses as she first entered the room.
My pillowcases I boil

and hang to dry
on tin curtain rods.
"The sun is the best disinfectant," she taught me.
I pull cords like hoisting ship sails
to open the blinds to let in the sun
but keep the windows closed

to keep out the neighbors' breathing
as they pass on the walk.
One calls for me through the screen.
That night I spray Lysol
at the window ledge and bricks.

The door is locked. "Nobody's coming in here,"
I yell to the Super when he complains
about a leak in the garage.

Pompeii's bodies in contortions
keep getting uncovered, one by one, two by two.
So far, not one has arms open to the sky in awe.
Not one embraces the inevitable.

We hold onto what we can
even now, sitting, here
surrounded by a world of virus.
Coronavirus has come, COVID-19
and we are running from the ash
sealing eyes in goggles
mouths and noses in filtered masks
but can anything keep the calamity out
or again am I just buying time? Feeding time?

What position do you want to be in for *l'eternità?*

I wish there was just one body dancing in all Pompeii in A.D. 79
one proof of embracing the clean scythe's eternal swing

Imagine being in position for all time
arms wide open, heart facing
the volcano ash plume's descent
lava swallowing me whole
Arms up to the sky, a child reaching for *Sanctus Madre*
Arms up to the sky, two prongs plugged into *Spiritus Sanctus*

I look to the sky
as beautiful today April 1st, 2020
as September 11th, 2001—as blue
COVID-19 shreds lungs
worldwide thousands on ventilators
numbers rising each day.
I wonder how the sky looked
that day in A.D. 79 before *Vesuvio*
put out the light

Can I raise my arms to the sky
like a baby wanting to be picked up by her mother?

What position do you want to be in for *l'eternità?*

I will make art

until I die

and then I will

paint the sky

ACKNOWLEDGMENTS

"My Map of Sicily is Wounded" includes excerpts first published as "Another Spring," in *Talking to the Girls: Intimate and Political Essays on the Triangle Fire,* edited by Edvige Giunta and Mary Anne Trasciatti. New Village Press, New York: 2022.

"Ladder of Time" appeared as "*Sistemazione*" in *Mediterranean Poetry,* www. Odyssey.pm, Anders Dahlgren, Editor. Sweden: 2021.

"*i 'Cpodde d'Acquaviv*" premiered as a video recitation on Neil Goldberg's podcast, "She's a Talker," 3/31/20, and was first published in *Paterson Literary Review (PLR)* #49, Editor Maria Mazziotti Gillan. Paterson: 2021.

"*Nerina*" was awarded an Allen Ginsberg Poetry Award Honorable Mention, sponsored by the Poetry Center at Passaic County Community College, published in *Paterson Literary Review (PLR)* #49, Editor Maria Mazziotti Gillan. Paterson: 2021.

"*Perché*" appeared as "Notes from Napoli 7," with "Caves" in *VIA: Voices in Italian Americana*, Volume 29, Number 1. Poetry Editor Peter Covino, Bordighera Press. New York: 2018.

"*I Muratori*" in *KGB Bar Lit,* an online literary review, Issue #13. Editor Patsy Zumhagen, New York: June 1, 2021. KGBBarLit.com. The story premiered in performance at Dixon Place in Lanzillotto's solo show, "Feed Time," New York: June 14th, 2018, and was developed at City Lore, directed by Marjorie LeWit, New York: November 15, 2019.

"An Overpopulation of Angels," "For Those Who Came with Nothing," and "Church Bells and Fishermen Yells," in *Paterson Literary Review (PLR) #47*, Editor Maria Mazziotti Gillan, the Poetry Center at Passaic County Community College, Paterson: 2019.

"Strangest Fruit" and "A Ladder of *Fiori*" and "In the Muscular Hills" in *Philadelphia Poets,* Volume 25, Editor Rosemary Cappello. Philadelphia: 2019.

"At Sea At Sea," "*Immacolatella*" and "*Il Cristo Velato* / The Veiled Christ," in Atelier Internazionale, Editor Eleonora Rimolo. www.atelierpoesia.it, Borgomanero, Novara, 2018.

"Rachel's Blue Onion Linoleum Floor, 1975-2016" and "Renaissance Heaven" in *Ovunque Siamo,* Editors Michelle Reale and Chad Frame. U.S.A: 2018.

"*Perché*" for Francesco Durante *(VIP: Vadi in Pace)*

"All She Wanted" for Amelia Trotter King *(VIP: Vadi in Pace)*

"Bubbles" for Stanislao Pugliese and Jennifer Romanello

"Tomorrow My *Cugini*" for Claudia Masiello and Antonello Sperti

"*I Fosforescenti,*" for Peter Covino and Giorgio Sica

"A Ladder of *Fiori*" for Diane Fortuna *(VIP: Vadi in Pace)*

"*L'Indifferenziata Lazzi*" for Joshua Fausty

"Joe Candy" for Antonello Rizzo

"Clothespins" for Libera Durante

"For Those Who Came with Nothing" for Natalie Marrone

"*Carissime Mamme Palermitane*" for young queers of Palermo.

GRATITUDE

GRAZIE MILLE

The miracle of a book being in your hands is the result of the hands-on work of a cadre of people. First and foremost, Bordighera Press founders Anthony Julian Tamburri, Fred Gardaphè and Paolo Giordano made an exquisite home for Italian American literature. Nicholas Grosso shepherded this book with an artist's eye and the light navigational touch of a gondolier. Bordighera is a literary home for many. Look at the list at the back of this book and you'll see a glorious mountain of work starting with Volume #1 by Bob Viscusi (*VIP: Vadi in Pace*, 1941-2020). Twenty-five years ago, just after Bob wrote that oration, I invited him to recite it on the sidewalk outside Our Lady of Mount Carmel Church on East 187th Street in the Bronx, where I was creating site-specific performance-art at the time in the old Italian pushcart market on Arthur Avenue. I remember the priest's hand pulling my orange extension cord in through the window to power-up a microphone for Bob who shocked the crowd and passers-by in a magnetic rant. That potent moment lives on . . . Bronx Italian performative life. This present book is woven together with that oration on the continuum of Bordighera publications. I tip my hat in reverence for my mentor, Joe Papaleo (*VIP: Vadi in Pace*, 1925 - 2004), who enlightened me on what it means to be a writer, and who first brought to my attention the work being done at Bordighera, and iawa: italian american writers association.

VI RINGRAZIO TANTO

Like my mother's scapular which I wear one saint on sternum and one on spine, guarding me front and back, these pages too are bookended by guardians. My dear friend Edvige Giunta wrote a loving foreword. She is the axle of the wheel of a community of Italian-American women writers through her scholarship, authorship, friendship, and organizing work. Over the decades, Giunta enfolded me into her family and the memoir communities of New Jersey City University, and Malìa: A Collective of Italian-American Women. The back cover is anointed with passionate blurbs by artists who I love and admire: Joe Mantegna, Marianne Leone, Tim Z. Hernandez, and Erica Cardwell. Joe Mantegna and I share a unique bond—our *piccolo paese,* Acquaviva delle Fonti, a connection of ancestral spirit and the *sorgente*—the ever-flowing source of sweet water. *Evviva Acquaviva!*

MOLTE GRAZIE

The genesis of this book was writing a poem a day in *Napoli* in the spring of 2018 when on a literary tour organized by Francesco Durante (*VIP: Vadi in Pace*, 1952-2019) and Stanislao Pugliese. Generous hosts presented and helped along the way. I am grateful to the following individuals and organizations in Italy: Stefania Taviano went above and beyond, organizing readings and inviting me into her home and family life. Angela Colonna translated "This is the Bronx" into Neapolitan. Libera Durante, Barbara Burdick, Angelo Cannavacciuolo, Iole Capasso, *Napoli Città Libro, Università degli Studi Suor Orsola Benincasa, Università Degli Studi di Salerno a Fisciano,* Giorgio Sica; *Festival Salerno Letteratura*: Ines Mainieri, Rosa Maria Grillo; *Fondazione SASSI,* Mariateresa Cascino, Elizabeth Jennings; *Letti di Sera, Potenza*: Paolo Albano, Pino Brindisi, Simona Bonito, Maria Giovanni Trotta, Angela Bochicchio, Andrea Galgano; *La Gazzetta del Mezzogiorno*: Virginia Cortese; *Sicilia Queer FilmFest*: Mirko Lino, Charlotte Ross, Silvia Antosa; *Museo Laboratorio della Civiltà Contadina*, Matera: Donato Cascione; *Toponomastica Femminile*: Ester Rizzo; Giorgia Bona, Antonino Rizzo, Vanni Salvio, Giuliana Pella, Rita Passeri, Carola Spadoni, Joshua Fausty, Dalila Urbano, Jacob Burkhardt, Ann Stupay, Mayor Mimmo Balsamo of Villafranca Sicula, Mayor Luca Cannata of Avola, Mayor Davide Francesco Ruggero Carlucci of Acquaviva delle Fonti.

To translate phrases into regional languages, I consulted friends, cousins, and contacts: Edvige Giunta, Stefania Taviano, Bibi Marin, Massimilliano Verde, Oronzo Montrone, Maria Serena Carella, Maurizio Fasano, Angelo Zeolla, Stanislao Pugliese.

I am especially thankful to all my cousins and the people of Acquaviva delle Fonti, Bitetto, and Cassano delle Murge.

GRAZIE

Editors and publishers of journals and anthologies in which versions of some of the texts in this book have previously appeared: Rosemary Cappello, Peter Covino, Anders Dahlgren, Lynne Elizabeth, Chad Frame, Maria Mazziotti Gillan, Edvige Giunta, Michelle Reale, Eleonora Rimolo, Mary Anne Trasciatti, Patsy Zumhagen (*VIP: Vadi in Pace*, 1944-2022).

Theaters, galleries, venues, and directors, where I first performed some of these stories on stage: Dixon Place: Ellie Covan; City Lore: Steve Zeitlin, and Molly Garfinkel; Moving Body Resources: Mary Abrams; Pace University's Media, Communications and Visual Arts: David Freeman, Lou Guarneri. Marjorie LeWit.

GRAZIE INFINITE

In the final stages of writing this book, I was diagnosed with a third cancer, which is common in the life of a long-term survivor of teenage Hodgkin's Disease. I am part of a cohort of the lucky ones who have lived long enough to develop iatrogenic cancers. Upon hearing of this diagnosis, author Nancy Caronia, walking in the *Spiritus Sanctus*, responded by setting up a GoFundMe campaign, inspiring a wellspring of tactical support. Nancy may never know the magnitude of her impact upon my *sopravvivenza*. I shouldn't have been as shocked as I was. Caronia, for years has performed acts of spiritual outreach; to me she has shared her mastery of Tai Chi, and her reach as a professor, giving me the boon of including my first book, *L is for Lion: an italian bronx butch freedom memoir*, on her syllabus at West Virginia University along with gay and lesbian icons: James Baldwin (*VIP: Vadi in Pace* 1924-1987), and Audre Lorde (*VIP: Vadi in Pace*, 1934-1992). Her syllabus hangs over my writing desk.

The GoFundMe created a health "Special Needs Trust" through the tremendous efforts and devotion of my beloved friend Rob Stupay, with the intercession of his contacts Sara Sugihara and David Dorfman, JD. Trustees include my beloved nieces Melissa Montagino Arkus, and Nicole Lanzillotto. The trust can be contacted and donated to: TrustForAnnie@gmail.com. This support takes care of the myriad of health-related expenses not covered by Medicare and Medicaid, including a life-saving nebulizer medication that is only covered in-patient or in nursing homes, two places I tap dance to avoid. Thanks to all who gave, for this literal breathing room.

GRAZIE DI CUORE

To create this book, I've relied upon family, friends, neighbors, and a world class medical team to stay alive and well. I am fortunate to say there are far too many to name. Thanks to you all—who accompany me on early morning pilgrimages to Sloan Kettering, who answer the phone, send food, and stay inspired to make this phrase true: THE SHOW MUST, MUST GO ON!

A few shout-outs of all-stars of constant generosity: Audrey Lauren Kindred, Neil Goldberg, Dr. Sandy Kempin, Joanna Clapps Herman, Ellynne Skove, Rabbi Simkha Y. Weintraub, Salley May, Kathleen Zamboni McCormick, Sean Meehan, Dr. Diane Pepe-Stover, Linda Tatum, Dr. William S. Breitbart, Dr. Lisa Donovan, Dr. Anna Marcelli, Dr. David J. Straus, Dr. Debra Mangino, Dr. Murk Hein Heinemann, Alexandra Hartmann, Ellie Covan, Martha Wilson, Harley Spiller, Ron Raider, Valerie Reyes-Jimenez, Adam Feingold, Barry VanSteenbergen, Tufara Waller-Muhammad, Jessie Kindred, LuLu LoLo, Mike Fiorito, Jude Rubin, Antonia Kirkland, Rob Barbera, Simba-Nyota Wa Katolo Mwangala Bushiku Ina Banza Wa

Luba Sandra Yangala, Gabriella Belfiglio, Marg Suarez, Hannah Marks, Al Hemberger, David De Luca, Dixie De Luca, Linda Reich, Steve Reich, Lucia Mudd, John Mudd, Linda Ciana, Joan Spota, John Denaro, Joel Van Liew, Rosemarie Montagino, Peter Montagino, Sean Meehan, Emily Jordan Agnes Kunkel, Debby Gorney, Lois Sceppaquercia, Karen Trifoli, Elise Bernhardt, Al Tacconelli, Maria Famà, Valerie Vitale, Joe Corcoran, Karen Cellini, Gina DiRenzi, Clare Ultimo, Ronnie Marmo, Marc Choyt, Will MacAdams, Joanne Graziosi, Shirley Kaplan, Allen Lang, John Gennari, Min Brassman, Rosette Capotorto, Sophia Capotorto, Roseann Tucci, Camilla Casaw and the MELODY study at Memorial Sloan Kettering, Trisha Gorman, Annie Hauck-Lawson, Chiara Montalto, Ruth Sergel, Sherry Kane, Mitch Del Monico, Sister Elain Goodell (*VIP: Vadi in Pace*, 1925-2022) and all the artists who participate in StreetCry writing and theater workshops.

I thank the following organizations who've supported my work: StreetCry Inc, Hedgebrook, Santa Fe Arts Institute, The Loft Recording Studios, Dixon Place, Franklin Furnace Archive Inc, St. Ann & The Holy Trinity Church, *Le Ortique, Strade Dorate*, I AM Books, City Lore, Theatre 68, Remember the Triangle Fire Coalition, Sarah Lawrence College Theater Outreach Program, Italian American Writers' Association, NYU *Casa Italiana Zerilli-Marimò*— profound thanks to Stefano Albertini, and Julian Sachs.

È MOLTO GENTILE DA PARTE VUOI

Rose Imperato was the last to pick peaches with me from Grandma Rose Peach Tree before they chopped her down.

ABOUT THE AUTHOR

ANNIE RACHELE LANZILLOTTO is a Bronx born poet, performance-artist, author, playwright, actor, director, songwriter, activist, *cantastoria*, whose stage presence has been called riveting and volcanic. Her work is inspired by the cacophonous opera of pushcart peddler street cries, the roots of theater in the agora, and the solo *cantastoria* in the piazza. She incorporates and puts metaphoric spins on iconic urban objects: the blue street corner mailbox, Spaldeens, the parking meter, traffic lights, block ice, casts of sewer caps. You can listen to her raw Bronx roar in *Annie's Story Cave* podcast, and her audiobooks on Audible.com. Visit AnnieLanzillotto.com, StreetCryInc.org.

Lanzillotto is the author of the books *Whaddyacall the Wind?* (Bordighera Press), *Hard Candy: Caregiving, Mourning and Stage Light*, and *Pitch, Roll, Yaw* (Guernica World Editions), *L is for Lion: an italian bronx butch freedom memoir* (SUNY Press, Finalist for the Lambda Literary Foundation Award), and *Schistsong* (Bordighera Press). She hosts the talk show *Tell Me a Story*, (CityLore, StreetCry). Albums include: *Never Argue with a Jackass, Swampjuice: Yankee with a Southern Peasant Soul, Blue Pill, Carry My Coffee*. Plays and performance works include: *Zerega Blues* (Bronx Museum of the Arts), *Feed Time* (Dixon Place, City Lore), *A Stickball Memoir* (Smithsonian Folklife Festival), *Confessions of a Bronx Tomboy: My Throwing Arm, This Useless Expertise* (Under One Roof, Manhattan Class Company), *La Scarpetta* (Guggenheim Museum), *a'Schapett!* at The Arthur Avenue Retail Market in the Bronx, (Dancing in the Streets OnSite/NYC; Rockefeller Foundation MAP Fund, Puffin Fund), *The Flat Earth: Wheredddafffhuck Did New York Go?* (Dixon Place

Mondo Cane Commission), *How to Wake Up a Marine in a Foxhole* (The Kitchen), *Pocketing Garlic* (Franklin Furnace), *The Hooking Place* (Theatre 68), *Lasagna Superstar*, a musical (St. Ann's Church). Internationally she's performed readings at *Napoli Città Libro*, *Fondazione Sassi*—Matera, *Sicilia Queer FilmFest*—Palermo, *Associazione Lette di Sera*—Potenza. Lanzillotto was a founding board member of Remember the Triangle Fire Coalition and conceived of the *146 Shirtwaist Kites*, which grew into a coalition-wide community art project emblematic of the fallen sweatshop workers of 1911.

Lanzillotto has garnered fellowships from the New York Foundation for the Arts in Non-Fiction Writing, and Multi-Disciplinary Performance, the Rockefeller Foundation Next Generation Leadership program, and commissions and grants from Dancing in the Streets, Franklin Furnace, Dixon Place, Rockefeller Foundation Multi-Arts Production Fund, and Puffin Foundation. Her poetry was awarded the Henry & Anne Paolucci Award from the Italian American Writers' Association, the Allen Ginsberg Award from The Poetry Center at Passaic County Community College, and the John & Rose Petracca Award from Philadelphia Poets. She's had writing residencies at New Jersey City University, Hedgebrook, and Santa Fe Arts Institute. She is 2022 *Creatives Rebuild New York* grantee.

VIA FOLIOS

A refereed book series dedicated to the culture of Italians and Italian Americans.

TAMBURRI. et al., Eds. *Italian Cultural Studies 2001*. Vol 33. Essays.
ELIZABETH G. MESSINA, Ed. *In Our Own Voices*.
Vol 32. Italian/American Studies.
STANISLAO G. PUGLIESE. *Desperate Inscriptions*. Vol 31. History.
HOSTERT & TAMBURRI, Eds. *Screening Ethnicity*.
Vol 30. Italian/American Culture.
G. PARATI & B. LAWTON, Eds. *Italian Cultural Studies*. Vol 29. Essays.
HELEN BAROLINI. *More Italian Hours*. Vol 28. Fiction.
FRANCO NASI, Ed. *Intorno alla Via Emilia*. Vol 27. Culture.
ARTHUR L. CLEMENTS. *The Book of Madness & Love*. Vol 26. Poetry.
JOHN CASEY, et al. *Imagining Humanity*. Vol 25. Interdisciplinary Studies.
ROBERT LIMA. *Sardinia/Sardegna*. Vol 24. Poetry.
DANIELA GIOSEFFI. *Going On*. Vol 23. Poetry.
ROSS TALARICO. *The Journey Home*. Vol 22. Poetry.
EMANUEL DI PASQUALE. *The Silver Lake Love Poems*. Vol 21. Poetry.
JOSEPH TUSIANI. *Ethnicity*. Vol 20. Poetry.
JENNIFER LAGIER. *Second Class Citizen*. Vol 19. Poetry.
FELIX STEFANILE. *The Country of Absence*. Vol 18. Poetry.
PHILIP CANNISTRARO. *Blackshirts*. Vol 17. History.
LUIGI RUSTICHELLI, Ed. *Seminario sul racconto*. Vol 16. Narrative.
LEWIS TURCO. *Shaking the Family Tree*. Vol 15. Memoirs.
LUIGI RUSTICHELLI, Ed. *Seminario sulla drammaturgia*.
Vol 14. Theater/Essays.
FRED GARDAPHÈ. *Moustache Pete is Dead! Long Live Moustache Pete!*.
Vol 13. Oral Literature.
JONE GAILLARD CORSI. *Il libretto d'autore. 1860 - 1930*. Vol 12. Criticism.
HELEN BAROLINI. *Chiaroscuro: Essays of Identity*. Vol 11. Essays.
PICARAZZI & FEINSTEIN, Eds. *An African Harlequin in Milan*.
Vol 10. Theater/Essays.
JOSEPH RICAPITO. *Florentine Streets & Other Poems*. Vol 9. Poetry.
FRED MISURELLA. *Short Time*. Vol 8. Novella.
NED CONDINI. *Quartettsatz*. Vol 7. Poetry.
ANTHONY JULIAN TAMBURRI, Ed. *Fuori: Essays by Italian/American Lesbiansand Gays*. Vol 6. Essays.
ANTONIO GRAMSCI. P. Verdicchio. Trans. & Intro. *The Southern Question*.
Vol 5. Social Criticism.
DANIELA GIOSEFFI. *Word Wounds & Water Flowers*. Vol 4. Poetry. $8
WILEY FEINSTEIN. *Humility's Deceit: Calvino Reading Ariosto Reading Calvino*.
Vol 3. Criticism.
PAOLO A. GIORDANO, Ed. *Joseph Tusiani: Poet. Translator. Humanist*.
Vol 2. Criticism.
ROBERT VISCUSI. *Oration Upon the Most Recent Death of Christopher Columbus*.
Vol 1. Poetry.

Milton Keynes UK
Ingram Content Group UK Ltd.
UKHW010618080823
426502UK00006B/241